COMPANIONS
in Christ
™

P9-DEN-621

DATE DUE

Gerrit Sc   an Hinson,
Rueben   M. Wright

Contents

Acknowledgments

Companions in Christ is truly the result of the efforts of a team of persons who shared a common vision. This team graciously contributed their knowledge and experience to develop a small-group resource that would creatively engage persons in a journey of spiritual growth and discovery. The authors of the chapters in the Participant's Book were Gerrit Scott Dawson, Adele Gonzalez, E. Glenn Hinson, Rueben P. Job, Marjorie J. Thompson, and Wendy M. Wright. Stephen Bryant was the primary author of the daily exercises and the Leader's Guide. Marjorie Thompson created the original design and participated in the editing of the entire resource. Keith Beasley-Topliffe served as a consultant in the creation of the process for the small-group meetings and contributed numerous ideas that influenced the final shape of the resource. In the early stages of development, two advisory groups read and responded to the initial drafts of material. The persons participating as members of those advisory groups were Jeannette Bakke, Avery Brooke, Thomas Parker, Helen Pearson Smith, Luther E. Smith Jr., Eradio Valverde Jr., Diane Luton Blum, Carol Bumbalough, Ruth Torri, and Mark Wilson. Prior to publication, test groups in the following churches used the material and provided helpful suggestions for improvement of the Participant's Book and the Leader's Guide.

Acknowledgments

First United Methodist Church, Hartselle, Alabama
St. George's Episcopal Church, Nashville, Tennessee
Northwest Presbyterian Church, Atlanta, Georgia
Garfield Memorial United Methodist Church,
    Pepper Pike, Ohio
First United Methodist Church, Corpus Christi, Texas
Malibu United Methodist Church, Malibu, California
First United Methodist Church, Santa Monica, California
St. Paul United Methodist Church, San Antonio, Texas
Trinity Presbyterian Church, Arvada, Colorado
First United Methodist Church, Franklin, Tennessee
La Trinidad United Methodist Church, San Antonio, Texas
Aldersgate United Methodist Church, Slidell, Louisiana

My deep gratitude goes to all these persons and groups for their contribution to and support of *Companions in Christ*.

—Janice T. Grana, editor of *Companions in Christ*
April 2001

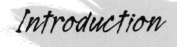

Introduction

Welcome to *Companions in Christ,* a small-group resource for spiritual formation. It is designed to create a setting where you can respond to God's call to an ever-deepening communion and wholeness in Christ—as an individual, as a member of a small group, and as part of a congregation. The resource focuses on your experience of God and your discovery of spiritual practices that help you share more fully in the life of Christ. You will be exploring the potential of Christian community as an environment of grace and mutual guidance through the Spirit. You will grow closer to members of your small group as you seek together to know and respond to God's will. And your congregation will grow when you and your companions begin to bring what you learn into all areas of church life, from classes and meetings to worship and outreach.

How does *Companions in Christ* help you grow spiritually? It enables you to immerse yourself in "streams of living waters" through the spiritual disciplines of prayer, scripture, ministry, worship, study, and Christian conversation. These means of grace are the common ways in which Christ meets people, renews their faith, and deepens their life together in love.

* Through *Companions,* you will explore the depths of scripture, learn to listen to God through it, and allow your life to be shaped by the Word.

- Through *Companions*, you will experience new dimensions of prayer, try fresh ways of opening to God, and learn what it means to practice the presence of God.

- Through *Companions*, you will reflect on Christ's call in your life and discover anew the gifts that God is giving you for living out your personal ministry.

- Through *Companions*, you and members of your group will grow together as a Christian community and gain skills in learning how small groups in the church become settings for spiritual guidance.

Although *Companions* is not an introductory course in Christianity for new Christians, it will help church people take up the basic disciplines of faith in renewing and transforming ways.

An Outline of the Resource

Companions in Christ has two primary components: individual reading and daily exercises throughout the week with this Participant's Book and a weekly two-hour meeting based on suggestions in the Leader's Guide. For each week, the Participant's Book has a chapter introducing new material and five daily exercises to help you reflect on your life in light of the content of the chapter. After the Preparatory Meeting of your group, you will begin a weekly cycle as follows: On day 1 you will be asked to read the chapter and on days 2–6 to complete the five daily exercises (found at the end of the chapter reading). On day 7 you will meet with your group. The daily exercises aim to help you move from information (knowledge about) to experience (knowledge of). An important part of this process is keeping a personal notebook or journal where you record reflections, prayers, and questions for later review and for reference at the weekly group meeting. The time commitment for the daily exercises is about thirty minutes. The weekly meeting will include time for reflecting on the exercises of the past week, for moving deeper into learnings from chapter readings, for having group experiences of prayer, and for considering ways to share with the congregation what you have learned or experienced.

The material in *Companions in Christ* covers a period of twenty-eight weeks divided into five parts or units, as well as a preparatory meeting and a closing retreat. The five parts are as follows:

1. *Embracing the Journey: The Way of Christ* (five weeks)—a basic exploration of spiritual formation as a journey toward wholeness and holiness, individually and in community, through the grace of God.

2. *Feeding on the Word: The Mind of Christ* (five weeks)—an introduction to several ways of meditating on and praying with scripture.

3. *Deepening Our Prayer: The Heart of Christ* (six weeks)—a guided experience of various forms and styles of prayer.

4. *Responding to Our Call: The Work of Christ* (five weeks)—a presentation of vocation or call: giving ourselves to God in willing obedience and receiving the fruits and gifts of the Holy Spirit.

5. *Exploring Spiritual Guidance: The Spirit of Christ* (five weeks)—an overview of different ways of giving and receiving spiritual guidance, from one-on-one relationships, to spiritual growth groups, to guidance in congregational life as a whole.

Your group may want to take a short break between units either to allow for some unstructured reflection time or to avoid meeting near Christmas or Easter. However, the units are designed to be sequential. It would be difficult and unwise for new members to join at the beginning of a later unit or for a group to skip a unit, since each unit builds on previous ones.

Your Participant's Book includes a section entitled "Materials for Group Meetings" that begins on page 293. This section includes some brief supplemental readings that you will use as a part of several group meetings. Your leader will alert you when you will be using this material. Also you will find an annotated resource list on pages 304–8 that describes additional books related to the themes of various parts of *Companions in Christ*.

You will need to bring your Participant's Book, your Bible, and your personal notebook or journal to the weekly group meeting.

The Companions in Christ Network

An additional dimension of *Companions in Christ* is the Network. While you and your group are experiencing *Companions in Christ*, groups in other congregations will also be meeting. The Network provides opportunities for you to share your experiences with one another and to link in a variety of meaningful ways. As you move through the resource, there will be occasions when you will be invited to pray for another group, send greetings or encouragement, or receive their support for your group. Connecting in these ways will enrich your group's experience and the experience of those to whom you reach out.

The Network also provides a place to share conversation and information. The Companion's Web site, www.companionsinchrist.org, includes a discussion room where you can offer insights, voice questions, and respond to others in an ongoing process of shared learning. The site provides a list of other Companions groups and their geographical locations so that you can make connections as you feel led.

The Companions Network is a versatile and dynamic component of the larger *Companions* resource. A Network toll-free number (1-800-491-0912) is staffed during regular business hours by a Resource Specialist who can assist you.

Your Personal Notebook or Journal

"I began these pages for myself, in order to think out my own particular pattern of living....And since I think best with a pencil in my hand, I started naturally to write." Anne Morrow Lindbergh began her beloved classic, *Gift from the Sea*, with these words. You may not imagine that you "think best with a pencil in hand," but there is something truly wonderful about what can happen when we reflect on the inner life through writing.

Keeping a journal or personal notebook (commonly called journaling) will be one of the most important dimensions of your personal experience with *Companions in Christ*. The Participant's Book gives you daily spiritual exercises every week. More often than not, you will be asked to note your thoughts, reflections, questions, feelings, or prayers in relation to the exercises.

Even if you are totally inexperienced in this kind of personal writing, you may find that it becomes second nature very quickly. Your thoughts may start to pour out of you, giving expression to an inner life that has never been released. If, on the other hand, you find the writing difficult or cumbersome, give yourself permission to try it in a new way. Because a journal is "for your eyes only," you may choose any style that suits you. You need not worry about making your words sound beautiful or about writing with good grammar and spelling. You don't even need to write complete sentences! Jotting down key ideas, insights, or musings is just fine. You might want to doodle while you think or sketch an image that comes to you. Make journaling fun and relaxed. No one will see what you write, and you have complete freedom to share with the group only what you choose of your reflections.

There are two important reasons for keeping a journal or personal notebook as you move through *Companions in Christ*. First, the process of writing down our thoughts clarifies them for us. They become more specific and concrete. Sometimes we really do not know what we think until we see our thoughts on paper, and often the process of writing itself generates new creative insight. Second, this personal record captures what we have been experiencing inwardly over time. Journaling helps us track changes in our thinking and growth of insight. Our memories are notoriously fragile and fleeting in this regard. Specific feelings or creative connections we may have had two weeks ago, or even three days ago, are hard to recall without a written record. Even though your journal cannot capture all that goes through your mind in a single reflection period, it will serve as a reminder. You will need to draw on these reminders during small-group meetings each week.

Begin by purchasing a book that you can use for this purpose. It can be as simple as a spiral-bound notebook or as fancy as a cloth-bound blank book. Some people prefer lined paper and some

unlined. You will want, at minimum, something more permanent than a ring-binder or paper pad. The Upper Room has made available a companion journal for this resource that you can purchase if you so desire.

When you begin the daily exercises, have your journal and pen or pencil at hand. You need not wait until you have finished reading and thinking an exercise through completely. Learn to stop and write as you go. Think on paper. Feel free to write anything that comes to you, even if it seems to be "off the topic." It may turn out to be more relevant or useful than you first think. If the process seems clumsy at first, don't fret. Like any spiritual practice, it gets easier over time, and its value becomes more apparent.

Here is how your weekly practice of journaling is shaped. On the first day after your group meeting, read the new chapter. Jot down your responses to the reading: "aha" moments, questions, points of disagreement, images, or any other reflections you wish to record. You may prefer to note these in the margins of the chapter. Over the next five days, you will do the exercises for the week, recording either general or specific responses as they are invited. On the day of the group meeting, it will be helpful to review what you have written through the week, perhaps marking portions you would like to share in the group. Bring your journal with you to meetings so that you can refer to it directly or refresh your memory of significant moments you want to paraphrase during discussion times. With time, you may indeed find that journaling helps you to think out your own pattern of living and that you will be able to see more clearly how God is at work in your life.

Your Group Meeting

The weekly group meeting is divided into four segments. First you will gather for a brief time of worship and prayer. This offers an opportunity to set aside the many concerns of the day and center on God's presence and guidance as you begin your group session.

The second section of the meeting is called "Sharing Insights."

During this time you will be invited to talk about your experiences with the daily exercises. The group leader will participate as a member and share his or her responses as well. Generally the sharing by each member will be brief and related to specific exercises. This is an important time for your group to learn and practice what it means to be a community of persons seeking to listen to God and to live more faithfully as disciples of Christ. The group provides a supportive space to explore your listening, your spiritual practices, and how you are attempting to put those practices into daily life. Group members need not comment or offer advice to one another. Rather the group members help you, by their attentiveness and prayer, to pay attention to what has been happening in your particular response to the daily exercises. The group is not functioning as a traditional support group that offers suggestions or help to one another. Rather, the group members trust that the Holy Spirit is the guide and that they are called to help one another listen to that guidance.

The "Sharing Insights" time presents a unique opportunity to learn how God works differently in each of our lives. Our journeys, while varied, are enriched by others' experiences. We can hold one another in prayer, and we can honor each other's experience. Through this part of the meeting, you will see in fresh ways how God's activity may touch or address our lives in unexpected ways. The group will need to establish some ground rules to facilitate the sharing. For example, you may want to be clear that each person speak only about his or her own beliefs, feelings, and responses and that all group members have permission to share only what and when they are ready to share. Above all, the group needs to maintain confidentiality so that what is shared in the group stays in the group. This part of the group meeting will be much less meaningful if persons interrupt and try to comment on what is being said or try to "fix" what they see as a problem. The leader will close this part of the meeting by calling attention to any patterns or themes that seem to emerge from the group's sharing. These patterns may point to a word that God is offering to the group. Notice that the group leader functions both as a participant

and as someone who aids the process by listening and summarizing the key insights that have surfaced.

The third segment of the group meeting is called "Deeper Explorations." This part of the meeting may expand on ideas contained in the week's chapter, offer practice in the spiritual disciplines introduced in the chapter or exercises, or give group members a chance to reflect on the implications of what they are learning for themselves and for their church. It offers a common learning experience for the group and a chance to go deeper in our understanding of how we can share more fully in the mind, heart, and work of Jesus Christ.

As it began, the group meeting ends with a brief time of worship, an ideal time for the group to share special requests for intercession that might come from the conversation and experience of the meeting or other prayer requests that arise naturally from the group.

The weeks that you participate in *Companions in Christ* will offer you the opportunity to focus on your relationship with Christ and to grow in your openness to God's presence and guidance. The unique aspect of this experience is that members of your small group, who are indeed your companions on the journey, will encourage your searching and learning. Those of us who have written and edited this resource offer our prayers that God will speak to you during these weeks and awaken you to enlarged possibilities of love and service in Christ's name. As we listen and explore together, we will surely meet our loving God who waits eagerly to guide us toward deeper maturity in Christ by the gracious working of the Holy Spirit.

Part 1

Embracing the Journey: The Way of Christ

Rueben P. Job and
Marjorie J. Thompson

The Christian Life As Journey

I was six years old when my family took a trip of more than one day. We traveled from North Dakota to Wyoming—my parents, two brothers, and I, along with clothes and food for many days—all packed into a 1929 Durant automobile. My parents had planned carefully for overnight stops, and daily meals were served from an old wooden apple crate. We ate lunches beside the road or in a shady village park. Breakfast and supper were shared where we spent the night at roadside cabins that preceded modern motels.

It was a long journey filled with uncertainties. The car was not always dependable. Poorly marked and inadequately maintained roads resulted in a rough and dusty ride. Moreover, we had never traveled this way before. Our simple road map needed frequent interpretation, gleaned from truck drivers and other fellow travelers.

But what a glorious trip it was! Every day was filled with new surprises and sometimes with delight beyond description. The entire journey informed and transformed us as we shared new perceptions, made discoveries, and learned from our experience together.

We learned, for example, to be patient when the engine stopped and we had to wait for help. We learned that adversity could be encountered and overcome as we experienced one flat tire after another. We learned how to face the unexpected as road construction forced detours

to areas we had not planned to see. We discovered the simple joy of bread, fruit, and sausage, and the incomparable refreshment of cool water shared in the journey's pause. We marveled at vast prairies and the majesty of mountains seen for the first time. Our little car shook from a violent summer thunderstorm on the plains, and we trembled at the awesome power of nature.

After more than sixty years, memories of that journey remain vivid. My brothers and I still reflect on it when we get together. Lessons learned in that experience continue to inform my life, especially my spiritual life.

Movements in the Journey

I can well understand why Christian spirituality is often described as a journey rather than a destination. The spiritual life is characterized by movement and discovery, challenge and change, adversity and joy, uncertainty and fulfillment. It is also marked in a special way by companionship, first with the One we seek to follow and second with those who also seek to follow Jesus Christ.

The Bible is filled with images of spiritual life as journey. Perhaps the most remarkable illustration of spiritual journey in the Bible is the story of the Exodus. For forty years the Hebrew people struggled to move from Egyptian bondage to the freedom of the Promised Land. Some trials were met with obedience, others with dismal failures of faith, yet God's constant faithfulness kept them safe through the wilderness sojourn.

Hebrew Bible scholar Walter Brueggemann suggests that the life of faith is a journey with God characterized by three basic movements: (1) being oriented, (2) becoming disoriented, and (3) being surprisingly reoriented.[1] The psalms give consistent evidence of movement through such phases. I suspect these movements are familiar experiences to most of us who have embarked on an intentional spiritual journey. There are times when our certainties about life seem seriously undermined, if not completely shattered. There are other times when, through conscious effort or quite apart from it, we move

The Christian life involves more than growth and development. It involves conversion and transformation, a radical turning of the Self toward the God who made us and who continues to sustain us. Christian faith is about an inner transformation of consciousness resulting from our encounter with the living Christ.

—James C. Fenhagen

from disorientation to a new constellation of meaning and wholeness. Life is not a stationary experience. New insights and developments continually challenge our understanding of life and our
experience of God. Yet if we see the spiritual life as a journey, these
cycles of change will not alarm us or turn us aside from our primary
goal—to know and love God.

The Journey of Jesus and His Followers

Jesus' life gives us a supreme example of spiritual life as journey. Like
us, Jesus began his earthly sojourn as a helpless, vulnerable infant,
completely dependent on the nurture of his parents and the provi-
dential grace of God. He grew from childhood to the maturity of
adulthood, all the while coming to fuller consciousness of his identity in relation to the One he knew as Father. Even at age twelve, he
was at home in his Father's house among the elders of Jerusalem. He
was firmly "oriented" in his unique relationship with God and received
divine affirmation for his vocation specifically in his baptism and at
his transfiguration. Jesus knew intensely personal communion with
God. He knew many high and holy moments of divine power manifested in and through himself; he knew the joy of community with
his disciples and with the crowds who revered him. But he was not
immune to struggle, disappointment, or the sting of rejection from
friend and foe alike. Surely the experience of temptation in the wilderness was one of disorientation and reorientation for Jesus. On more
than one occasion, Jesus expressed his frustration with disciples and
others who repeatedly misunderstood his teachings and his basic purpose. Even more, the agony of Gethsemane, the experience of betrayal
and denial by his closest human companions, and the ultimate hor-
ror of feeling abandoned even by God reveal a depth of disorientation in Jesus' life journey that defies our comprehension. Yet Jesus
pioneered for us the ultimate reorientation to God's loving purpose
in the glory of his resurrection. God's final word is life, not death;
communion, not separation!

Jesus' journey is in some sense a model for each of his followers,

*A spiritual life is
simply a life in which
all that we do comes
from the centre, where
we are anchored in
God: a life soaked
through and through
by a sense of [divine]
reality and claim, and
self-given to the great
movement of
[God's] will.*

—Evelyn Underhill

although each will experience the particular pattern of the journey in a different way. We have glimpses of that pattern for the twelve disciples who began their journey by accepting Jesus' call to follow him. Along with many days of wearying travel, punctuated by ridicule and rejection from some, came stunning moments of revelation and wonder: impossible healings, the miraculous feeding of the multitudes, the calming of a sudden storm on the lake. The disciples learned only gradually and imperfectly who Jesus was. Whatever certainties they had about him were thrown into crisis at their last Passover supper and in the devastation of the crucifixion. Yet beyond this profound disorientation came experiences of the risen Lord. One of the most powerful stories is the one of two disciples on the road to Emmaus. Here, two little-known men discovered the risen Christ as companion and teacher on their path of confusion and sorrow. The completely new orientation to life and meaning those disciples received remains a powerful promise for our own experience of life in faith.

The Nature of Our Journeys

Perhaps we have been fortunate enough to have been given a secure orientation to God's love early in life. Even so, we cannot long escape the disorienting blows life inevitably brings: the death of a loved one; flagrant injustice in the world or in our own lives; the sins of prejudice, greed, and power-grasping that result in so many evils. It is often difficult to perceive the reality of God's presence, much less the goodness of divine grace, in these profoundly disturbing experiences. Yet God's grace comes in more shapes than security in danger or comfort in the midst of painful disjunctures.

True devotion to God means seeking the divine will in all things. Over time, life teaches us that not getting what we want in prayer may be just what we need. It is part of God's gift that we are weaned away from false notions of who God is, as well as false understandings of what God wants us to be. To imagine that God is here simply to console, affirm, heal, and love us is to deny the holiness of a God who requires righteousness, who challenges our illusions, who con-

fronts our idolatries. When we are being "disillusioned" from false perspectives, the spiritual journey feels arduous—more like climbing a steep mountain than like driving the great plains. Indeed, at times it feels like going over the edge of a cliff on nothing but the thin rope of faith. Sometimes we are called to endure in hope when we can see nothing positive on the horizon at all.

Reorientation to a deeper, richer, and less brittle faith is the potential that lies within truly disorienting life experiences. But this gift does not always come as soon as we would wish or necessarily in the way we hope for. God's ways are profoundly mysterious to us. It is only by faith that we can claim boldly the promise of Romans 8:28: "We know that all things work together for good for those who love God, who are called according to his purpose."

The Promise of Our Faith

God is good and works continually for good in the world, especially in and for and through those who love God. However, the goodness of God's purposes in the world is not accomplished without suffering. We see this truth most clearly in the life of Jesus Christ. Jesus himself promises his followers that they too will suffer in this world if they choose to be his disciples. Yet the greater promise is joy, the incomparable joy of a life lived not for our own sake or from our own center, but for God and centered in Christ. Life in Christ is life abundant! It is possible to know this joy even in the midst of turmoil and suffering. The enduring practices of scriptural reflection, prayer, worship, and guidance within the community of faith help us discover and live these spiritual truths personally and corporately. Exploring such practices together is the purpose of this resource.

Throughout Jewish and Christian history, life with God—the spiritual life—has been seen as a journey. It will be natural, then, during the course of these weeks of reflection and formation to look at our own spiritual life this way. Each of us is on a journey personally, but we will also be covenanting to journey together for a time in the process of deeper exploration represented by this small-group experience. We can help one another remember that the spiritual life is not complete maturity but growth in Christ. We have not arrived but are moving toward God and, therefore, toward the fulfillment of our potential as children of God.

The writer of Ephesians calls us "to maturity, to the measure of the full stature of Christ" (4:13). Such maturity is connected to sound teaching, for it is characteristic of the spiritually immature to be susceptible to "every wind of doctrine" (v. 14). To "grow up in every way into him who is the head, into Christ" (v. 15), signifies a capacity for unity in Christ, an ability to show in our individual lives that we are part of a healthy, unified, life-giving organism called the church. When members of the church are properly equipped with God's truth in Christ, when each part of the whole works as it should, the church grows by "building itself up in love" (v. 16). And the more we build the church up in love, the more like our Lord we become. "What we will be has not yet been revealed. What we do know is this: when he is revealed, we will be like him" (1 John 3:2). This is the goal of the Christian life, a topic we will explore further in the next section.

In everything, keep trusting that God is with you, that God has given you companions on the journey.

—Henri J. M. Nouwen

DAILY EXERCISES

Be sure to read the first chapter, "The Christian Life As Journey," before you begin these exercises. Keep a journal or blank notebook beside you to record your thoughts, questions, prayers, and images. In preparation for each exercise, take a few moments to quiet yourself and let go of particular concerns from your day. Release yourself to God's care, and open your heart to the guidance of the Holy Spirit. In the exercises this week you will be given the opportunity to reflect on your experience of the spiritual life as a journey of faith.

EXERCISE 1

Read Genesis 12:1-9. This story is about an unsettling event in Abram's life that marked the beginning of the faith journey of the Hebrew people. What marked the beginning(s) of your faith journey—your conscious movement from the "land" you knew to the "land" that the Lord would show you? Write down your remembrances, reflections, and feelings about what got you started. Pause to share your feelings with God.

EXERCISE 2

Read Genesis 28:10-22. This story is about God's waking Jacob up to the divine presence and promise in his life. If you were able to walk back through your personal history, where would you marvel with Jacob, "Surely the Lord is in this place—and I did not know it"? Take a mental tour of your early, middle, and recent years, prayerfully repeating this phrase in connection with each memory. Jot down remembrances and any new awareness of God's presence. Close by expressing your gratitude to God.

EXERCISE 3

Read Exodus 17:1-7. This story tells of the Israelites' faith struggles as they "journeyed by stages" from slavery in Egypt through the wilderness. Identify a stage in your journey when you were spiritually thirsty, discouraged, or empty. What happened? What brought you through

the desert? Write your reflections. Close by sharing your questions and wonderings with God.

EXERCISE 4

Read Psalm 126. This psalm expresses the Israelites' joy upon returning home after years in exile. When have you experienced the joy of reunion with a person, place, or community of deep significance to you? When in your spiritual journey have you felt restored in your relationship with God? Record your reflections. Give thanks to God for always welcoming you home.

EXERCISE 5

Read Luke 24:13-35. This story is about two disciples who experienced rapid movements from being oriented (before Jesus' crucifixion) to being disoriented (vv. 13-24) to being reoriented (vv. 25-35). Their story mirrors our own as we grow in our walk with Christ. Which of these movements best describes where you find yourself right now? Record your insights. Spend a few minutes in prayerful conversation with Christ about where you perceive his presence or inward prompting in your life.

Remember to review your journal entries for the week in preparation for the group meeting.

Part 1, Week 2

The Nature of the Christian Spiritual Life

What is the Christian spiritual life? It is simply life lived in Christ—that is, a life where Christ rather than our own self-image constitutes the center of who we are. It is a Spirit-filled, Spirit-led, Spirit-empowered life like the one Jesus embodied with every fiber of his being. Empty of self-importance and self-interest, human life is free to be what God intended: holy, humble, joyfully obedient, radiating the power of love. Paul describes this state of being succinctly in Galatians 2:20: "It is no longer I who live, but it is Christ who lives in me." This, at least, is what a mature Christian life looks like. Most of us feel quite acutely how far we fall short of such spiritual maturity. While it offers a beautiful vision of human capacity and a noble goal, it may seem a daunting, if not impossible, ideal.

That is why we need to begin with grace. The spiritual life is not even remotely possible for us apart from God's grace. And grace is precisely what God gives to us in Jesus Christ. We find some of the most helpful writing in all of scripture on the subject of grace in the letter to the Ephesians. This brief letter contains a treasure trove of truths to help us understand and live the Christian spiritual life. Indeed, many scholars count Ephesians as the "crown jewel" of the church's theology.

The accent on grace is present from the opening greeting: "Grace to you and peace from God our Father and the Lord Jesus Christ." But

We humans, who are a due part of your creation, long to praise you.... You arouse us so that praising you may bring us joy, because you have made us and drawn us to yourself, and our heart is unquiet until it rests in you.

—Augustine of Hippo

the full scope and content of grace become especially evident in chapter 1:3-14. I invite you to read this passage through now at a reflective pace before we continue.

The author of Ephesians[1] begins by blessing the God who has gifted us "with every spiritual blessing" in Christ. It is really quite awesome to think that God "chose us in Christ before the foundation of the world to be holy and blameless before him in love." The rich blessings that come with this gift are many: We are forgiven and redeemed from sin, adopted as children of God, given the inheritance of salvation and knowledge of the mystery of God's will. This is our destiny, chosen not by us but by God for us. And all this abundance of grace is a sheer expression of God's goodwill toward us in Christ. We are being drawn irresistibly to the purpose for which we were made: to praise God with joy!

The Book of Ephesians gives us here a sweeping and convincing portrait of God's tremendous goodwill toward us. It pictures a comprehensive plan for all creation, gathered up in Christ, the Word made flesh. The mystery of this plan is Christ's sacrificial love: Though we have fallen far from grace by sin, in him we are forgiven, reconciled, restored to holiness. God's greatest desire and good pleasure are to bless us in Christ Jesus! Nothing will be withheld from those who live in him by faith. The single word that sums up the central truth of this passage is *grace*.

Grace: An Illustration

Grace is one of those words that floats around in the vocabulary of religious conversation with little examination. No doubt each of us has had an experience of grace, and no single experience is defining for everyone. Grace is hard to define, yet we often recognize what it is by experience. The following illustration comes from a childhood memory. Perhaps it will help you to discover and name your own experiences that give meaning to the word *grace*.

Receiving a slingshot was a big event when I was a child. I remember well when my father made my first one. He cut the Y from a chokecherry tree and used rubber bands from an old truck inner tube, and leather from the tongue of a discarded shoe to hold the stone. When he finished, my father took a few practice shots with little pebbles and then handed the slingshot to me with some low-key but firm instructions about its use. He told me never to shoot at a window, animal, or bird, and never to aim at anything that I did not intend to break, injure, or kill.

It all started well. I was the happiest five-year-old in the county! Ammunition was without limit, and targets were everywhere. Trees, leaves, fence posts, rocks, and water puddles all received well-aimed stones from my slingshot.

One spring evening just after we had finished eating, I was out playing with my slingshot when a mourning dove caught my attention. I knew I was not supposed to shoot at the bird, but I also knew the chances of a "hit" were very, very small. So I pulled up the slingshot and let a stone fly in the direction of the dove. Much to my shock and dismay, the bird fluttered, wounded and helpless, to the ground. I was frightened and heartbroken because I did not want to anger or disobey my father.

I ran indoors and went straight to bed with my clothes on! Soon I heard my father enter the room, and the next thing I knew he was sitting on the side of my bed. He asked me why I was in bed; and through my tears, I blurted out the story of my failure to act responsibly with the slingshot he had made for me. He pulled me to himself and held me as I cried. We talked about the danger of breaking rules designed to keep us and all of God's creatures safe. In his arms I found forgiveness and the promise of another chance. Soon we were walking out the door hand in hand rehearsing what it meant to be a responsible owner of a slingshot.

Grace often comes in unexpected ways and unexpected places. However it comes, it is always unmerited, pure gift. We cannot earn it, purchase it, or even destroy it. The writer of Ephesians makes this clear in the second chapter: "For by grace you have been saved through faith, and this is not your own doing; it is the gift of God—not the result of works, so that no one may boast" (vv. 8-9).

Why would God choose to gift us so lavishly when all of us have been disobedient—sometimes willfully and sometimes unknowingly? As the letter explains, it is simply "so that in the ages to come [God] might show the immeasurable riches of his grace in kindness toward us in Christ Jesus" (Eph. 2:7). It is God's nature to love with overflowing kindness. Indeed, in a deeper sense, grace is the gift of God's own presence with us, "freely bestowed on us in the Beloved" (Eph. 1:6). Jesus is the Beloved, a name revealed in his baptism (Matt. 3:17). Every spiritual gift—love, purity, mercy, peace, truth, fidelity, simplicity, joy—is an offering of God's own nature to us in Christ Jesus. Such grace is given for our comfort, healing, guidance, and transformation. It is given so that we might have life in abundance.

Grace transforms our dreadful failing into plentiful and endless solace; and grace transforms our shameful falling into high and honourable rising; and grace transforms our sorrowful dying into holy, blessed life.
—Julian of Norwich

The Goal of the Spiritual Life

Now we can return to the "impossible ideal" of the Christian life. It is by the grace of God in Christ that we are enabled, very gradually, to become what God has destined us to be.

We are destined to be conformed to the image of Christ, who is himself "the image of the invisible God" (Col. 1:15); the divine image in which we were originally created is restored to us in Jesus Christ. But this process of being reshaped according to God's intended pattern takes time. It is the work of the Holy Spirit and is called sanctification in Christian theology. After turning our hearts back to God and receiving the justification that comes through faith in Christ, then begins the work of bringing our whole character in line with that of Christ. We begin to mature in knowledge, wisdom, and love. Our growth in the Spirit is marked by movements up and down, forward and backward, and sometimes even in circles! For human beings, the spiritual life is no straight line of unimpeded progress. It is, however, by God's unwavering goodness, always undergirded by grace. This is what gives us the hope and courage to persevere. Persevering on the journey is illustrated quite simply by the response a monk once made to a curious person's question, "What do you do up there in that monastery anyway?" The monk replied, "We take a few steps, then we fall down. Then we get up, take another step, and fall down again. And then we get up…." As someone has observed, "It is not falling in the water that drowns us, but staying there."

Precisely because God is so gracious and generous toward us, in the face of all our waywardness, the Christian life is especially marked by gratitude and trust. Gratitude is the hallmark of the heart that knows its Redeemer personally and intimately. Grasping the true significance of God's gift overwhelms the soul with thanksgiving. And a thankful life is naturally a generous life, desiring ways to give something back to God, however small the gesture may seem.

The grace of God also teaches us to trust God's goodness and power. Only divine love is strong enough to transform the most unlovely of us into companions of our living Lord. Grace enables our cynical, burned-out spirits to see life with new eyes—eyes fresh with wonder like a child's. We continue to see evil, sin, and pain in the world. In fact, we see these things more clearly and feel them more acutely. But we see them encompassed by God's presence, purpose, and greater power of love. When we begin to see with the eyes of faith, we can accept God's power to heal, redeem, and transform each of us personally and all of us together.

The letter of Ephesians describes Paul's prison circumstances in this light. The apostle knew firsthand the suffering of persecution. He is portrayed writing this letter as "an ambassador in chains" (6:20), imprisoned for his faith yet feeling only deep affection and gratitude for the church, desiring above all that his new Christian flock might know the hope and inheritance to which it was called. Paul knew that God's power is made perfect in our weakness (2 Cor. 12:9) and that new life is unleashed through the suffering of crucifixion. It would be perfectly consistent for him to pray that the Ephesians would come to know "what is the immeasurable greatness of [God's] power for us who believe" (1:19).

Certainly the Apostle Paul knew from experience God's power to bring life out of death. His experience of the risen Lord turned him from persecutor to proclaimer of Christ. He perceived that his life as a Pharisee, "righteous under the law," was a form of spiritual death.

He knew the taste of life in Christ, the spiritual freedom of one who had received "grace upon grace." He saw that since he did not have to earn salvation by good works, he could give himself joyfully to good works as an offering of gratitude.

A Life of Continued Conversion

In essence, the writer of Ephesians comprehends the spiritual life as a life of conversion—conversion from falsehood to truth, from bondage to liberty, from death to life. Moreover, it is not just a one-time conversion, although Paul himself had a profound and specific conversion experience on the road to Damascus. The Christian life is one of continual conversion, daily turning from the old way of life to the new way we have come to know in Christ. That is why the writer urges the Ephesian converts to "lead a life worthy of the calling to which you have been called, with all humility and gentleness, with patience, bearing with one another in love, making every effort to maintain the unity of the Spirit in the bond of peace" (4:1-3).

Conversion is part of the process of maturing toward the full stature of Christ. The Ephesians have already received grace so that they no longer follow "the course of this world" (2:2). But they still need reminders not to "live as the Gentiles live" in greed and impurity. They need to hear about speaking truth to one another, working honestly, and using words to build one another up. "Put away from you all bitterness and wrath and anger and wrangling and slander, together with all malice," he says (4:31). This is not what they have learned of Christ! "You were taught to put away your former way of life, your old self…and to clothe yourselves with the new self, created according to the likeness of God in true righteousness and holiness" (4:20-24). What does the new life look like but to "be kind to one another, tenderhearted, forgiving one another, as God in Christ has forgiven you" (4:32)?

Like the Ephesians, we are "in process" in our faith. We have already received grace in more ways than we can name or even be aware of. Yet we also need to be reminded regularly of what a Christian life

> *The adventure with God is not a destination but a journey. The never-ending journey begins when you open the door and invite the Presence to come into your consciousness in an abiding way. Beginning the journey is like a wedding that takes places at a definable time; but the journey itself is like a marriage—it takes time to know and understand each other.*
>
> —Ben Campbell Johnson

looks and acts like. It takes practice to become "imitators of God." It takes freedom from self-interest to "live in love, as Christ loved us and gave himself up for us" (5:1-2). We need a great deal of support, encouragement, and practice in "clothing ourselves with the new self." Seeking God's continued grace for our practice is critical. But this is also where we discover that the community of faith is crucial to our sanctification.

The New Community

We cannot travel this path into new life alone, and we are not expected to. The risen Christ, who promised to be with us "to the end of the age," travels with us. But often it is through his body, the church, that we experience his presence with us most powerfully. We do not always experience the church this way, but it is undoubtedly what Jesus calls the church to be: a filling out of his presence in the world through the work of the Holy Spirit.

Ephesians makes it clear that the spiritual life is life in community as members of the body of Christ. It must be so because such life in community expresses the reconciliation and peace Christ died to give to us. Please read Ephesians 2:11-22 in connection with this discussion. The writer of Ephesians wishes the reader to understand that Paul, a Jew, is speaking here to Greek Gentiles. The cultural divide between Jews and Gentiles in his day was enormous, scarcely to be bridged by the best imagination or goodwill. While commerce might occur between them in a civil way, Jews perceived no connection with Gentiles at the level of religion. Gentiles had no part in the covenant promise. Yet Paul clearly preaches that in Jesus Christ, the wall of hostility and division between them has been dissolved. In his own body, Jesus has reconciled the two peoples into one, "that he might create in himself one new humanity" reconciled to one another and to God.

The community of faith in Jesus Christ is now the temple where God dwells: "In him the whole structure is joined together and grows into a holy temple in the Lord; in whom you also are built together spiritually into a dwelling place for God" (2:21-22). Indeed, the gifts

No one can develop a mature spirituality alone. To be a Christian is to be called into community. It is to become a functioning part of the body of Christ.

—Steve Harper

of the Spirit are given to individual members of the body only to build up the strength, integrity, and witness of the church. Gifts are "to equip the saints for the work of ministry, for building up the body of Christ, until all of us come to the unity of the faith and of the knowledge of the Son of God" (4:11-13).

The Christian spiritual life cannot be lived apart from community. Elizabeth O'Connor writes, "This is the most creative and difficult work to which any of us will ever be called. There is no higher achievement in all the world than to be a person in community, and this is the call of every Christian."[2] It is in the various communities of the church (including our families) that we should be able to share love, forgiveness, reconciliation, and a unity of spirit deeper than our surface differences. Naturally, we do not always experience these things in our congregations or families. Sin continues to have its hold on us, and it is hard to see that the victory of love has already been won. Yet the church is called to be the very community where we learn to live out the love of Christ in spite of and through our conflicts. We need to allow Christ to be our peace and to find our unity in him, since we will never achieve unity through our opinions!

Our task, ultimately, is to practice living the Christian life wherever we are. To enable this practice God gives us the great gift of grace. But we begin by receiving particular means of grace from the church to help us understand and live our faith. Historically these have included hearing God's Word preached and receiving the sacraments. The means of grace extend to praying in community, serving one another in humble love, receiving mutual guidance, and learning to discern the movement of the Spirit together.

The adventure upon which we are embarked in this course of experiential learning, as a small community of faith within the church, will help us begin to explore some of these means of grace both personally and corporately.

DAILY EXERCISES

Read the second chapter, "The Nature of the Christian Spiritual Life," before you begin these exercises. Keep your journal at hand to record reflections. Remember to quiet yourself, release your concerns to God, and open both mind and heart to the work of the Spirit. During this week, you will be reading from the Book of Ephesians and reflecting on the gift of God's grace in your life.

EXERCISE 1

Read Ephesians 1:1-14. The opening of this letter is like a downpour of blessing. Pay attention to the expressions of praise and prayer, allowing the many spiritual blessings with which God has blessed us to soak into the soil of your mind and heart. Which aspects of what God has done for us in Christ are most important for you? Reflect in your journal. Note any aspects that remain a mystery for you. Take time to offer your praise to God and to list other ways God has blessed and sustained you with grace.

EXERCISE 2

Read Ephesians 2:11-22. In your world of family, friends, church, or community, where is there a "dividing wall" with "hostility between us"? Offer the situation to God in prayer. Imagine Christ standing in peace between you and the one with whom you're in conflict, opening a way to live together in love. Write or draw what you see and feel about the gift Christ gives. What difference could it make, and what action does it call for on your part?

EXERCISE 3

Read the prayer in Ephesians 3:14-19 several times slowly as a way of internalizing its promise for you. First, read it as a prayer for you personally. Then pray it as a prayer for your family; next, as a prayer for your church; finally, as a prayer for the whole human family. After each reading, reflect in your journal on how the prayer opens your way

of seeing God's transforming grace in you. Take to memory a favorite phrase and carry it prayerfully in your heart throughout the day.

EXERCISE 4

Read Ephesians 5:6-20. These verses describe what it means to emerge from darkness and "live as children of light." As you read, reflect on where you find yourself saying "yes," "no," or "yes, but" to the counsel of these verses. In your journal, record a letter to the writer of Ephesians. Describe what you are learning about living as a child of light in our time and about the challenges for which we need guidance today. Read what have you written and see if God is speaking to you through your own words.

EXERCISE 5

Read Ephesians 6:10-17. To "take up the whole armor of God, so that you may be able...to stand firm" means to remain "rooted and grounded in love" (3:17). What inner and outer forces routinely uproot your faith, sap your inner strength, or undermine your courage to "stand firm" in Christ's love? What personal and communal practices nourish your roots in love and strengthen the life of God in you? What "armor" do you need to "take up"? Who can assist you in standing firm?

Remember to review your journal entries for the week in preparation for the group meeting.

Part 1, Week 3
The Flow and the Means of Grace

As we have said, the Christian life is possible only by the grace of God. Every awakening to God within us is the result of the Holy Spirit's action in and upon us. We are awakened to God and sustained in God by the initiative that the Holy One takes toward us and on our behalf. Just as life is pure gift, unrequested and beyond our power, so the spiritual life is offered to us from the heart of God long before we ever think of our walk with Christ.

The letter to the Ephesians proclaims that God's grace was flowing out to us before the foundation of the world. At the very beginning of creation we were chosen in Christ to live in love and peace with God (Eph. 1:4). God's grace precedes, follows, surrounds, and sustains us always. It is a constant and completely consistent gift. We cannot stop, alter, or change it. We are eternally cradled in God's abundant and life-giving grace.

While the initiative and the invitation to companionship are entirely God's, response lies with us. God gives us grace to respond to the awakening call of the Holy Spirit, but we can choose to turn away and refuse the invitation. Or we can choose, by the Spirit's help, to walk in faithfulness and harmony with God. By doing so we claim our true and full inheritance as children of God. Choosing to open ourselves to grace means receiving life's greatest gift and walking the path of spiritual abundance.

God's grace is not divided into bits and pieces,…but grace takes us up completely into God's favor for the sake of Christ, our intercessor and mediator, so that the gifts [of the Spirit] may begin their work in us.

—Martin Luther

This week we will explore further the nature of grace, the flow of grace, and the means of grace. How do we receive this gift for our redemption, joy, and fruitfulness as disciples? In what ways does grace shape and mold our lives as we move from being strangers to intimate companions of God?

The Nature of Grace

In my first year of school, I contracted scarlet fever. I became very ill and did not return to school for an entire year. For weeks I was delirious and unable to be out of bed. Then when I became strong enough to sit up, my mother prepared a special place for me to get well. We lived in a modified sod house with walls nearly three feet thick. Each window had a large, boxlike well inside the house, where my mother often kept plants through the winter.

When I was strong enough to sit up, my mother made a little nest of pillows for me in a south-facing window well. Then she carried me from my bed to this place of healing comfort. Perhaps she intuited the healing virtues of sunlight. Certainly, she knew I would be safe, warm, and near to her. While the illness was long and in many ways devastating, one of my happiest childhood memories is being nestled there in the light and warmth of the sun. I could look outside and see my father working. I could see and hear my mother nearby, cooking, mending, and doing what mothers of growing families did.

The winter sunlight, pouring through that south window, warming, giving light and hastening my healing, is for me a wonderful image of God's grace. The gift of grace is always present to give light, warmth, comfort, and healing.

The Christian concept of grace is rooted in scripture and always reflects God's redemptive love reaching out to us. The Bible tells the story of God's saving work on behalf of all people. This work is always undeserved, an expression of God's unconditional love for humankind. God offers love, redemption, covenant community, and companionship to each and all of us without precondition.

Christians see grace most clearly in God's act of self-giving through

The music of divine love plays uniquely in each person's life. Through individual personalities and personal life events, the goodness of God takes on a melody all its own. The song of God needs an instrument to give it shape and voice....We are all called to be instruments through which the melody of God takes shape. Through our lives God's love seeks to dance and make music for the world.

—Joyce Rupp

the person of Jesus Christ. In the suffering love and forgiveness of the cross, we perceive grace in all its fullness. Faith in Christ becomes the way we discover and apprehend this incredible gift (Rom. 5:1-2). From the beginning of creation we were meant to know ourselves as God's children, enjoying all of the benefits of our full inheritance (Eph. 1:5). Having lost our native inheritance through sin, we now receive these benefits through Jesus Christ. God's love and favor in Christ bestow them upon us.

The Flow of Grace

Our experience of grace represents a certain natural progression in the Christian life. Initially divine grace surrounds us without our conscious knowledge. We are simply immersed in God's unconditional, ever-present love. God works to protect us from spiritual danger and "woos" us in the unconscious infancy of our faith, calling us to be aware of grace. Once we have become fully conscious of a faith decision and choose to receive God's forgiving love in Jesus Christ, we experience the grace of justification. At this point the experience of grace helps us know that we belong not to ourselves but to our faithful Savior, Jesus Christ. We understand that righteousness before God is not something we earn; it can be received only as gift. As the Spirit builds on the foundation of justification, we gradually grow in holiness of life, or sanctification. This experience of grace leads us to bear the fruits of the Spirit and to exercise the gifts of the Spirit.

Creation is shot through with the self-gift of God. The divine life, the divine self-giving called grace, is the secret dynamism at the heart of creation.

—Maria Boulding

In one great strand of historic Christianity (the Wesleyan/ Methodist), these experiences of grace have been called prevenient (or preceding) grace, justifying grace, and sanctifying grace. They are understood to represent a certain "flow" or progression from our introduction to God's grace to our completion in it. We move from unawareness toward intentional cooperation with God that enables us to accept our justification and grow into Christian maturity. According to John Wesley, the fruit of justifying grace is the "blessed assurance" of belonging to Christ; and the fruit of sanctifying grace is growth in holiness and perfection in love.

However, progression from one expression of grace to another is not automatic or as methodical as it may sound. Many areas overlap throughout our lives. God's pervasive and persuasive grace always upholds us. And God is continually at work to help us accept fully the gift of our justification, as well as to shape us into the perfect design for which we were created. Thus various expressions of grace operate at the same time, yet it is always one and the same love spilling out eternally from the heart of God, sweeping over us even when we are unable to appreciate or receive God's activity on our behalf.

Divine grace continues to draw us from death toward life, to provide the healing and cleansing of forgiveness and restoration, and to offer the strength and courage to move toward a more perfect life. We may receive these spiritual gifts through the means of grace.

The Means of Grace

Recalling how my mother placed me in the sunny window well so I could recuperate from deadly illness helps me make sense of the means of grace. Placing ourselves in a position where we may benefit most from the life-giving light of God's love is the purpose of every means of grace. The means of grace are methods and practices we use to "put ourselves in God's way." They help us adopt a posture of receptivity.

Although we cannot manipulate or control what God will give us through various means of grace, we can trust that grace will be given and that what we receive will be tailored to our specific situation. For instance, we may be "caught" by a passage of scripture today that we have read for years without ever being challenged, nurtured, or formed by it. Suddenly a certain text or story comes alive for us, and we will never be the same.

Grace comes to us in many ways as we make our journey Godward. While the ways are countless, certain means of grace have been practiced almost universally in the history of the church. Some are as old as humankind. Even if many or all are known to you, they require disciplined practice to make them your own.

The traditional means of grace include worship, the sacraments of baptism and the Lord's Supper, prayer, fasting, scripture reading,

and community. Each is a well-tested means to receive and appropriate God's life-giving grace. The means of grace have no merit in themselves, but they can lead us toward wholeness and deeper communion with God.

Worship

Corporate worship is an essential means of grace for any serious traveler on the Christian way. Worship has been identified as humankind's most profound activity. Nothing that we can do equals the act of worship in significance for us, the world about us, or the God before whom we come to offer worship. To gather with others who seek God's will and way is in itself a marvelous way of placing ourselves in a position to receive grace.

Protestants generally affirm the two sacraments of baptism and the Lord's Supper as means of grace. In baptism we recognize that God's active love on our behalf precedes our birth and surrounds us eternally. The psalms declare that we would not exist were it not for God's grace (Pss. 119:73; 139:13). In the covenant of baptism we accept our adoption as God's children by grace and promise our faithful response. We are incorporated into the body of Christ and become a part of the church, the covenant community of faith (1 Cor. 12–13).

For most Christians, the Eucharist, or Lord's Supper, is the central act of worship. There we declare who God is and who we are in God's presence. At the table of the Lord all are needy and hungry; all are invited to come for healing and sustenance. No believer is turned aside; all equally receive God's unmerited forgiveness, peace, and presence. Our unity in humility with our Lord, who emptied himself in sacrificial love for us, spiritually unites us with one another in this meal. The grace of communion with Christ is simultaneously a grace of communion with one another in the fellowship of faith.

Prayer

Prayer is often recognized as the most central and profound means of grace. Prayer is native language to all of us, young and old, of every

> *The sure and general rule for all who groan for the salvation of God is this,— whenever opportunity serves, use all the means [of grace] which God has ordained; for who knows in which God will meet thee with the grace that bringeth salvation?*
>
> —John Wesley

race and creed. Prayer is a language we learn as we explore the mystery of life, often prompted by gratitude that craves expression or by pain that cries for relief. It is a language learned through questions without answers and life-giving discoveries that arise over the course of our journeys. It is a language learned while searching for guidance on the way and in response to direction clearly given.

While we may never have formally decided to pray or may forsake the way of prayer for a time, most of us have some experience with this means of grace. For many people, prayer is as natural as breathing; for others, it requires intense effort and concentration. For some, prayer is joyful companionship with Jesus Christ; for others, it is a struggle to keep the relationship with God vital. Some nurture their relationship with God through prayerful living; others are so consumed with living that they have little time or energy left for prayer. Regardless of our situation, prayer remains a primary means of grace.

A loving, living relationship with God is impossible without prayer. We cannot know the mind and heart of Christ, receive God's direction, hear God's voice, or respond to God's call without this means of grace. We may enter God's kingdom without the benefit of some of the means of grace but not without prayer. Prayer is so important that Jesus left even the needy crowd to pray (Mark 6:31). His entire life and ministry were set in the context of prayer. Those who choose to follow him can do no better than to take up his example.

The disciple on an intentional spiritual journey will discover prayer to be an indispensable means of nurturing intimacy and companionship with the living Christ. A classic writer of Christian spirituality once noted that prayer is the mortar that holds our life together. Prayer is really not so much about us as it is about God. Prayer is simply our response to the invitation of grace to come home and live with God all the days of our lives, in this world and the next.

Richard Foster lists twenty-one kinds of prayer! Others identify fewer types. The number of forms is less important than the faithful practice of whatever form you are led to. Those who have gone before us in faith have left much wise counsel on how to pray. The third part of this resource will look at prayer in more depth as a means of grace.

Fasting

Dallas Willard identifies fasting as a spiritual discipline of abstinence.[1] From ancient times onward, fasting has been understood as a practice that opens our lives to receive God's gifts. Fasting has had two primary purposes for those seeking to walk with God: first, repentance; and second, preparation to receive God's strength for faithful living.[2] Fasting has often been connected with prayer to form a powerful way of receiving the gifts of grace.

Fasting suggests a laying aside of our personal appetites, desires, and even felt needs in order to hear more clearly the call of God. It is a way of emptying our hands and our lives so that they may be filled with God. Food, entertainment, sex, possessions, activity—all good gifts in their time and place—can be focused upon to the exclusion of God. You might ask yourself what now fills your life to the point of crowding God out. The answer will likely lead you to the kind of fast that could be a special means of grace for you.

When beginning to fast for the first time, you do well to move slowly. Try a short fast to see how you respond. If you have physical problems, it is best to seek medical advice when fasting from food.

A fast can be made more meaningful if it is shared with another person or a praying community. It is important that each person in the group agree on the purpose of the fast and to the kind of fast being undertaken. Take time to discuss these matters. After such decisions have been made, you will be ready to move on to the details, such as duration and starting and ending times.

Many contemporary Christians report fasting to be a wonderful means of grace that brings clarity and direction to the spiritual life. Some people fast one day a week; others, for special occasions only. You will want to pray for guidance when you consider fasting as a means of grace for yourself and those with whom you journey.

Scripture

Next to prayer, scripture reading is the most profound means of grace for most persons on an intentional spiritual journey. To read and to meditate upon the scriptures every day raises our awareness of God's presence in our lives in remarkable ways. The transforming experience of living daily with scripture will, over the course of a lifetime, shape our hearts and minds more and more into the image of Christ.

Scripture records God's mighty acts, including creation and God's ongoing relationship with humankind. It is a record of God's self-revelation. For Christians, this revelation finds its apex in the Incarnation when God chose to become flesh in the person of Jesus of Nazareth. Some have said that God has given us three books of revelation: nature, history, and the Bible. Most Christians would probably agree that the Bible speaks most clearly of God's person and purpose. The second part of this resource will focus directly on the spiritually formative power of the Bible.

Other Considerations

The community of faith is also a means of grace. Since the entire fifth week of Part 1 is devoted to Christian community as a means of grace, it is mentioned here only to note its importance.

Sometimes we speak of the means of grace as spiritual disciplines. The word *discipline* may have harsh connotations for us. True spiritual disciplines are never externally imposed. Rather, they are "practices that help us consciously to develop the spiritual dimensions of our lives. Like an artist who wishes to develop painting skills, or an athlete who desires a strong and flexible body for the game, a person of faith freely chooses to adopt certain life patterns, habits, and commitments in order to grow spiritually."[3]

Spiritual disciplines are practices that have proven to be effective in opening the windows of our lives to the refreshing, life-giving breath of God. There are many spiritual practices, but none has merit in itself. The value lies in one simple test: how effectively the disciplines turn our lives toward God and open our hearts to the Holy Spirit. Countless faithful witnesses to Christ assure us that we may trust the Spirit to guide us to those means of grace that will be most transforming for us. May we have the faith and courage to follow.

DAILY EXERCISES

Read the third chapter, "The Flow and the Means of Grace." Keep your journal at hand to record your reflections. Remember to take time for silence, turn your attention to God, and open yourself to the guidance of the Holy Spirit before each exercise. This week's exercises will guide you to reflect on the movements of grace in your life and the means by which God has touched you.

EXERCISE 1

Read Luke 15:11-32. Jesus tells a parable about the loving father of two sons. With which of the sons do you identify, and how? Reflect on how the younger son "came to himself." When have you come to yourself, recognized your need, and begun a return to God? How have you experienced the seeking love of God's prevenient grace?

EXERCISE 2

Read Luke 15:11-32 again. Jesus' parable portrays a forgiving father who is <u>foolishly</u> in love with his two sons. Reflect on the father's response to his younger son's return, even "while he was still far off." When have you experienced such compassion, acceptance, and forgiveness (whether you were far from God in a way more like that of the younger or the elder son)? How did you respond? How have you experienced the saving love of God's justifying grace?

EXERCISE 3

Read Luke 15:11-32 again. Jesus seems to have told the parable primarily to address the "elder brother" tendencies in the Pharisees and in us, confronting our smallness of heart. How do you think you would have responded to the return of the younger son? Where do you believe that you are growing in your ability to love and forgive, and where do you still feel blocked? In other words, where are you experiencing the call and challenge of God's sanctifying grace?

EXERCISE 4

Read Luke 15:11-32 once more. Jesus' parable is full of actions that serve as outward and visible signs of each character's inward and spiritual condition. Go back and note each action of the father as an outward means of expressing the inward grace of his welcoming heart, his readiness to forgive and fully restore the son's wasted life. Through what means of grace (traditional or nontraditional) has God touched you, restored you, and encouraged your growth? Reflect on your baptism as a means by which God runs to us while we are "still far off" to embrace and kiss us and to clothe us in newness. Reflect on your experience of Holy Communion as a means by which God continues to celebrate our movement from death to life.

EXERCISE 5

Read Luke 15:11-32 a final time. Look at Jesus' parable as an unfinished story about a family on a journey of healing and wholeness. Use your imagination to continue the story from the perspective of one of the three characters or as an imaginary observer, such as a neighbor watching through a window. For instance, what does the father say to the younger son the day after the party about what it means to be back in the family? Does the elder son remain resentful, or does the father's love prevail in transforming his attitude? Do the sons grow to share the life and love of their father? How does your way of completing the story reveal your assumptions about God, people, and yourself?

Remember to review your journal entries for the week in preparation for the group meeting.

Sharing Journeys of Faith

We began this small-group study with some reflections on the image of journey as a metaphor for life and growth in faith. A younger generation apparently has tired of hearing the term *journey* applied to human emotional and spiritual maturation; yet it remains a remarkably apt metaphor. In a very deep sense, life is pilgrimage. Its earthly expression moves from a beginning to a distinct destination. It traverses a great deal of terrain psychologically, intellectually, and physically. There are certain markers on the journey, common stages we go through in the process of development. But there are also unique experiences that mark our individuality, sometimes in indelible ways. The timing of one's particular life path is always deeply personal, directed by many forces beyond one's control—family, circumstances, environment, location in history and place—as well as by the choices one makes in relation to these forces.

It helps to recognize, at least to some extent, the character and contours of the spiritual journey. When we see some of the main routes and major turning points along the life-path, we may begin to articulate their meaning for us and, if we choose, to share that meaning with others on the path.

A helpful way to become more conscious of the shape of the spiritual path over time is to look at the lives of some great and faithful

Powerful stories throughout history… teach us what it means to be a follower of Jesus. Our own life stories and the stories of our communities of faith serve as icons that help to shape our ways of being and doing.

—Dwight W. Vogel and
Linda J. Vogel

forebears in the faith. What motivated their search for God? How might we characterize their spiritual journeys? What were some significant turning points, and how did they interpret the meaning of these for themselves?

Models of the Faith Journey

Perhaps Augustine of Hippo (354–430 C.E.) was the first to write a true spiritual autobiography. His *Confessions* is a remarkable testament to searching self-examination, and it remains engaging reading for Christians sixteen centuries later! Augustine had a formidable intellect, so it is not surprising that his quest for God took the form of an intellectual search for truth. While his writing is filled with passion, deep feeling, and spiritual depth, it is the sheer power of his mind to penetrate, analyze, and describe the character of his inner life that is so impressive. For a man of a "prepsychological age," Augustine had an astute capacity to diagnose his own mind and heart in a way that astonishes modern readers.

Augustine's personal obsession with finding truth led him through several philosophies popular in his day. But gradually, his mind led him away from the doctrines of the Manichees and Neoplatonists. He complained that the Manichean orators continually talked about truth, "although the truth was nowhere to be found in them." Addressing God directly, as he does throughout the *Confessions*, Augustine exclaimed, "Truth, truth: how in my inmost being the very marrow of my mind sighed for you!"[1] In the very next paragraph he acknowledges, "But my hunger and thirst were not even for the greatest of your works, but for you, my God, because you are Truth itself *with whom there can be no change, no swerving from your course* (James 1:17)."[2] Although not capturing all the complexity of Augustine's journey, it would be fair to say that his path to God was one of intense inquiry, a path through the gift of the mind.

Martin Luther, twelve centuries later, embodies another kind of journey. Luther, who was (ironically) part of an Augustinian order as a young man, was driven by a different need in his search for God.

Possessed of a vibrant, expansive, tempestuous personality and an agonized conscience, Luther felt inwardly that he could never be sure of his salvation. A common maxim of his time was "Do that which is in you to do, and leave the rest to God." Even though the maxim was intended as a counsel of comfort to help overly scrupulous monks find release from self-imposed efforts to win divine grace, Luther felt he could never be sure that he had done all that was in him to do! What was meant as a word of grace was, for him, an impossible demand and a heavy weight of judgment. The need to be righteous before God was like an albatross around his neck.

The deep issue for Luther was that while he knew of God's grace intellectually, he could not assimilate it emotionally. Young Martin grew up as a child of medieval German lore. Influenced by old beliefs in capricious water sprites and malevolent forest spirits, he harbored something of a terrorized soul. Here are his own words from the Preface to his *Latin Writings*: "Though I lived as a monk without reproach, I felt that I was a sinner before God with an extremely disturbed conscience. I could not believe that he was placated by my satisfaction. I did not love, yes, I hated the righteous God who punishes sinners, and secretly…I was angry with God."[3]

Interestingly, both Augustine and Luther had conversion experiences that were connected to passages in Paul's letter to the Romans. For Luther, the passage was Romans 1:17, in particular the phrase, "The one who is righteous will live by faith." The dawning recognition that righteousness is a gift we receive simply by faith was, for Luther, an enormous release from the emotional burden of believing that he was somehow required to fulfill what he considered an impossible expectation. Listen again to his own words: "I felt that I was altogether born again and had entered paradise itself through open gates.…And I extolled my sweetest word with a love as great as the hatred with which I had before hated the word 'righteousness of God.'"[4]

Luther's spiritual journey was not so much a quest for intellectual truth as a quest for heartfelt assurance of God's grace. It was the path of an anxious heart in search of comfort. Not infrequently, a fearful or deeply wounded heart impels us toward God.

We see quite another kind of journey in the life of Mother Teresa of Calcutta, a beloved saint of our own era. She had the capacity to see Christ in the faces of the poor. Born to Albanian parents who named her Agnes, the woman later known as Mother Teresa had no great intellect or any apparent deep emotional need. Agnes was a simple and rather unpromising nun in the eyes of some of her superiors. But she felt deeply called to a very focused task: that of caring for the poorest of the poor—the sick and dying of Calcutta's ghettos who were despised and forgotten by everyone else. Mother Teresa had a vision of giving herself to Christ by loving each person created in God's image, no matter how unloved or unlovely: "Whoever the poorest of the poor are, they are Christ for us—Christ under the guise of human suffering."[5] Her mission was not to save as many as possible or to change social structures. It was to love one person at a time— each a beautiful soul, a child of God, a person of unique and irreplaceable value to God. "I feel called to serve individuals, to love each human being. My calling is not to judge institutions....If I thought in terms of crowds, I would never begin my work. I believe in the personal touch of one to one."[6]

Mother Teresa and the Missionaries of Charity she founded were driven Godward by a hunger for holiness expressed in relationships of service to the needy, what John Wesley called "social holiness." It is a path to God marked by active love. While rooted in worship and contemplation, this journey is neither primarily intellectual nor emotional but essentially physical. With the body one lifts and soothes and touches the sorely wounded of the world. Here is a path to God through the gift of the physical being.

Still a different kind of journey is represented in the life and ministry of Evelyn Underhill, another spiritual giant of the modern era. Widely read during the first half of the twentieth century, her prolific writings on the spiritual life are a relatively unknown treasure of Christendom today. Evelyn was born in England and raised in the Anglican Church. By the early 1920s, this brilliant woman was earning a reputation as an expert in the field of mystical theology, yet her own spiritual life felt to her like an intolerable burden of loneliness and isolation. She could not find herself fully at home either in the Church of England or in the Roman Catholic Church. Sharing her prayer life with no one, Evelyn was "cut off from sacramental life and the possibility of community that might have sustained her."[7]

A major turning point came with Evelyn's first retreat at an Anglican retreat house called Pleshey. There in the quiet beauty of the Essex countryside, Evelyn began to experience a sense of being at home in the church of her birth for the first time. She wrote to her spiritual director Baron von Hügel, "The whole house seems soaked in love and prayer. To my surprise a regimen of daily communion and four services a day with silence between was the most easy unstrained and natural life I had ever lived."[8] Interestingly enough, this retreat had the effect not of leading her into further withdrawal from others but of curing her solitude: "I lost there my last bit of separateness....My old religious life now looks...thin and solitary."[9]

It was not long before Underhill began conducting spiritual life retreats for others at Pleshey. A gifted spiritual guide and retreat leader, she gave more than a decade of her life to this ministry for which she is as much beloved as for her many books. She understood from experience that a true retreat reconnects us with our living Source, so that we find ourselves more truly connected with one another. Time spent in worship, silence, and communion refreshes our spirits at a depth no other activity can match.

Evelyn's path to God was marked by hunger for union with Reality (her favorite name for God). She journeyed home by way of contemplation. Contemplation is essentially the wordless path to union with God. Yet her life was filled with writing, lecturing, and active service to the homeless in her community. Just as Mother Teresa's path was primarily active but rooted in contemplation, Evelyn's was primarily contemplative but expressed in a balance of activities. Like the journey of Teresa of Avila or Thomas Merton, Evelyn Underhill's journey was a remarkable blend of action and contemplation. A mystic at heart, she championed the path of interior quiet and listening.

Finding Connections

To oversimplify the matter, these four figures represent in turn a primary path to God through mind, heart, body, and spirit. Many other persons of faith could illustrate these basic pathways just as well. These particular figures are offered to help "prime the pump" for thinking about your own spiritual path. Do you tend to approach God by struggling with theological issues and intellectual questions? Through conflicted feelings and deep wounds? With a compelling desire to love others in simple service? Through the yearning for inward peace and a sense of being at home in a spiritual tradition? Is there some other path you would identify as your own?

God draws each one of us to the heart of life in a time and manner uniquely suited to our own nature and circumstance. Your journey and mine cannot be the same, even if we are identical twins! Yet our many journeys share remarkable commonalities, points where we find comfort in human identification and common ground. The signs of God's grace at work in us are often strikingly similar: perhaps a sense of being overwhelmed by prayer answered beyond our best hopes; the experience of anguish over prayer not answered the way we had hoped, yet in retrospect answered in an unexpected and perhaps deeper way; the intuition that God has called us to a task we felt was beyond our gifts or capacity, yet through faith and perseverance, we discovered it to be a genuine call for which God equipped us.

I hope these suggestions have whetted your appetite for looking at your own spiritual journey more closely. Where or how did you start out? Who most influenced your spiritual growth? When did you discover a new sense of direction, and where did it take you? What major experiences have shaped your journey, and how? These are just a few of the questions that can help you attend to the course of your spiritual development.

Telling Your Story

One way to observe and tell your faith journey is to write a simple spiritual autobiography. It need not be as profound or comprehen-

It is absolutely crucial…to keep in constant touch with what is going on in your own life's story and to pay close attention to what is going on in the stories of others' lives. If God is present anywhere, it is in those stories that God is present.

—Frederick Buechner

sive as Augustine's *Confessions*, but it should be as honest and clear-sighted as you can make it. Such a document would be for your eyes only. Begin with your earliest memories of anything related to your faith, and carry the story forward to the present. Note the influence of your religious tradition or lack of it, your family's way of relating to faith, and mentors and peers along the way. Pay attention to the deep motivations behind your searching and finding. Look at the balance between your need for solitude and your desire for community, the inward aspects of your faith and their outward expressions. Describe your experience of prayer. Notice the significant turns, conversions, and changes along the way. See if you can identify a "primary path" in your story.

You might also choose to draw your spiritual journey. Take a large sheet of blank paper, or tape several together for adequate space. Draw a line that represents your life, showing the ups and downs, turns, circles, or whatever pattern seems right to you. Mark particularly significant events with symbols that represent what they have meant in your faith life. Be creative with this process, using colors to express your feelings at various times or gluing onto the paper other materials that expand and interpret your symbols.

You may prefer to write a poem or a series of poems that give voice to the more interior and intangible aspects of your spiritual life. See if you can identify several experiences or circumstances that have been keys to your spiritual path in life. They might be things such as a significant move in childhood; a traumatic, challenging, or inspiring time in adolescence or young adulthood; the loss of a deep relationship; a change of career direction; an experience of another culture. Allow the feelings, images, and metaphors connected with the experience to surface in your reflection. Write a poem about each one that expresses for you the spiritual dimension of that experience. Often our experience of God does not lend itself to descriptive prose writing. Art, music, dance, and poetry are the language of the soul.

Remembering our stories helps us perceive ways God has shared in our personal history. We remember incredible answers to prayers and grace moments, times when God helped us through what seemed impossible crises.
—Richard Morgan

DAILY EXERCISES

Read the fourth chapter, "Sharing Journeys of Faith," before beginning these exercises. Keep a journal of your reflections. Settle yourself in openness and expectancy before God as you begin each one. These exercises will help us consider various models of the faith journey and prepare us to articulate our own spiritual stories.

EXERCISE 1

Read Galatians 1:11–2:1. We see that Paul's transformation in Christ was not immediate but took place over time. In time, he received a revelation of Christ, went apart to seek understanding, conferred with the other apostles, and worked out his calling in community.

Review the section called "Models of the Faith Journey." With which person described do you most identify? Why? What affinity or resistance do you feel toward each of the four persons? Share your feelings with God and listen. Can you name another "model of faith" with whom you particularly identify? Why? Note your reflections.

EXERCISE 2

Read Mark 12:28-30. Jesus reaffirms that the first commandment is to "love the Lord your God" with your whole being—heart, soul, mind, and strength. Which of these four aspects represents your primary path to God? For example, has your search for a deeper relationship with God been more related to your heart (affection and hunger for love), soul (intuition and desire for union with God), mind (inquiry and search for truth), or strength (action and serving the common good)? Which motivation is strongest? weakest? Has your motivation or manner of searching changed over the course of your journey? Capture your reflections in your notebook.

EXERCISE 3

Read Psalm 116. Complete verse 1 for yourself: "I love the Lord, because...." Write your own expression of what connects you with God and what God has done for you. Then take a few minutes to read back through your written reflections on the exercises from the first three weeks. Try to name the pivotal moments in your spiritual history, chapters in your story, and even a title for your unfinished story. What would be the name of the chapter you are now writing for God? Give thanks to God for the uniqueness of your journey.

EXERCISE 4

Read Psalm 107. This psalm, like many other psalms, tells faith stories of people. Were you to add to this psalm a stanza for your story, how would it read? Spend some time today and tomorrow thinking about the various ways you might describe or tell your spiritual life story. Choose a way that suits you to portray, express, or picture your story. For example, you might "draw" your journey, using an image or metaphor that captures the uniqueness of your spiritual history. You might write a poem or a brief autobiography that tells of formative influences and experiences. You could sketch a graph of high and low moments, diagram the paths you have followed, draw a "tree" of the people through whom God has shaped you, or make a collage of significant images. Be creative; let the Spirit guide you. Take these two days to work on your spiritual life story. Then be prepared to share your journey with the group in whatever way is comfortable for you. You will have ten to fifteen minutes to share whatever you choose about your story.

EXERCISE 5

Read Psalm 136. Spend a few minutes giving thanks for the steadfast love of God in your life and all the ways you have experienced it. Finish the work you began yesterday. Invite the Spirit into your efforts!

Remember to review your journal entries for the week in preparation for the group meeting.

Part 1, Week 5
Living As Covenant Community

*L*ife-threatening situations often reveal the character of people involved in them. My first adult bout with life-threatening illness revealed as much about the character of those around me as it did about my own. The first person to offer support, outside of family, was a member of the covenant group that I had been part of for more than a decade. While I was struggling to stay conscious, I knew that along with my family my covenant group had thrown a cloak of love and prayer around me. At this critical time, when I had great difficulty with rational thought or prayer, trusted colleagues were praying for and with me. To know that I was held in the light of God's presence by the prayers of God's faithful servants gave me great peace and comfort. The unqualified support of those in covenant relationship with us is but one important benefit of community. There are many more; some are hinted at in the following paragraphs, and others can be discovered only as you explore the richness of living in mutual covenant with others.

Christians are called into a community of mutual servanthood, and covenant groups are an ideal place to live out this calling. Each of us has a unique gift to offer to others. Small communities of covenant commitment are places where we can share and strengthen our gifts. In this group we discover our need for acceptance, growth, and accountability; here we may also see that need met.

We were not created to live in isolation ....While no one questions the need for periods of solitude and refreshment in our lives, faith tends to thrive most readily when shared and experienced with others.

—Mary Lou Redding

Tilden H. Edwards says that community is "what everyone wants but almost no one is able to sustain well for long."[1] Edwards is right. To form a genuine community takes intentional and committed effort. That is precisely what a covenant represents. Covenant community does not happen by accident. To sustain such community requires consistent attention and commitment. Perhaps that is why there are so few of us in long-standing covenant communities today. We may not know how to begin such a community, and we are often reluctant to pay the price of time and effort to sustain it.

But we do yearn for the benefits of covenant community, for meaningful relationships with others who intentionally set their faces and life journeys toward God. It is lonely to be serious about the spiritual life in our time. Those who are aware of their hunger for a deeper life with God often feel isolated and misunderstood. We need others to help us see and hear ourselves clearly. We need others to explore with us the edges of our fear and faith. We grow spiritually only in and through our relationship with God and with others.

We know that Jesus' life revealed a vital balance of solitude and community, the kind of wholeness and balance that we yearn to experience in our own lives. The twelve disciples became a trusted and beloved community, even though it was made up of persons like us with less than perfect understanding or character. Jesus valued community, finding both time and occasion to cultivate personal relationships with those who were his followers and closest friends (John 15:15). He also valued solitude, finding time and place to cultivate his inner life and relationship with God. Jesus was whole, with precisely the balance and rhythm of life we so desire for ourselves.

But how do we begin? Where do we look for such community? Who will companion us, and will we be compatible? Will we have the courage to form a community built on shared covenant? Can such a community be sustained in our culture? Do I personally have the capacity to live in covenant with others? What will it cost, and what are the rewards of covenant living? These are some of the questions that will undoubtedly come to us as we think about our participation in more intimate Christian community.

of our life in faith will we be able to accept this dimension of Christian community. Again, it is important that any group seeking to fashion a working covenant take the time to explore the meaning and benefit of accountability, feelings about it, and how it will be practiced in the group.

Naturally, an element in every search for community is the desire to experience the joy of mutual caring, sharing, and discovery in the Christian journey. When Christians form a covenant community, they have every right to expect unparalleled support and acceptance. But such support and acceptance do not happen automatically. Early discussion and planning can prompt each member to be alert to opportunities for care and ministry to one another.

Weighing Costs and Benefits

Now, what of the cost? Is covenant community worth the price? In our society we have become such bargain hunters that we are reluctant to "buy in" to anything that may ask too much and offer too little. A careful analysis of cost and benefit is a worthy endeavor. Saints who have traveled the path of life in community before us encourage us to count the cost and encourage us as well with report of the rewards. The cost includes relinquishing some portion of our autonomy, giving up a false and contrived self, giving our time, practicing a cultivated and careful listening, and being willing to do the hard work of holding one another close and accountable in love.

What are the benefits? Those who have journeyed on ahead of us would answer, "A taste of heaven." They are joined by the voices of many today who have experienced firsthand the fruits of covenant community. One participant in a women's group described the people she had come to love with a simple sentence: "They are like an extended family, one that you don't have to keep explaining yourself to over and over again."[5] Another man who felt constructively challenged by his group described the benefits this way: "The group makes me uncomfortable every week because I'm being challenged to give a little more and grow a little more and become a little more honest

with myself and a little more intimate with God or other people. And that's what I need very much."[6]

God has called us into being as a community and our life as a community, though fraught with struggles and failures, is a powerful act of revelation, testimony, and service.

—Rule of the
Society of St. John
the Evangelist

Entrusting oneself—body and soul—into the care of a loving, faithful community is one of the most rewarding and blessed experiences possible. To know that there is a praying, listening community ready to help me discern God's will and way in every eventuality of life offers me great assurance. To be reminded that every day my life is held close to the loving heart of God by those who seek only God's best for me is a wonderful gift. And to have the protection of a community that has the courage and faith to offer correction when I stray or a helping hand when I stumble is pure gift. Simply knowing that this caring and committed community stands with me, holds me, cares for me, and will not let me fall is enormous security and blessing in a world where such gifts are rare.

Morton Kelsey says, "Walking with others on their spiritual pilgrimages is an art."[7] How might each of us become an artist helping to create the beautiful mosaic of a living, growing, and life-giving community? Great artists have many native skills, but their work is the result of disciplined effort and a willingness to try and try again. Each of us has the capacity to live in covenant with other children of God. And each of us has native gifts to foster faithful living within the community. However, just as the artist constantly works at employing native gifts, so we constantly invest our skills and gifts in the effort to create community that more and more reflects the divine image.

Take courage and explore the meaning of covenant community with those sent by God to discover with you a fuller and richer discipleship than you have ever known. Remember, God calls, gathers, and forms every faithful community. This awareness alone gives us hope and courage to go on.

DAILY EXERCISES

Read the fifth chapter entitled "Living As Covenant Community," keep your journal handy, and open yourself to God's spirit as you begin each exercise. The exercises this week are in preparation for discerning a group covenant at your next meeting. You are already part of a covenant group, since you have committed to the readings, daily exercises, and weekly meetings of *Companions in Christ*. This is just one more step in clarifying the type of small-group experience that you are seeking and what practices you would choose to support this community.

EXERCISE 1

Read Mark 3:13-19. The Twelve appointed by Jesus gathered around him in community, not simply to get to know one another, but to respond to a common call and a promise of shared life in God's kingdom. Take time to listen deeply to your heart now. What call do you hear, and what promise do you sense in being part of this group? What would you like to see the group become as you continue to journey together in Christ? Offer your hopes in all honesty to God. Capture significant thoughts, insights, and questions in your journal.

EXERCISE 2

Read Luke 22:21-34. This passage offers evidence both of joy and conflict in the community of disciples that Jesus called together. In his book *The Active Life*, Parker Palmer observes that one of the purposes of community is to "disillusion" us; that is, to dispel our illusions about God, others, and ourselves so as to bring us closer to the joy of truth. How have you experienced both joy and struggle as part of this group so far? Have you experienced disillusionment? If so, listen to what God may be saying to you through it. Write your thoughts.

EXERCISE 3

Read Philippians 2:1-4. Paul's counsel to "look…to the interests of others" calls us to a larger sense of who we are and, at the same time,

challenges our grip on personal autonomy. Get in touch with your feelings of attraction and resistance to a covenant by which you agree to live in light of others' interests. Try to name what you like about that covenant and what you fear. Listen to what the Spirit may be saying to you about your feelings. Remember to capture your thoughts in writing.

EXERCISE 4

Read Psalm 133. Reflect on the relationship between the joy of community expressed in this psalm and the Hebrew context for community—covenant with God and one another. What in your experience are the agreements and practices needed for human community to be "good and pleasant" and a foretaste of God's "blessing, life forevermore"? What agreements and practices are needed for your small group to grow as a community in which everyone can persevere in grace and truth?

EXERCISE 5

Read Mark 6:30. Support and accountability both for the outward and the inward aspects of the spiritual journey were integral parts of the disciples' community with Jesus. What kind of support for practices, decisions, or changes would you welcome from this group? What kind of support would you resist? What kind of support would you be willing to offer others in the group? Prayerfully imagine yourself giving and receiving positive support in the group. What does such mutual support look like? Write your thoughts.

Remember to review your journal entries for the week in preparation for the group meeting.

Feeding on the Word:
The Mind of Christ

E. Glenn Hinson

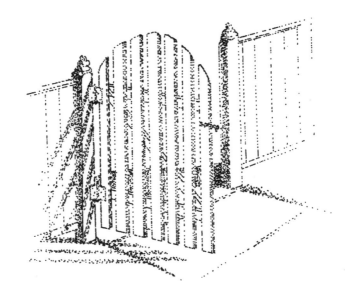

Why Do We Call the Bible God's Word?

My grandmother left me my earliest memories of this fascinating book, the Bible. I can still see her sitting on the porch in her rocking chair, rocking back and forth, Bible open on her lap. Sometimes she went to sleep. But more often than not, I remember seeing tears dripping down onto the pages of her well-worn and well-marked Bible. I often asked her what was wrong. She usually replied, "Shh! I'm just seeking a word from God."

As a four- or five-year-old, I got my first personal exposure to the Bible in a Lutheran Sunday school in St. Louis, Missouri. A teacher told us Bible stories, and we colored pictures illustrating them. Born into a family of conflict with already painful memories, I found some heroes in those stories—Joseph, Moses, David, Jesus. I could scarcely wait to read the Bible for myself. In the sixty some years since then, I've read it many times. Well, I must confess that I have fudged a bit on the Baptist counsel to read straight through. Not once have I made it through Leviticus in that way.

Perhaps you have been drawn to the Bible but, apart from the structure of a church school class, you may have felt that it was difficult to understand and relate the Bible to your daily experience. You may have become confused by what seemed to be contradictions in the Bible. Or perhaps you have wanted to establish a pattern of daily scripture reading but found that other activities continually usurped

If you want true knowledge of the Scriptures, try to secure steadfast humility of heart, to carry you by the perfection of love not to knowledge that puffs up, but that enlightens.

—John Cassian

the time. In thinking together about the Bible as God's Word to us, I invite you to examine your attitudes toward scripture and your patterns of reading it. Prayer and Bible reading are deeply interwoven and offer us a discipline to listen to and meet the God who loves us.

How the Bible Came to Be

What a fascinating book the Bible is! Actually, to make it more intriguing still, I've had to recognize that it is not one book but many. It consists of different kinds of writings composed over several centuries and collected little by little, first by the Jewish people and later by Christians. The Hebrew Bible, what Christians have commonly referred to as the Old Testament, consists of accounts of the history of the Jewish people, stories of saints (Ruth, Esther), a masterpiece on human suffering (Job), a collection of songs (Psalms), an anthology of proverbs (Proverbs and Ecclesiastes), a narrative of a love tryst of newlyweds (Song of Solomon), and writings of prophets.

The Christian scriptures (the New Testament) are composed of four accounts of the story of Jesus (Gospels), an account of the early spread of Christianity (Acts of the Apostles), letters of Paul and other apostles, an early Christian sermon (Hebrews), and an apocalypse (Revelation). Until the Reformation of the sixteenth century and among Roman Catholics even today, the Christian scriptures have also included a group of writings called the Apocrypha. The Protestant reformers excluded them from their scriptures because they lacked Hebrew originals and did not belong to the Jewish canon. Today, however, many Protestant Bibles include the Apocrypha.

Given such diversity and time span, you may wonder how the Bible came to be. Obviously, its formation came in several stages. Stage one involved an oral account, for instance, of the exodus of the Hebrew people from Egypt and of the ministry, death, and resurrection of Jesus. Ancient peoples relied far more on memory than we do today. After a considerable period of time, certain people began to write down the stories people told, the songs they sang, the proverbs they quoted.

Stage two thus had to do with writing. Modern scholarship has shown that this was not a simple process with only one author composing one writing. In the case of the historical books, for instance, scholars have discerned the hands of several editors and revisers to produce writings such as the first few books of the Bible as they now stand. In the case of the Gospels we can see that both Matthew and Luke used Mark and another "source" in composing their accounts of the good news. Luke, in fact, speaks about "many" before him, who had "undertaken to set down an orderly account of the events that have been fulfilled among us" (Luke 1:1).

Stage three entailed reproduction and transmission. In the biblical period people did not have printing presses that could make this a simple task. They copied manuscripts by hand and circulated them to people who would read them. They could set up a copy business in which several scribes recorded what another person read, but as you would guess, handmade manuscripts cost dearly and did not circulate widely.

Stage four concerned the authoritative use of certain writings. The Hebrew people, for instance, did not immediately recognize the worth of a prophet like Jeremiah. Indeed, as he complained, some contemporaries laughed at him, denounced him, and reproached him when he spoke (Jer. 20:7-10). Only later did others see that he spoke the truth. They put his prophecies in a special category, reading them in public worship. Christian communities always considered the Old Testament authoritative, just as Jews did. Little by little, different churches singled out Christian writings they knew for use in public worship. Rome, for example, probably used Mark's Gospel; Antioch used Matthew's; Corinth used some of Paul's letters to them. In time collections of writings were recognized as authoritative (canonical), at first small ones and later larger ones.

Stage five involved the forming of authoritative collections on a wider scale. For the Old Testament we can see three blocks: the Law (the first five books), recognized as authoritative by around 400 B.C.E.; the Prophets (including some historical writings), by 150 B.C.E.; and the Writings (the rest of the Hebrew scriptures), not until rabbis acknowledged them in meetings at the rabbinic school at Jamnia

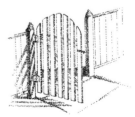

around 100 C.E. Degree of authority varied too. The Law stood well above the Prophets and other Writings.

Although the first Christians recognized the Hebrew Scriptures as their Bible too, by the second century C.E. they were ranking Christian writings alongside them. The four Gospels, the letters that went under Paul's name, First Peter, and First John quickly attained authoritative status in most churches. Other writings now in the New Testament were used in public worship in some churches but not in others. What most Christians would recognize today as the New Testament canon of twenty-seven books was not decided until the end of the fourth century in councils held at Carthage in North Africa.

The final stage is translation and circulation. Old Testament writings were composed mostly in Hebrew with a few Aramaic passages; the New Testament was written in the popular (*koine*) Greek, which was used commercially throughout the Roman Empire when Christianity came on the scene in the first century C.E. As an intensely missionary faith, Christianity soon translated both Hebrew and Christian scriptures into the dozens of popular languages of peoples who lived in or near the Roman Empire—such as Latin, Coptic (for Egypt), Armenian, and others. This stage continues even today.

The Relationship between the Hebrew and the Christian Scriptures

What is the relationship between the Hebrew and the Christian Scriptures? Christians have given different answers to that question. Although Christianity began as a sect of Judaism, by the late first century the child separated from the parent. The Christian Scriptures, however, raise here a very urgent question: How can they be understood unless we see the integral connection they have with the Hebrew Scriptures? The answer is, they cannot be. They are filled with citations and allusions from the Hebrew Scriptures and arguments based on them. The earliest Christians obviously lived by the Hebrew Scriptures just as Jesus and other Jews did. Consequently, Christians are bound to keep the two sets of scriptures inseparably linked to each

other. The Jewish people can live out of the Hebrew Scriptures as they have down through the centuries, but Christians cannot find their path using only Christian Scriptures. By themselves their scriptures will not be intelligible or speak with authority.

Responding to the Bible as God's Word

Both Jews and Christians have referred to this compilation of writings as the Word of God. What do they mean? Some contend that the scriptures are the Word of God in the sense that every syllable is inspired and therefore free from human error and infallible. They believe that God, the Holy Spirit, guided each author to write exactly what God intended.

Naturally, many others have not agreed with this theory of direct verbal inspiration. As an alternative, they believe that the Word of God is revelation, God's self-disclosure. The scriptures contain revelation, but not every word within them is that revelation. They believe God did not dictate the writings but, through the Holy Spirit, enabled human beings to discern God acting in nature, history, and the ordinary affairs of human life. The scriptures are thus the Word of God in the sense that they record God's self-disclosure in these ways. Scripture is also the Word of God in that, through its words, God searches, invites, challenges, and comforts us. Through the Bible, we hear God speaking a personal word to us.

> *Our own curiosity often hinders us in reading the Scriptures, because we wish to understand and argue when we should simply read on with humility, simplicity and faith.*
>
> —Thomas à Kempis

When we refer to the Bible as the Word of God, we recognize the authority of scripture for our faith and practice. Scripture presents a living portrait of God and God's will for human beings. As such, it carries authority. To be quite honest, we human beings struggle to yield ourselves to that authority. Our pride often prevails. There is a sense in which the scriptures do not become the Word of God until we take them into our hearts and live the message they have for us. In recognition of the complex process by which that may happen, one church that I know follows the Sunday readings with the statement: "May these words become to us the Word of God."

Here is where the Holy Spirit must come to our aid. The Spirit

Where the Spirit does not open the Scripture, the Scripture is not understood even though it is read.
—Martin Luther

illumined minds to see what God was disclosing in nature, history, and human experience. The Spirit guided the complicated process of forming the collections of scriptures. Now the Holy Spirit must help us interpret and apply the Word of God. As Paul reminded the Romans with reference to prayer, "the Spirit helps us in our weakness" (Rom. 8:26). The Spirit searches our hearts, clarifies our understanding, and further directs us in our effort to apply biblical insights to everyday life. The Spirit also enables us to yield our wills to God's will, enticing and inspiring us to obedience. The Spirit gives vitality to the Word of God that, as the author of Hebrews concluded, "is living and active, sharper than any two-edged sword, piercing until it divides soul from spirit, joints from marrow" and "is able to judge the thoughts and intentions of the heart" (Heb. 4:12).

God's Word will speak to us and transform our lives if we will come to it in a spirit of prayer and expectancy. The invitation is for us to seek the living presence of God in the Bible and to come ready to listen and respond. When we read the scriptures with openness and trust, we will not be disappointed. Thomas Merton, a profound and influential writer of the twentieth century, reminds us that we will know and experience the Bible as God's Word because it will change and liberate our lives. He writes, "The 'word of God' is recognized in actual experience because it does something to anyone who really 'hears' it: it transforms his [or her] entire existence."[1]

DAILY EXERCISES

Be sure to read the chapter before you begin these exercises. Keep a journal or blank book beside you to record your thoughts, questions, prayers, and images. In preparation, quiet yourself and reflect on the following quotation by Robert Mulholland:

> Christian spiritual formation is the process of being conformed to the image of Christ.…The scripture stands close to the center of this whole process of being conformed to the image of Christ. As we shall see, the scripture is one of the primary channels through which God encounters us…and awakens us to the dynamics and possibilities of a new way of being.[2]

EXERCISE 1

Read Psalm 119:97-105. What is your favorite Bible story or scripture passage? Reflect on why and how you came to cherish it. Identify any special role it has played in your life, its meaning for you, and how God has spoken to you through it.

EXERCISE 2

Read Genesis 1. Again and again we read, "And God said.…And it was so." Our words and actions do not always correspond, but God's word and action are one and the same. What God speaks becomes reality—if not immediately, then eventually. Keeping this in mind, reread 1:26-31. Contemplate the promise of opening wide your life to the Word: "And God said.…And it was so." What could happen? Record your reflections in your journal.

EXERCISE 3

Read Psalm 1. This psalm was placed at the beginning of the Psalter to be a preface and to convey a promise: those who study God's law and live by God's Word will be "like trees planted by streams of water." Sketch a picture of two trees—one on each side of a page. Make one tree a depiction of your life as it is. Make the second tree a depiction of your life as it could be. Beneath and between the trees, list or write

out two or three passages of scripture that have been for you streams of nourishment and growth. Spend a few moments quietly reflecting on what God is saying to you. Capture your thoughts in writing.

EXERCISE 4

Read John 1:1-18. The prologue to John's Gospel makes the remarkable claim that the Word of God is not limited to words and letters in a book, but that "the Word became flesh and lived among us" in Jesus Christ. When have you seen Christ as living Word? What is the promise of receiving the "Word made flesh"? How could this revelation change the meaning of Bible "study"? Record your reflections in your journal.

EXERCISE 5

Read 2 Corinthians 3:1-6. The Apostle Paul, being a proficient letter writer, calls his faithful disciples "a letter of Christ, prepared by us, written not with ink but with the Spirit of the living God…on tablets of human hearts." What a commendation! Think about your life as a letter that you write with your words, attitudes, and actions. What does your "letter"—this week's letter—say or not say about Christ and his life in you? What word from Christ would the Spirit like to write on the tablet of your heart for all to read? Record your thoughts and offer them to God.

Remember to review your journal entries for the week in preparation for the group meeting.

Studying Scripture As a Spiritual Discipline

*F*or the words of scripture to become the Word of God we will need to use our minds to hear what God is saying to us. This involves serious attention to and study of scripture. The English word *study* derives from the Latin word *studere*, "to busy or apply oneself." Its contemporary definition is "the act or process of applying the mind in order to acquire knowledge" or "careful attention to, and critical examination and investigation of, any subject, event, etc." It especially involves the intellect, faith seeking understanding through the body of writings that contain testimonies to God's self-disclosure in nature, events, and persons.

Study as Essential to Understanding

Through the centuries the faithful have recognized that spiritual growth requires disciplined and steadfast attention to scripture. During the period of the Exile (589–20 B.C.E.) and after, as the Law increased in importance, skilled students and interpreters of the Law called scribes arose to lead the way in the study of scriptures.[1] In Jesus' day Jewish religious leaders searched the scriptures because they believed "that in them you have eternal life" (John 5:39).

The first Christians recognized how essential it was to apply their minds to scripture. For one thing, convincing those who lived in a

> *It is the duty of all Christians diligently to search the scriptures....How useful soever this book of books is in itself, it will be of no use to us if we do not acquaint ourselves with it, by reading it daily, and meditating upon it, that we may understand the mind of God in it, and may apply what we understand to ourselves for our direction, rebuke, and comfort, as there is occasion.*
>
> —Matthew Henry

> *We will only be happy in our reading of the Bible when we dare to approach it as the means by which God really speaks to us, the God who loves us and will not leave us with our questions unanswered.*
>
> —Dietrich Bonhoeffer

Jewish context of the truth of their message required it. Luke paints a graphic picture of the application of the mind to scripture in his story of Philip's assisting the Ethiopian eunuch. "Do you understand what you are reading?" Philip asked. The eunuch replied, "How can I, unless someone guides me?" This exchange opened the way for Philip to proclaim the "good news about Jesus" (Acts 8:26-40). None, however, surpassed the Apostle Paul, a converted rabbi, in establishing an argument for Christianity by searching the scriptures "to see whether these things were so" (Acts 17:11). He worked careful arguments based on scripture into every letter. As the churches drew more and more converts from among the Gentiles, they held steadfastly to the importance of studying scriptures. "All scripture is inspired by God," the Apostle explained to Timothy, "and is useful for teaching, for reproof, for correction, and for training in righteousness, so that everyone who belongs to God may be proficient, equipped for every good work" (2 Tim. 3:16-17).

Many have asked why it is necessary to use the intellect in biblical interpretation. "If scriptures are the Word of God, of what use is critical scholarship? Why don't we just rely on the Spirit?"

First of all, we study scriptures because, as one early Christian discovered about Paul's writings, "some things in them [are] hard to understand" (2 Pet. 3:16). Like other complex and profound writings, the scriptures will scarcely reveal their insights to us unless we learn all we can about the author, purpose, date, place, circumstances of writing, and many other things. Different kinds of literature will pose different challenges. To wrestle the deep truths that we seek from these writings requires disciplined study using the best methods and information available.

More important, we put forth this effort because we want to have in ourselves the mind of Christ (Phil. 2:5), a love-guided, servant-oriented, humble mind. How do we develop such a mind? We do not just sit back and wait for the Spirit to bring about this change in us. Although God alone can effect such transformation in us, we know that we have to open ourselves to God and learn of God's will for us. Study involves us in the same eager searching of scriptures in which the saints have engaged through the centuries. As the popular author Richard Foster has said, "The Discipline of study is the primary vehicle to bring us to '*think* about [whatever is pure, whatever is lovely, whatever is gracious, if there is anything worthy of praise'" (Phil. 4:8).][2]

A group of devout Roman women set an example for us during the late fourth century. They gathered in the palace of Marcella on the Aventine Hill in Rome to study scriptures. Most of them were probably fluent in Greek, but they also learned Hebrew. When they learned that Jerome, the most noted biblical scholar of the day, had come to Rome in 382, Marcella persuaded him to lead them in their study. He did so reluctantly at first, but soon learned that Marcella and some of the others challenged even him in his thought and understanding. She plied him with questions and shared her interpretations. When he had to flee Rome and go to the Holy Land in 385, some of the Aventine Circle went with him. There they continued their eager search of the scriptures. Jerome dedicated much of his work in preparing the Vulgate Bible to one of them named Paula.

Tools for the Study of Scripture

In our study of scriptures we have to concern ourselves with two contexts—the original author's and our own. To interpret properly, we want to avoid reading our ideas and impressions into the document we are studying. Meaningful interpretation of the scriptures depends to a great extent upon proper understanding of each writing in the original language, culture, and context.

Language. An abundance of excellent English translations and paraphrases is available to serious students. A good translation is not literal. Rather, a careful translator will take the thoughts used by the original authors in their cultural setting and put them in modern terms that express the same ideas in our own cultural setting. Reading several versions of the same passage often helps us grasp its meaning.

As we choose various translations of scripture, we ought to exercise special care. Older translations can be misleading because even modern languages become dated. Words change. Take, for instance,

[In the community formed by Benedict], time was given for study and a more systematic approach to holy scripture and other writings but not as a prerequisite to letting God speak through a text or verse of the Bible. Accurate, academic dissection of the material was not the primary aim of being with the word. Instead the approach was to sit quietly in the presence of God and with open heart and mind to wait until the text touched a deep place within and invited the listener into conversation with its Author.

—Elizabeth J. Canham

the King James Version of 1 Thessalonians 4:15: "That we which are alive and remain unto the coming of the Lord shall not prevent [that is, precede or go before] them which are asleep." While perfectly intelligible in the seventeenth century, this translation will cause no small amount of confusion today because of the evolution of English. More important, the texts on which translations are based have improved with the discovery of new manuscripts and changes in technology. Also, the skill and knowledge of the translators will play an integral role in the quality and readability of the translations.

Culture. Language is only one part of culture with which interpreters need to deal in order to understand the scriptures and let them speak to the modern condition. Others include the psychology, physics, political perspective, and worldview of an author. Hebrew psychology, for example, contrasted quite noticeably with the Greek. Where the Greeks thought in terms of human beings in three parts—body, soul, and spirit—the Hebrews emphasized unity. Hebrew physics did not separate matter and spirit.

Context. Most of the books of the Bible were written in a simple enough style that we can understand the text as it stands, but they are clearer when we know their context. Context has to do with date, place, circumstances of writing, and other factors that help us interpret. The more you understand the context of a particular writing, for instance, that a certain text is actually a letter, the more likely you are to interpret accurately what the author was saying.

As an example from the Hebrew Scriptures, most scholars think that the eighth-century prophet Isaiah (742–701 B.C.E.) wrote only chapters 1–39 of Isaiah. Chapters 40–66 belong to the time of Cyrus of Persia (539 B.C.E.) and after. Proper interpretation of the message of Isaiah is helped by distinguishing these different contexts.

Determining the context of the Gospels and other New Testament writings poses a major challenge, but one that helps us glean their insights for us. It takes only a casual reading to see that John differs markedly from Matthew, Mark, and Luke—what are usually called the synoptic Gospels. John obviously wrote out of another context. Careful study of Matthew, Mark, and Luke shows that each of them fashioned his account of the good news in a different time and place, for a different audience.

The Limits of Study

The challenges of interpretation should not make us timid about reading scripture. A good study Bible will supply most of the basic information. The critical study of the scriptures, moreover, is not the most significant concern of spiritual formation. Historical and linguistic knowledge of scripture has its limits. Study helps us to use our minds to focus on God; but more important, it provides a framework for meditation, which is a kind of listening with the heart. Study is what Thomas Merton has called the "front porch" of meditation. "By study we seek the truth in books or in some other source outside our own minds. In meditation we strive to absorb what we have already taken in," he says.[3] The metaphor is helpful, for it reminds us that we must do more than learn about the Word of God. We want, rather, to know the God of the Word. Meditation, Merton adds, "seeks to possess the truth not only by knowledge but also by love."[4] In meditation, we seek to enter into God's presence, to listen to God's voice, and to respond in faithful and loving action. It is not accidental that monks were the copiers and illuminators of manuscripts, translators, and interpreters of scripture throughout much of Christian history. They had a desire for God that fostered a love of learning.[5] That love of learning focused, above all, on scriptures, and it was a learning both for mind and heart.

The reading of scripture is a spiritual discipline. One of the problems we have, however, is that when our reading of scripture becomes dry and doesn't seem to "do" anything for us any more, we tend to look somewhere else.…There is also the need to be willing to wait upon the Word, the necessity of offering up our reading of the scripture to God to be used as God chooses and when God chooses.

—M. Robert Mulholland Jr.

DAILY EXERCISES

The core of studying scripture is mental attention and careful listening. We listen with a desire to hear God's voice and do God's will. In this way, reflection on scripture becomes a means by which God leads us in becoming the persons we are called to be. This week prepare yourself with prayer, asking to be open to God. On first reading, ask yourself questions such as, "What do I need to know in order to hear this passage in its context? What general truths does this passage convey about God, me, and my relationships?" If you have a good study Bible, look at the notes on each passage. On second reading, ask yourself questions such as, "What aspect of this passage invites me to deeper exploration? What does God want me to hear or call me to do?"

EXERCISE 1

Read Genesis 3:1-13. This story speaks to the challenge of paying attention to God. On first reading, you might consider what the story reveals about the qualities of relationship that God desires, or blocks that we experience in listening to God. On second reading, you might pause at points along the way to allow words and images to search you. For example, with verse 8, how has God been "walking" in the garden of my life lately? With verse 9, how do I respond to God's searching call, "Where are you?" With verse 13, what gets stirred up in me when God asks, "What is this that you have done?" Record your thoughts and feelings.

EXERCISE 2

Read Genesis 32:22-32. This story is about Jacob's going to the river where he wrestles with God and is changed. On first reading, you might explore the larger context: What was Jacob worried about, and why did he go to the river alone? (This larger context can be seen in chapter 27 and chapter 32:3-21.) Or what does the story suggest about solitude and what one must do to gain time alone with God? On second reading, you might get in touch with parts of you that identify with Jacob's situation or your need to be away from others for a while. What must you do to gain that time alone with God? What will you and God wrestle about? How do you respond to God's question, "What is your name?" How might God express the promise of your life: "You shall no longer be called _____, but _____"?

EXERCISE 3

Read Psalm 81. This summons to worship turns into an expression of God's deep disappointment over our spiritual deafness. God appeals to us to listen and enjoy the benefit of divine guidance. On first reading, you might consider what this psalm reveals about the heart of God and about the hearts of the Hebrew people. On second reading, you might pause to listen to the "voice I had not known" regarding the condition of your own heart. What is the character of your heart when it is stubborn, and what have been some of the consequences? What is the character of your heart when it is listening, and what difference would a listening heart make in your life?

EXERCISE 4

Read Mark 10:17-22. This story is about a rich man who wanted to do what was required—within limits—to inherit eternal life. On first reading, you might note the contrast between the man's favorable words to Jesus and his reluctance to obey, or reflect on what limited this man's response to Jesus' call. On second reading, you might explore what keeps you from fully living your profession of faith in the "Good Teacher." Listen for what Jesus is saying about the one thing you lack. As you do so, see Jesus looking at you with love, nonetheless.

EXERCISE 5

Read John 10:1-10. This passage is about Jesus as the Good Shepherd. On first reading, note the differences Jesus describes between the shepherd and the thief. On the second reading, explore your own

awareness of the Good Shepherd's voice. What are its qualities? What other voices imitate God, appeal for your attention, and take over your life? How do you tell the difference between them and the voice of God in you?

Review your journal entries for the week in preparation for the group meeting.

Part 2, Week 3

Meditating on the Word

There are many kinds of Christian meditation, but above all it is listening to God through the scriptures, ruminating on the Word, a deep conversation of hearing and responding. In meditation we read not just for information; we probe, ponder, and explore so that the words of scripture become for us the Word of God in our lives.

The Practice of Meditation

The Hebrew tradition that centered on the Law encouraged meditation. In Deuteronomy, the "book of the Law," Moses instructed the people to "keep these words that I am commanding you today in your heart" (Deut. 6:6). He also commanded Joshua to "meditate on [the Law] day and night, so that you may be careful to act in accordance with all that is written in it" (Josh. 1:8).

The Book of Psalms opens, "Happy are those…[whose] delight is in the law of the Lord, and on his law they meditate day and night" (Ps. 1:1-2). Another psalmist entreated, "Let the words of my mouth and the meditation of my heart be acceptable to you, O Lord, my rock and my redeemer" (Ps. 19:14; see also 49:3). Another asked, "How can young people keep [God's statutes] pure?" and answered, "By guarding [them] according to your word.…I treasure your word in my heart, so that I may not sin against you" (Ps. 119:9, 11).

The gospel is not a doctrine of the tongue, but of life. It cannot be grasped by reason and memory only, but it is fully understood when it possesses the whole soul, and penetrates to the inner recesses of the heart.

—John Calvin

In the second century B.C.E. the Jewish scribe Jesus ben Sirach spoke about the searching attention scriptures must receive well beyond what we would call study. "Happy is he who gives his mind to wisdom and meditates on understanding; happy is he who reflects on her ways and ponders her secrets" (Ecclus. 14:20-21, REB). Meditation on the Law means "not only thinking about the Law, studying the Law, but living it with a full, or relatively full, understanding of God's purpose in manifesting to us [God's] will."[1]

Jesus of Nazareth doubtless spent many hours meditating on the Hebrew Scriptures, just as the rabbis did. His use of scripture in engaging his critics would seem to make this clear. And the rabbi Saul (turned apostle Paul) urged his converts to meditate: "Finally, beloved, whatever is true, whatever is honorable, whatever is just, whatever is pure, whatever is pleasing, whatever is commendable, if there is any excellence and if there is anything worthy of praise, think about these things" (Phil. 4:8; see also Col. 3:2). He uses the word *think* in the sense of reflection or pondering.

Christian meditation blossomed uniquely in the deserts of Egypt and Arabia among the hermits and monks of the fourth through the sixth centuries who sought purity of heart in order that they might see God. In these early centuries of the church, few of the desert fathers and mothers would have owned complete Bibles or been able to read them, but the Sayings of the desert monks speak often of the benefits of meditating on scripture. Both individually and communally, the monks said the words of a particular text orally, mulled them over in the mind, chewed on them, and slowly digested them. Such practices helped them abandon themselves to God for the strengthening and transforming of their lives.[2]

The meditative wisdom of the desert fathers and mothers stood behind the Benedictine spiritual tradition. In the sixth century, Benedict of Nursia founded one of the notable monastic orders. The Rule of Benedict divided the monks' day into three parts: six hours of manual labor, four hours of the daily office (chanting the psalms), and four hours in spiritual reading and prayer. The time of reading might include other devotional writings such as the lives of saints, but it

focused, above all, on the scriptures. The objective was "a more intimate communion with God not only in the future *but also here and now.*"[3] Such communion requires not just knowledge but also love.

Approaches to Meditation

What does meditation involve? Your approach will depend to some extent on your personality. Some persons want to listen slowly to the words of scripture. They may prefer to break the text down into its component parts, pausing to reflect on each thought that comes to mind. Some passages lend themselves to such an approach. The Beatitudes, for instance, halt you in your tracks with their reversal of logic and make you think. "Blessed are the meek, for they will inherit the earth" (Matt. 5:5). You might ask, "Hmm? How could that be? What we usually see is the triumph of the powerful, not the meek. How could the meek inherit the earth? Did Jesus inherit the earth? What did Francis of Assisi or Gandhi or Martin Luther King or Mother Teresa accomplish by gentleness? Don't people gain more by aggressiveness?"

The meditation of Scripture centers on internalizing and personalizing the passage. The written Word becomes a living word addressed to you.
—Richard J. Foster

That is one level of meditative reading: asking what the scripture could have meant to the people of Jesus' day and could mean to us in general. There is, however, another level: to ask, "What is it saying to me? Does the text have a 'word' for me in this day and time? All too often I am anything but meek or gentle—in driving, in pressing my argument, in replying to someone whose words have hurt me. And where has that led me? How has this affected my relationships? The meek seem to get run over. But what is the consequence of the power games we play? Constant conflict? Violence completely out of control? Am I willing to hear Jesus' revolutionary challenge to a lifestyle of meekness? 'Lord, gentle me. Help me to understand what it means to be meek.'"

Some persons' way of meditating with scripture may rely more on intuition, "apprehending it in its wholeness as beauty rather than as truth."[4] Take Psalm 139, that wonderful psalm about God's inescapable nearness. The author seemingly wants to escape God, but then finds God in the midst of all creation. In the first seven verses the writer speaks of God's intimate knowledge of us. God knows us better than we know ourselves.

The psalmist goes on to reflect on the fact that there is no place to flee from God's presence. Verse 8 states the disturbing yet comforting truth: "If I ascend to heaven, you are there; if I make my bed in Sheol, you are there." Two words jump out at me in my meditation on the last half of the verse—*make* and *Sheol*. The psalmist doesn't say, "If I trip and fall in." He says, "If I make." That says to me, "Glenn, you cannot mess your life up to the extent that God will abandon you." In Hebrew thought, Sheol is by definition where God is not. For our psalmist, God is to be found everywhere. "If I take the wings of the morning and settle at the farthest limits of the sea, even there your hand shall lead me, and your right hand shall hold me fast" (139:9-10).

In the next chapter, we will explore how the use of imagination can help us in our meditation on scripture. The more vividly we can enter into the scripture in imagination, the better. If we are meditating on a story in which there are animals, says Ignatius, smell the manure! Meditation allows for diverse approaches that will help us be attentive to God.

A Basic Pattern of Meditation

Benedict of Nursia urged his communities to practice a regular rhythm of spiritual reading of scripture. Over the following centuries, the Benedictines gave the practice of meditation on scripture a more defined form. They outlined a simple but profound pattern that integrates reading, meditation, and prayer. This pattern or method has been widely used through the centuries both by Roman Catholics and Protestants. It is often referred to by its Latin title, *lectio divina* (which means "sacred reading or holy reading"). In *lectio divina*, the seeker is invited to choose a place and time conducive to reflection and prayer, where he or she can be comfortable and undisturbed. Typically, *lectio divina* is described in four phases or stages. These reflect

Lectio is undertaken in the conviction that God's word is meant to be a "good" word; that is, something carrying God's own life in a way that benefits the one who receives it faithfully.

—Norvene Vest

different dynamics of our praying and reading and could be more accurately described as movements of the mind and heart.

The first stage is a slow reading of the scripture passage. Usually one selects a short passage since the focus is not on the amount of text to be covered but on the depth and concentration of the reading. Frequently it helps to read the passage more than once. Images and words can easily go unnoticed in only one reading. We must be willing to stay with portions of the text that seem to be speaking to us and allow for times of silence and rereading as they seem helpful.

The second stage focuses on meditation. We begin to reflect intently on the scripture passage. This is the heart of meditation where we seek to hear and explore the special words, images, or phrases through which God may be speaking. We allow the words to sink into our consciousness and help us look at ourselves and our relationship with God.

A contemporary author, Elizabeth Canham, has written of this experience during a meditation on Mark 1:35-39. In this text, Jesus has gotten up early to pray, but Simon and the others find him and tell him that they have been hunting for him. In fact, they report, "Everyone is searching for you." Jesus answers that he is ready to go to the neighboring towns and continue to proclaim the message for which he has come. And so he goes to continue his ministry of preaching and healing. In Elizabeth's meditation, this passage immediately reminds her of how much pressure she experiences in her own life and helps her see how the demands on her time have generated resentment in her. She begins to think of Jesus, how he set his priorities with his early rising for prayer and yet, in response to the words of the disciples, how readily he took up again his ministry to a hurting world. She finds herself longing to be present to God in prayer so that she can sense more clearly her call to service. She wants to receive new energy and vision to go to those places of service and to overcome the resentment that colors her perspective. Her meditation has enabled her to see what is happening in her life and also to see what God may be offering to her.[5]

The third stage of *lectio* is prayer. After meditation we move naturally into a time of prayer, expressing our response to what we have heard. We speak directly to God of our needs and struggles, our repentance and our gratitude. We open ourselves to the new life God is offering and ask for the grace to do what we are being called to do. The scripture passage has moved from an external reading to a word that dwells within us.

In the last stage, we come to an experience of contemplation, a time of quietness and resting. Our words cease, and we simply abide in God's presence. We trust ourselves to the One who loves us. It is a time of letting go and being receptive to what God seeks to give us at that moment.

Of course, these stages or phases do not always progress in such an orderly, sequential way. We may move easily among the various stages—sometimes "caught" by a word and immediately wanting to pray or desiring to pause and rest in an awareness of God's enfolding love. Sometimes our prayer may take the form of writing. Whatever the movement, we are expressing our desire that God will give us a word of life and that we will be able to hear and respond.

Helpful Guidelines

Thomas Merton has given some guidelines to help us in meditation. One important consideration is "the proper atmosphere of prayer," which basically means you need a quiet place away from normal distractions—a room in your home, a chapel, a garden, a park. You can meditate with others or by yourself. "The most important thing," Merton says, "is to seek silence, tranquillity, recollection and peace."[6]

Some of us may have to give ourselves permission to meditate. We belong to a society that values activity and views time spent in solitude as laziness. If you hold this view, argue a case for yourself. Say, "I need this for my re-creation. Others can't stand to live with me if I don't do this! I will become more collected and get more done in the long run if I do this. I may 'burn out' if I don't. After all, I am not doing nothing!"

As for the meditation itself, the crucial point is sincerity. You will get something out of scripture even when the exercise becomes routine, but the routine will be a far cry from what you want. The desert monks and the Puritans spoke often about "compunction." Compunction has to do with a recognition that we are in need of God. Like Paul, we confess, "We do not know how to pray as we ought" (Rom. 8:26), and we call on the Spirit to help us in our weakness.

As we wrestle sincerely with the words of scripture, they begin to speak to our condition. Abba Isaac, one of the desert saints, explained how he and others related the psalms to their life situations: "When we use the words, we remember, by a kind of meditative association, our own circumstances and struggles, the results of our negligence or earnestness, the mercies of God's providence or the temptations of the devil, the subtle and slippery sins of forgetfulness or human frailty or unthinking ignorance."[7]

Meditation requires concentration. Teresa of Avila, the sixteenth-century Carmelite reformer and mystic, offered a homely image of meditation for beginners. For those unaccustomed to the practice, she warned that meditation may tire the mind, for it is like lifting water out of a cistern with a bucket. Sometimes we may find the cistern dry, and always we will have distractions.[8] Indeed, we may experience our minds flitting around "like a hummingbird on holiday."[9] The advice of Teresa, who struggled for twenty years to learn how to pray, was that you not give up. Just wait for the Spirit to lift you.[10] If distractions come, be aware of them and then let them go in order to resume your listening.

Dietrich Bonhoeffer, the German theologian who opposed Nazi ideology, sounded like a Benedictine monk when he required the seminarians at Finkenwalde to meditate thirty minutes every morning for a week on the same passage of scripture. In *Life Together* he explained what should take place:

> In our meditation we ponder the chosen text on the strength of the promise that it has something utterly personal to say to us for this day and for our Christian life, that it is not only God's Word for the Church, but also God's Word for us individually. We expose ourselves to the

It might also be of use, if, while we read [the Bible], we were frequently to pause, and examine ourselves by what we read, both with regard to our hearts and lives.... And whatever light you then receive, should be used to the uttermost, and that immediately. Let there be no delay....So shall you find this word to be indeed the power of God unto present and eternal salvation.

—John Wesley

specific word until it addresses us personally. And when we do this, we are doing no more than the simplest, untutored Christian does every day; we read God's Word as God's Word for us.[11]

We should not expect to get through the entire passage in one sitting. One sentence or even one word may arrest us. We need not express our thought or prayer in words or discover new ideas or have unexpected, extraordinary experiences. What matters is that the Word "penetrates and dwells within us."[12] We want to ponder these things in our hearts, as Mary pondered what the angels told the shepherds (Luke 2:19). Bonhoeffer's encouraging word is this: "We must center our attention on the Word alone and leave consequences to its action."[13]

DAILY EXERCISES

This week you will begin to practice a pattern for reading scripture prayerfully (or praying with scripture) called *lectio divina* (pronounced LEX-ee-oh dih-VEE-nuh), which is Latin for "divine or sacred reading." Classic descriptions of *lectio divina* list a sequence of four movements: *lectio* (reading), *meditatio* (ruminating and reflecting), *oratio* (responding to God), and *contemplatio* (receiving and resting in God).

Lectio—Slowly read a brief passage of scripture. Read it as though you are hearing it read to you. Read it silently and aloud. Experiment by reading it with different emphases and inflections.

Meditatio—Mull over the text; internalize the words. Listen for the phrases that stand out for you as you read the passage. Turn them over in your mind. Reflect on why these words catch your attention, what they bring to mind, and what they mean for you today. Jot down in your journal the meaningful words, noting associations, reactions, feelings, or challenges.

Oratio—Turn your meditation from dialogue with yourself to dialogue with God, which is prayer. Share with God in all honesty your reflections, questions, or feelings. Offer your thanksgiving, confession, petitions, or intercessions as they arise within during your dialogue with God. Listen for God's response and inner nudging.

Contemplatio—Rest your mental activity and trust yourself completely to God's love and care. Relax in God's presence. Pick a phrase from the text to which you can return again and again as you keep your attention on God. Allow this prayer-phrase to sustain your presence to God throughout the day. After a few minutes of "practicing the presence of God" in this way, you might close with the Lord's Prayer, a song, or a final moment of grateful silence.

Capture your meditation, prayer, and the new insights and possibilities God gave you through your journal. Consider one token—one small act—you can offer today in grateful response to God's life-giving word to you during this special time with the scripture.

Classical writers have compared this process to eating. In reading, you bite off a small chunk of text. Through meditation, you chew on it, extracting the nutrients and juices. In prayer, you swallow, incorporating the results of your meditation and allowing them to nourish your life. And in contemplation, you savor the good taste left in your mouth, celebrate the gift of God's word to you, and embrace the new life you have received. *Lectio divina* is more than a method; it is a way of life rooted in daily listening to the Word of God.

As you move through the daily exercises this week, you will be using the four movements of *lectio divina*. Before you begin, prepare yourself for a period of time to be with God. Quiet yourself by breathing slowly and deeply. Prepare to be personally addressed by a word from God. Pray before you begin your *lectio* each day, "May these words become to me the Word of God." Enter into each passage with the question, "What is God saying to me through this text?" Honor the natural movements of the words from the eyes and lips (in reading) to the mind (in reflection) to the heart (in prayerful responses to God) to the spirit of your life (in receiving God's gift and resting in God's love). Let the Spirit guide you in your journey to God through each text. Consider the written suggestions below as just that—suggestions if you need help getting started.

EXERCISE 1

Read Psalm 23 silently and then aloud as though for the first time.

Meditate slowly on each verse. Linger with images that are rich in meaning. Explore why these images attract you.

Pray to God with your thoughts and feelings (gratitude, joy, or longing). Tell God where you need what the words of the psalm convey. Open your heart in all honesty, then listen.

Contemplate the gift of God's care. Trust your life to God in situations that concern you.

Record your experience.

EXERCISE 2

Read Psalm 27 through once, then again—one line at a time slowly.

Reflect on meanings for you in each phrase; for example, "The Lord," "is my light," "and my salvation."

Respond to the question, "Of whom shall I be afraid?" Tell the Lord the fears that control you. Personalize each verse as a way to talk with God; then listen.

Rest in God's light with an affirmation such as verse 14: "Wait for the Lord; be strong, and let your heart take courage."

Record your experience.

EXERCISE 3

Read Matthew 16:13-16 and any study notes that your Bible may provide.

Reflect on Jesus' questions as though they were addressed to you. Who do people today say Jesus is? Who do you say Jesus is? Explore your affirmations and questions.

Respond to Jesus directly. Dialogue with him in prayer, and listen for his responses and promptings.

Rest in Jesus' remarkable trust in us to be his church. Resolve to act as you are led.

Record your insights.

EXERCISE 4

Read Luke 12:22-32 several times, and repeat the verses that draw you in more deeply.

Meditate on verse 25. Name your worries, needs, or preoccupations about the future.

Converse with Jesus about any of your reservations concerning his counsel "not to worry" and "strive only for the kingdom." Listen for his response.

Soak in the assurance of how much God values you and of how free you are to let go of those things that cause you worry.

Record your insights and thoughts.

EXERCISE 5

Read Romans 8:31-39. Return to a verse that best captures for you the meaning of the passage.

Reflect on what it means to live with such faith in God's love and care.

Respond in prayer by telling God of circumstances where you or other people do in fact feel separated from an awareness of God's love. Pay attention to the leading of the Spirit.

Rest in God's presence as you offer each circumstance to God, asking for faith to say in each, "For I am convinced that neither death, nor life,...nor anything else in all creation, will be able to separate us from the love of God in Christ Jesus our Lord" (vv. 38-39).

Record your insights.

Review your journal entries for the week in preparation for the group meeting.

Part 2, Week 4
Directing Imagination

*A*s the preceding lesson mentioned, meditation on scripture can also benefit from the use of imagination, entering into scriptures in the way a child listens to a good storyteller. You have witnessed that, haven't you? Children will get up and act out part of the story. They will answer questions that haven't been asked. They make the story their story.

The more vivid your imagination, the more deeply the story will fix itself in your memory and thought and the more deeply it will penetrate into the unconscious, to use the terminology of Jungian analysts. What takes place resembles what happens when you dream, except that you are awake. You are dealing with scripture both at the conscious level—seeing, hearing, touching, tasting, smelling, and reflecting—and at the subconscious level. As a result, meditation can leave its mark on both levels.

In the Jungian understanding, our human psyche is much larger and more complex than the part that operates on the conscious and rational levels. The unconscious level accounts in many ways for who we are and how we act as persons. We experience all kinds of things from outside ourselves at the unconscious level. Life experiences, some good and some bad, burrow their way into the unconscious and remain hidden until another event causes them to spring into consciousness again.

Imagination is the capacity to make connections between the visible and the invisible, between heaven and earth, between present and past, between present and future. For Christians, whose largest investment is in the invisible, the imagination is indispensable, for it is only by means of the imagination that we can see reality whole, in context.

—Eugene H. Peterson

Imagination, like dreams, comes into play not only in our observing and thinking processes but also in the vastly larger unconscious. Human imagination is highly complex. Like dreaming, it deals in symbols that often have far greater effect than words or thoughts. They touch us subtly at the deepest levels of our being. Take, for example, Paul's experience recorded in 2 Corinthians 12:1-10. Fourteen years earlier, he said he had experienced being caught up into heaven or paradise. Whether that happened in or out of the body, he couldn't say. There he saw and heard things that no mortal can repeat—visions and revelations of the Lord. Repeatable or not, they affected him profoundly. They transformed his life forever. Visionary experiences like Paul's are generally conveyed through symbols and images.

Entering Scripture with Imagination

How does imagination with scripture work? First, it works best with narrative portions of the Bible: stories with characters, dialogue, and movement. Passages from the Gospels or Acts are ideal for this kind of meditation. By using the imagination, we carry on a conversation with biblical figures and events through which God chose to speak. We try to become a part of the story, picturing it and identifying with the persons described. As we enter into the story this way, it can open up insight, inspire us, and enliven us.

Two remarkable Christian leaders viewed the proper direction of imagination in biblical meditation as a key to the holy life. One was Ignatius of Loyola (1491–1556), the great Catholic reformer and founder of the Society of Jesus (Jesuits). The other was Richard Baxter (1615–91), a very influential Puritan English pastor and writer. These two differed in the way they expressed the goal of imaginative meditation. For Ignatius, the goal was to prepare the soul "to free itself of all inordinate attachments" and to seek and discover God's will for one's life.[1] For Baxter, it was to attain "the saints' everlasting rest."[2] Today perhaps we would express the goal in terms of intimacy with God.

Surprisingly, Ignatius and Baxter agreed as to the method of meditation—entering into scriptures imaginatively and allowing them

> *Frequency in heavenly contemplation is particularly important, to prevent a shyness between God and thy soul. Frequent society breeds familiarity, and familiarity increases love and delight, and makes us bold in our addresses. The chief end of this duty is, to have acquaintance and fellowship with God; and therefore, if thou come but seldom to it, thou wilt keep thyself a stranger still.*
>
> —Richard Baxter

to touch and shape one's life. Scriptural meditation assumes an intimate and deep familiarity with the Bible, not just casual acquaintance. Devout Puritans, convinced that they would find answers to life's most urgent questions only in the scriptures, spent hours in study and meditation, poring over the Bible and memorizing all they could. John Bunyan, the seventeenth-century author of *The Pilgrim's Progress*, said that, during his traumatic battle with manic depression, he "was never out of the Bible, either by reading or meditation." [3] Puritans expected familiar scripture texts to dart into their minds and hearts and give them needed guidance.

To prepare for this meditation, Baxter gave similar advice to that of Thomas Merton. Find a place where you can become quiet and consider carefully the disposition of your heart. The heart must be freed from as many distractions as possible. Then, set about this work "with the greatest solemnity of heart and mind." [4] The key to directing the heart toward "heavenly rest" or intimacy with God lies in exercising the affections: love, desire, hope, courage, and joy. Since emotions can be tricky and misleading, however, we must take care that they move us closer to God. That is the task of "consideration." [5]

For Baxter, consideration as a form of meditation relied on imagination and could draw from the deep well of memorized scriptures. He painted word pictures in which he contrasted scenes of heaven with scenes on earth to help the devout aspire to heaven. Like Ignatius, he wanted vivid imagination of the glories of heaven and the trials of earth. In order to inspire Christians to consider the glories of heaven with deep feeling, Baxter encouraged sensory imagination in much the same way as Ignatius. Listen to Baxter's own words as he encourages a meditation on the vision of heavenly glory from the Book of Revelation. It is adapted here into modern English so we may understand it more clearly (remember that to "suppose" is essentially to imagine):

> Draw as strong suppositions as you can from your senses for the helping of your affections....Suppose yourself now beholding the city of God; and that you have been companion with John in his survey of its glory; and have seen the thrones, the Majesty, the heavenly hosts, the

[In meditation,] get thy heart as clear from the world as thou canst. Wholly lay by the thoughts of thy business, troubles, enjoyments, and every thing that may take up any room in thy soul. Get it as empty as thou possibly canst, that it may be the more capable of being filled with God.

—Richard Baxter

shining splendor which he saw: suppose…that you have seen the saints clothed in white robes, with palms of victory in their hands: suppose you have heard the song of Moses and of the Lamb; or do even now hear them praising and glorifying the living God.…Get the liveliest picture of them in your mind which you possibly can. Meditate on them, as if you were all the while beholding them, and as if you were even hearing the hallelujahs while you are thinking of them, till you can say, "I think I see a glimpse of the glory! I think I hear the shouts of joy and praise! I think I stand by Abraham and David, Peter and Paul…I think I even see the Son of God appearing in the clouds.…I think I hear him say, Come, you blessed of my Father!"[6]

We can see how Baxter encourages his readers to place themselves imaginatively into certain settings described in the Bible. Later, while illustrating this method with one of his own meditations, Baxter breaks into a spontaneous dialogue between Christ and his own soul, a device Ignatius also frequently commended for taking personally to heart the message of scripture.

Baxter cautiously suggested that the devout might assist their meditation with the use of sensory objects if they were careful not to actually draw the objects, as Roman Catholics did. In our day most Protestants are less hesitant to use paintings, icons, stained glass windows, statues, and other symbols for meditation. In an age of visual learning many are rediscovering how traditional Christian icons may draw us "into closer communion with the God of love."[7]

Example of Meditation

Here is an example of one of my own meditations on Jesus' encounter with Zacchaeus in Luke 19:1-10. In my mind's eye I imagine myself as Zacchaeus that day as Jesus passed through Jericho on his way to Jerusalem. I am a "head tax collector," not a nice position to be in. Tax collectors are not highly regarded in our own society today, even though they work for us, "the government of the people." I can just imagine what those people clamoring around Jesus think about me, a Jew, when I collect taxes for the Romans who occupy our country. To make matters worse, I have been known to skim money off in order to get rich.

Also, I am small. I am so short that I have to run and scramble up a big sycamore tree just to see Jesus. Little people often have to be inventive to survive. I get there just as Jesus starts to pass by.

But to my amazement, he doesn't go on past. He stops, looks up, and says, "Zacchaeus, hurry and get down from there, for I've got to stay at your house today." Oh, wow! I almost fall out of that tree. I expect him to look every which way but up, to look right on past me lest people think he associates with the likes of me, or to give me that withering look so many others do. But he doesn't. He looks me right in the eye and invites himself to my house.

What do I feel? What else but inexpressible joy? Joy! Joy! Jesus has given the precious gift of attention and acceptance. Not only does he look me in the eye; he asks me to serve as his host. But does he realize what he is doing?

Now I pause for a little "meditative association." I begin to think about times when I have experienced the hurt of inattention the way Zacchaeus did. One time I went to a party and struck up a conversation with someone, and she kept sweeping the room with her eyes looking for someone more interesting to talk to. Another time I tried to present a new proposal to my colleagues and found that they did not share my excitement. They listened politely but showed little response to my ideas. Then I also thought of the times that I had experienced the pain of rejection.

But here, at last, is one whose love is wide enough to embrace even a tax collector. Whom will he not accept? If I doubt his acceptance, I need only look at what happens next.

See the price Jesus pays immediately. He no sooner gets to my house than the muttering starts, the pretended cries of disbelief: "He has gone in to have lunch with a sinful man."

I might start to worry again. But by now I have had a change of heart and I say, "See, sir, I will give half of everything I own to the poor. And if I have defrauded anyone, I will repay fourfold." I imagine the thoughts and feelings that have led to this change of heart in me.

Now I observe Jesus' response. Once again, he does not disappoint. Not only has Jesus accepted me, a universally despised person;

The scriptures are a vast repository of human dramas, and offer us endless scripts for exploring our feelings, understandings, and commitments. Only a little imagination makes them come alive with power and efficacy for contemporary living.
—John Killinger

I learned to listen while I read. Sometimes I would hear nothing except the words of my reading. More often, I was simply conscious that the passages were entering mind and heart and becoming part of me. But increasingly there were times when some aspect of what I was reading came home to me with such sudden strength and clarity that I was left with no doubt that God had something to say not just to the psalmist, the prophet, or the disciple— but to me.

—Avery Brooke

he even affirms me. No, not because of my promises, but because of his love. "Today salvation has come to this house, because he too is a son of Abraham. For the Son of Man came to seek out and to save the lost." Oh, good thing Jesus was inside the house when he said that. These people who adored him just a little while before would have murdered him! The very idea, calling me, a despicable tax collector, "a son of Abraham."

Your meditation on this passage might lead you to different feelings and images, based on your lived experience in relation to the scripture text. The meditation has led me to hear again the affirmation in this story, the same affirmation we get from the cross. As one hymn puts it, "There's a wideness in God's mercy like the wideness of the sea." And as Paul reminds us in Romans 8, nothing in all the world can separate us from the love of God. Ponder that assurance a while. I invite you to transfer it from your head to your heart. That is the goal of meditation.

DAILY EXERCISES

Before you begin the exercises for the week, remember to read the new chapter and write your notes, responses, questions, and concerns in your journal. This week's passages move through Luke's version of the Christmas story and help us to use our imaginations in meditating on scripture. Please try to follow the instructions even if you find them difficult or uncomfortable. Remember to write in your journal as you ponder the questions and/or after you have finished your contemplation.

EXERCISE 1

Read Luke 1:5-23. Go back through Zechariah's story and put yourself in the place of the man who was "getting on in years." Visualize what you are doing in the sanctuary, then what you see and feel when the angel first appears. How do your feelings change when the angel tells you that "your wife Elizabeth will bear you a son"? Imagine an honest conversation with the angel about the news. Capture the dialogue in writing, if possible. Imagine holding the news in silence for several months. Note what your imaginings with this story churn up in you—about unrevealed promise in your life, long-held prayers, or your ability to change. Pray to the Lord, and rest in God's promise.

EXERCISE 2

Read Luke 1:24-25. Try to put yourself in the story in the place of Elizabeth, a woman beyond childbearing years. Imagine how you learn of Zechariah's experience and discover what has happened. What is your reaction? Why do you decide to go into seclusion, and how does it help you? Imagine how you spend your time and what you are pondering and praying about during those five months apart. Reflect on the ways you identify with Elizabeth. For example, is God trying to tell you about something new happening in your life? Would some time apart help it become a reality?

EXERCISE 3

Read Luke 1:26-38. After reading the story of the Annunciation, go back through the story slowly in your imagination, putting yourself in Mary's place. Try to imagine yourself as Mary, hearing the angel's message. Where are you? What do you see and hear? What range of emotions do you feel? How do you respond to the angel? How does the "Holy Spirit...come upon you"? Reflect on what your imaginings with the story stir within you. What connections do you make with the divine promise in your life? Compare your response to Mary's response.

EXERCISE 4

Read Luke 2:8-20. Identify with the shepherds' story and their changes of emotion. What is the good news that you hear from the angel? Let your heart fill with song: carols, choruses, or portions of Handel's *Messiah*. Write your own words of praise. Trace your search for Mary and Joseph and the child. When you find them, what do you see, smell, or feel? What do you actually say to them? Reflect on what surprised you as you experienced the story in your imagination.

EXERCISE 5

Read Luke 2:22-38. Imagine yourself as a bystander in the crowd when Mary and Joseph bring Jesus to the Temple. Close your eyes and picture the scene as vividly as you can, using all five senses. Watch the story unfold as Simeon and Anna play their parts. Feel free to refer to the text, but hold the scene in your mind. If you would like to interact in some way—speak to Simeon, hold the baby and offer your own praise—go ahead. Afterward, write about any actions you took in the scene, your reactions, feelings, thoughts. Spend a few moments reflecting on what your meditation may mean for your life.

Remember to review your journal entries for the week in preparation for the group meeting.

Part 2, Week 5
Group Meditation with Scripture

Although Protestants have held firmly to the conviction that every individual who seeks the Word of God may find it in the scriptures, they have had to recognize also the values of listening to God in the company of other believers. Corporate meditation can contribute in a number of ways to listening for the Word of God in scripture.

I can find my true identity, my true name, only by sharing in the life of the community, the people of God, and taking my proper place there.

—Mary Jean Manninen

The Benefits of Group Meditation

Group meditation on scripture broadens perspectives. Culture exerts a powerful influence over the way we listen and what we hear. It beats, hammers, molds, and engraves us to such an extent that we may hear what the culture says rather than what God says through scripture. The more restricted our cultural experience, the more limited our ability to hear God through the scriptures. A group may also exhibit a narrow perspective. The more diverse the group, the more likely it is that the members will be able to broaden one another's outlook. It is amazing how many and diverse are the perspectives that participants hear in a gathering of the World Council of Churches where more than three hundred denominations from 120 nations are represented. Although few of us have opportunities to share in such meetings, we can find groups that will expand our individual outlook.

Group meditation can correct individual idiosyncrasies. People who are serious about meditation on scripture have sometimes come up with far-fetched interpretations of scripture and have blamed God as well as the devil for all sorts of questionable thoughts. Taken out of context, individual passages of scripture often yield curious conclusions. When John Bunyan used the Puritan method of relying on scriptures to dart into his mind and heart and tell him whether he was one of the "elect," for instance, it put him on a roller coaster emotionally. Sometimes he heard a reassuring word, "Whoever comes to me I will in no wise cast out." Most of the time, however, he did not get a positive word. The passage about Esau selling his birthright kept springing up. He became convinced that he was a modern Esau who had sold not his natural but his Christian birthright. He feared that he had committed the unpardonable sin. His moods rocketed up and down. He could never come to an even keel. What helped most to rescue him was the pastor John Gifford and participation in a little group at Gifford's home.[1] In his classic allegory *The Pilgrim's Progress*, Bunyan's main character Christian identified this church at Bedford as Interpreter's House, where he had seen "things rare and profitable; things pleasant, dreadful, things to make me stable in what I have begun to take in hand."[2] Group interaction forces participants to think more deeply and carefully about what they hear and how they apply insights.

Sharing insights with others should increase our confidence that we are listening well and hearing correctly. It is possible that only one person may hear God rightly and that a whole crowd may be wrong. Otherwise, we would have no prophets. Think of Martin Luther, father of the Protestant Reformation, standing against the entire German Parliament declaring that he could not act against his conscience:

> Unless I am convicted by Scripture or by right reason (for I trust neither in popes nor in councils, since they have often erred and contradicted themselves)—unless I am thus convinced, I am bound by the texts of the Bible, my conscience is captive to the Word of God, I neither can nor will recant anything, since it is neither right nor safe to act against conscience.[3]

But each of us, no matter how learned or spiritually mature, must shudder when we find ourselves in such a position and admit that we might be wrong. Group members who take seriously their corporate listening will, more often than not, come nearer the truth than an isolated individual.

We should get some joy out of discovering an insight with others. What pleasure in knowing that we are not alone in the search! Another's insight may amplify, clarify, or add new perspective to our own. Someone else in the group may put into words the experience we have but cannot express.

Description of Group Meditation

How does group meditation with scripture work? There are undoubtedly various ways to do it, but most would need to include the following elements: (1) an opening period of silence or some other centering exercise, (2) a reading aloud of a particular passage of scripture, (3) a second period of silence to permit each person to meditate long enough to enter the passage with the most vivid imagination or serious reflection, (4) a time of sharing insights that came to each person, and (5) some sort of closure.[4]

Initiating group meditation with a time of silence permits participants to get away from the day's distractions, become attentive to God, and direct their minds to what God may communicate through the text. Most will arrive still jangling from the day's activities, driving through traffic, memories of unpleasant encounters or other distractions that get in the way of listening. A period of silence will let people refocus before they try to listen. If members have trouble getting settled, the group leader may want to use some kind of relaxation exercise or other centering process, such as a song or simple spoken prayer; but silence is often the best preparation for listening.

Christian meditation has focused especially on the Gospels because in them we have "the story of stories," the story of Jesus.[5] This would not preclude the use of other scriptures, of course, for they form part of God's self-disclosure to us. Many have received deep nourishment

When we limit truth to our way of seeing, we often fail to receive the many surprises God offers us each day. When we open our eyes, and seek to see— through the eyes of a child or from perspectives different from our own— we are often able to experience God's world (and God) in ways we never imagined.

—Dwight W. Vogel and Linda J. Vogel

meditating on the psalms. If a group continues week by week, they might go consecutively through one of the Gospels or follow the lectionary readings for the Christian year. The group leader might choose to use different versions of the Bible, but preference should be given to clear, contemporary translations.

As noted earlier, we may do our meditating in different ways. Some will be more reflective, others more intuitive, and still others more imaginative. Different types of scripture will need different approaches. Meditation on Proverbs will probably rely more on logic than on imagination, whereas meditation on biblical stories invites active imagination. North American adults are probably more skilled in the use of reason than in the use of imagination; they have developed their rational aptitude more than their intuitive or feeling capacities. Consequently, the latter may need special emphasis. It may be helpful to encourage participants to listen to the text like a child who has never heard it before. This kind of listening does not need to conflict with study of scriptures, although some people trained in critical approaches may struggle to use their imaginations. The object of meditation is to go from intellectual processing to letting our inner selves be transformed by the Word.

A fifteen- or twenty-minute period of silence after the reading will give each person time to explore the passage thoroughly. The African-American spiritual "Were You There?" raises the right question. In imagination we put ourselves into the scene. The vast revolution from a more wordy to a more visual culture as a result of recent technological developments may help here. One of my students told me that she was "a more visual person." Are you visually oriented, too, or do you learn better through hearing, reading, or enacting?

In the concluding time when insights are heard, the leader can ask participants, "What jumped out at you? What spoke to your condition?" These are good starters, but people usually don't need much priming. After some minutes of silence, they are ready to let conversation flow. One caution: It is important not to plan an outcome. It is the Word that we want to hear and to which we want to respond.

Example of a Group Meditation

To illustrate, let me give a digest of the sharing from a student group I have led in meditating on the parable of the loving father or the prodigal son (Luke 15:11-32).

Mutual sharing about intimate experience of God—when offered freely and not demanded—enables us all to become more fully who we are.

—Norvene Vest

Leader: "What jumped out at you? What spoke to your condition?"

a: "The elder brother. I guess I would be more like the brother who stayed home, did everything the father expected, and felt a lot of resentment when the prodigal came home."

L: "What struck you about the elder brother?"

a: "The father's love toward him, notwithstanding his pouting and anger. See, he didn't want to go in, but it says, 'The father went out and urged him.' I've needed to hear that, because I've felt guilty for being angry."

b: "I identified more with the prodigal. I've had a pretty rough life. I didn't have an inheritance to claim, but I cut myself off from my family, just like he did. I couldn't stand my old man. He was always on my back. Never let up, so I got out of there. But I hadn't grown up enough to manage life on my own. I fell in with the wrong crowd—drank like a fish, smoked pot, shacked up with women, and did just as he did. Finally, I hit bottom."

L: "What did you do then?"

b: "I didn't do what the prodigal did. I couldn't go home. Not until after my dad died. But I did find God through AA. You know how that program works, don't you?"

L: "Yes."

c: "What strikes me in this parable is the father's watching and going out. It's in both halves. In the part about the prodigal it says, 'While he was still a long way off, the father saw him.' In that part about the pouty, elder brother, when he refused to come in, it says, 'The father went out and urged him.' That just hit me so hard. That is so unlike what my dad would have done."

L: "It's also unlike a Mid-Eastern father. He had to throw off all dignity."

c: "Well, what does that say about God?"

d: "To me it suggests extraordinary love, but it seems a little strange that God would take the initiative in reconciliation. Human parents would want the prodigal to come crawling back and the elder brother to apologize before they accepted them."

L: "I think you have seen the point there. God is not an ordinary parent. God's love is not an ordinary love."

e: "Yeah. If you think about it, you will recognize why God has to take initiative. Physicists now tell us that our universe is made up of more than a hundred fifty billion galaxies. How could we human beings get God's attention if God didn't take the initiative?"

d: "Oh, yes, I see your point. We couldn't shout loud enough, put out a long enough antenna, or send a spaceship far enough to get God's attention if God didn't do that."

f: "As we talk about the parable, it puzzles me that it came to be called 'the parable of the prodigal son.' It's really about the loving father, isn't it?"

L: "Yes, it begins, 'A certain man had two sons.' That's a tip-off."

c: "Right. The father is really the central character who ties both parts of the parable together. I can see now that Jesus was trying to tell us something about God, about the wideness of God's mercy."

a: "I've heard that Jesus told most of his parables in response to critics of his ministry. Whom do you think he was replying to here?"

b: "Probably some of the religious leaders who were critical of his connection with outcasts and sinners like the prodigal."

d: "Oh, that makes it all the more powerful, doesn't it? You can see Jesus confronting those who wanted to claim God only for the respectable. God's love knows no bounds."

L: "Well, that would be a good note to sound for each of us: 'God's love knows no bounds.' Can you hear that word deep inside, confirming what is deepest in you?"

The group meditation would be much more extensive than this summary of high points. However, participants will want some kind of closure. The leader might bring the meditation to a close by having another brief time of silence, reciting the Lord's Prayer, praying a brief verbal prayer, singing a stanza of a familiar hymn, or whatever way would be most appropriate to what has been shared.

Group meditation is another way to feed on the Word of God. It will add to our study of scriptures and listening to God through them. As we use these approaches, however, we keep in mind that our goal is not simply to know the scriptures but to enter into an ever deeper relationship with the living God. May our prayer be like the psalmist's: "As a deer longs for flowing streams, so my soul longs for you, O God. My soul thirsts for God, for the living God" (42:1-2).

DAILY EXERCISES

Read the chapter before you begin the daily exercises. You have learned several different ways to meditate on scripture. This week feel free to use whatever approach feels most comfortable or appropriate as you pray with these stories from the life of Christ. Record your thoughts and experiences in your journal.

EXERCISE 1

Read Mark 3:1-6—Jesus heals a man with a shriveled hand.

EXERCISE 2

Read Luke 13:10-17—Jesus restores a bent-over woman.

EXERCISE 3

Read Mark 6:45-52—Jesus walks on water.

EXERCISE 4

Read John 13:1-17—Jesus washes his disciples' feet.

EXERCISE 5

Read Luke 22:39-46—Jesus prays in Gethsemane.

Remember to review your journal entries for the week in preparation for the group meeting.

Part 3

Deepening Our Prayer: The Heart of Christ

Adele Gonzalez

Part 3, Week 1

Prayer and the Character of God

Has anyone ever asked you about your prayer life? If so, how did the question make you feel? What did you answer? Over the years I have discovered how difficult it is for most Christians to talk or even think about their prayer life. Some of this hesitation may come from the cultural assumption that prayer is a private matter. It may also be that we feel inadequate to comprehend our prayer life or speak clearly about it. Whatever the reason, it appears that prayer, one of the foundational elements of our faith, remains unclear or uncomfortable for many Christians. This week we will look at some of our basic beliefs and assumptions about prayer.

The English word *prayer* comes from the Latin verb *precari*, which means "to entreat or beg." This definition indicates that we always stand in need before God, even when petition is not our intent. In prayer we do not speak *about* God; we speak *with* God. We choose to become present to God who is always present to us and to respond to the One who continually seeks to communicate with us. Prayer is offering God hospitality and opening ourselves to a deepening, personal relationship. In prayer we communicate with God verbally or silently, and we allow time and space for God to communicate with us. To pray is to surrender ourselves to God and to open our hearts, understanding, and wills to God.

The God to Whom We Pray

Without a clear conception of what God is like, where God is to be found, and how God relates to the world, we are likely to be hesitant and limited in prayer. So the starting place for a discussion of thinking about prayer can very reasonably be some reflection on how we can think about God.

—Martha Graybeal Rowlett

In order to understand better the nature of Christian prayer, we need to understand something of the One to whom we pray. Who is God? What we believe about God shapes our prayer profoundly. Christian theology affirms that God is awesome in majesty, splendor, and power. The whole vast and intricate order of creation testifies to this. Indeed, the portrait we receive from the biblical record shows us God as the supreme source of all life whose power to create and recreate is complete. "For nothing will be impossible with God" (Luke 1:37). Yet God is also wise, just, and above all, loving. Therefore, God's power is exercised only in relation to love, "for God is love" (1 John 4:8). So God chooses to use power in a way that is completely consistent with the nature of divine love. Only such love can enable us to say without reserve, "God is good." Divine love frees us to approach the awesome power of God without being overcome by fear.

God's wisdom is an expression both of power and love. Wisdom includes justice and righteousness along with lovingkindness and compassion. God's wisdom is a source of deep consolation to us. Although we cannot understand its depths, we can trust that God knows what is best. God's understanding encompasses infinitely more than we can see, allowing God to act for the good of many persons simultaneously and even for the whole of creation.

A unique affirmation for Christians is that God is Trinitarian. That is, God is known in three persons: Father, Son, and Holy Spirit. The beginning of this doctrine lies in belief in the Incarnation. We believe that in Christ, the ineffable God has been revealed. Christ is the visible "image of the invisible God" (Col. 1:15), and "in him all the fullness of God was pleased to dwell" (Col. 1:19). Jesus Christ reveals to us a God who is essentially relational, who breaks through history, who loves passionately, and who empties God's self (Phil. 2:1-11). The Holy Spirit reveals and confirms these truths in our hearts (1 Cor. 2:6-16). By the Spirit we come to believe that Christ is the power and wisdom of God (1 Cor. 1:24) and the very love of God with us "in the flesh" (John 1:14; 3:16).

The three persons of the Trinity are united in a communion of perfect, mutual love. As persons made in the image of the Trinitarian God, we are created to be in communion with God and with one another. Prayer, in this context, is entering into the communion to which God calls us, a natural response of the heart to the One for whom we were made. Such prayer is definitely personal, but never private. Communion gathers us all into the heart of God.

These understandings of God's nature affect our perception of the act of prayer and how we enter into it. However, our personal histories and ideas also shape how we see and relate to God. Christians through the centuries have learned that as we discover more of God in prayer, we also find more of our true selves. What we are before God *is* what we are and nothing more. Prayer brings forth humility and truthfulness, revealing both our giftedness and our limitations. True prayer is always honest and authentic.

As prayer clarifies our self-understanding, we often discover discrepancies between the reality of God and our images of God. Our ideas about God affect deeply the ways we choose to communicate with God. Who is God for me? Do I see God as parent, judge, friend, or lover? What memories are connected to my images? If I perceive God as friend, I will probably desire to spend quality time in prayer. If I see God as unrelenting judge, I will probably avoid spending much time alone in God's company.

Some years ago, a friend of mine lost her three-year-old daughter to cancer. A well-meaning friend encouraged her to take heart because now "her little girl was in a better place." The friend explained that God had needed "a little angel in heaven" and had chosen her daughter. The grieving mother instantly rejected this "god" who did not seem to care about human suffering and loss. Any God who could take away her child in order to have another angel in heaven resembled more the thief who "comes to steal and kill and destroy" rather than the shepherd who has come "that they may have life, and have it abundantly" (John 10:10). For years, this woman searched for God in a variety of religions. Today she seems to have found some peace in praying to Mary, the mother of Jesus, as the only one able

If we are to grow up into Christ, we must be willing to push out the boundaries and accept the possibility of change—not change in the immutable God who was and is, but change in our perception and understanding of who this God is and who we are in relationship to God.

—Margaret Guenther

*O Lord, I have been
talking to the people;
Thought's wheels have
round me whirled a
fiery zone,
And the recoil of my
words' airy ripple
My heart unheedful
has puffed up and
blown.
Therefore I cast myself
before thee prone:
Lay cool hands on my
burning brain, and
press
From my weak heart
the swelling emptiness.*

—George MacDonald

to understand a mother's grief. In this specific case, the inadequate and false image of God as "thief" became an obstacle to her relationship with the living God.

During a faith-sharing meeting, a young man declared how tired he was of "chasing God," of trying so hard to reach God. A group member asked him who he thought God was. The man replied that as he grew up, God was always a judge, authoritative and remote. He went on to claim that his image had since changed to that of a merciful, loving God. Another group member suggested that perhaps he was trying too hard and that God still somewhat intimidated him. The man responded that he had not tried hard enough, that everyone knew how essential religious practices and disciplines were to attain a relationship with God. This man's early image of God was so deeply ingrained in him that he did not see how it continued to limit his perception of God's desire to be in communion with him. Oftentimes our images of God need to be healed before we can open ourselves to a life-giving prayer relationship.

Classic Postures of Prayer

If our images of God are rooted in grace and truth, we will pray out of our trust in God's goodness and faithfulness. We will open our hearts to this relationship because we believe ourselves to be beloved and wish to respond to this love in prayer.

As a relationship, prayer is dynamic and takes various expressions. The classic postures of prayer in the Christian tradition are adoration and praise, confession or contrition, thanksgiving, and supplication (petition and intercession). John Cassian, one of the early fathers of the church, wrote several treatises on the way prayer was organized in the monasteries at the end of the fourth and beginning of the fifth centuries. He explained, "There are as many types of prayer as there are different persons praying, nay as many as there are different states of mind" (*Collationes* 9.8). Cassian tried to present in an ascending order the kinds of prayers that Paul mentions briefly in 1 Timothy 2:1 (supplication, prayers of commitment, intercession, and thanksgiving).

Whether we consider these postures of prayer in ascending order, or simply as different expressions of our relationship with God, the important point to remember is that all these postures are interconnected and that each prayer contains some expression of the four. In prayer we acknowledge our neediness and our limitations. We are born helpless. As infants we cried when we were hungry or uncomfortable; we depended on others to meet our needs. As adults, particularly in our culture, we strive to become independent and self-sufficient. Sometimes this attitude impedes our awareness that before God we are always in need. Acknowledging our neediness does not mean a posture of slavery or dysfunctionality, but prayer reveals the truth of the creature before the Creator. It is an act of faith as we acknowledge that creation belongs to God and that God's creative presence is in everything. When we confess our limitations or ask for help, we reflect our grateful trust in a God who cares for us and who wishes to hear the deepest desires of our hearts. Thus, petition and confession contain elements of adoration and thanksgiving. As we discover God's presence in our lives, we joyfully adore the divine mystery and grandeur and at the same time thank God for the liberating action of Jesus Christ in human history.

To Pray as Jesus Did

As we consider the importance of prayer in the Christian life, the example of Jesus' own prayer life and his teachings concerning prayer are instructive. For Jesus, prayer was always an encounter with Abba, Father, a name of extraordinary intimacy in Hebrew. In this communion, Jesus gradually learned more fully the meaning of his own identity and God's plan of salvation. In the Gospels we see the centrality of prayer to Jesus' way of life from beginning to end. Jesus prayed at the beginning of his public ministry when he was baptized by John (Luke 3:21-22), and it was in prayer at the end of his earthly life that Jesus fully yielded his will to the Father's will (Luke 22:41-42). At important moments in his life, Jesus devoted special time to prayer. For example, he spent the night in prayer before choosing his

twelve disciples (Luke 6:12), and he went to a deserted place to pray after a long day of healing ministry (Luke 4:42). He prayed a prayer of gratitude and praise when the disciples returned from one of their missionary journeys (Matt. 11:25-26). While praying he was transfigured before Peter, James, and John (Luke 9:28-29). Jesus turned to God in his moment of profound pain and loneliness (Mark 15:34) on the cross, and finally, with his last breath, surrendered everything to God (Luke 23:46).

Jesus taught the necessity of prayer when confronting evil (Mark 9:29), and he taught about the power of uniting with others in prayer (Matt. 18:19-20). Jesus always asked for honesty in prayer. He called all who would listen to pray sincerely from the heart and to validate their prayer in action (Matt. 7:21-23; 15:8-9; Mark 12:40; Luke 18:11-13). Our Lord encouraged his followers to pray with confidence (Matt. 21:21-22). Just as prayer was at the core of Jesus' life and ministry, so it is for us as his followers. Our prayer should be marked by the same qualities as his: trust in God, intimacy, sincerity, honesty, integrity, and gratitude.

Prayer and Commitment

Jesus' prayer in Gethsemane reveals to us most clearly his willingness to trust utterly in God's goodness and higher wisdom. On that night, before his arrest, Jesus was distressed and agitated, experiencing deep grief (Mark 14:34). Jesus has begun his public life with God's profound baptismal affirmation "You are my Son, the Beloved; with you I am well pleased" (Mark 1:11). Now his sonship will be tested to the full. Gethsemane shows us a time of intense inward struggle in Jesus' heart and soul. The messianic task seems too painful to endure. In this final hour, Jesus, in an agony of spirit, prays once again: "Abba, Father, for you all things are possible; remove this cup from me" (Mark 14:36). Then his surrender and commitment to God prevail: "Not what I want, but what you want" (Mark 14:36).

The Gospel of Mark, the shortest and the earliest of the four Gospels, presents a hurried, human Jesus. It has been said of this

Growth in the life of faith demands a constant willingness to let go and leap again. Prayer is not always a smooth, peaceful progress, but a series of detachments from everything…that is not God.

—Maria Boulding

Gospel that if Jesus ever sat down, Mark failed to record it! The Gospel writer presents Jesus' grief and acceptance of God's will in a single verse, giving the impression that it took only seconds for Jesus to move from intense suffering to total abandonment to God. Regardless of the length of the struggle, the depth and vitality of Jesus' prayer enabled him at this critical moment to hold fast to his vocation and remain faithful to God even unto death (Phil. 2:8; Heb. 5:7-10). Jesus had a stronger commitment to God's reign than to his own life.

Similarly, when we pray, we make an implicit commitment to the vision of God's reign offered by Jesus and express our decision to follow in his footsteps. This is particularly evident in the prayer we commonly call the Lord's Prayer. Luke tells us that one day when Jesus was praying in a certain place, one of the disciples said to him, "Lord, teach us to pray." Jesus' response is the heart of Christian prayer:

Father, hallowed be your name.	*Adoration*
Your kingdom come.	*Surrender*
Give us each day our daily bread.	*Supplication*
And forgive us our sins,	*Confession*
for we ourselves forgive everyone indebted to us.	*Commitment to Follow*
And do not bring us to the time of trial.	*Supplication*
(Luke 11:1-4)	

We can pray such a prayer with a grateful heart when we truly believe that "neither death, nor life, nor angels, nor rulers, nor things present, nor things to come, nor powers, nor height, nor depth, nor anything else in all creation, will be able to separate us from the love of God in Christ Jesus our Lord" (Rom. 8:38-39). Only as we grow into a deep assurance of God's faithful love and care for us can we commit ourselves without reserve to the reign of God.

Our relationship with God is multifaceted. At times, it is like a parent-child relationship. Sometimes it has the character of a master-servant relationship; at others, it is like the relationship between friends. It may even resemble the intimacy between lovers. As we mature in faith, we tend to grow from the child or servant relationship into the friend or lover relationship. Jesus tells his disciples at the end of three years together that he no longer calls them servants but friends because he has shared with them his own intimate knowledge of God (John 15:15). The more we know God personally in the relationship of prayer, the more that relationship becomes friendship between God, who is Love, and ourselves, God's beloved.

In prayer we are invited to respond to God's initiative with attentiveness, openness, humility, and honesty. As we grow into deeper intimacy with the divine Friend, our prayer becomes more trusting. We trust in God's presence even when we cannot perceive or feel it, even when we cannot pray or do not know how to pray. We are confident in God's steadfast love in our pain and in our joy. We come to see that our God asks us not for perfect prayers, whatever we may imagine them to be, but for fidelity to the relationship that God, the lover of our souls, so deeply desires. The ultimate goal of the Christian life is union with God through Christ. It is a union of wills, in love, expressed symbolically and beautifully in the poem known as the Song of Solomon.

> I am my beloved's,
>   and his desire is for me.
> Come, my beloved,
>   let us go forth into the fields,
>   and lodge in the villages....
> There I will give you my love (7:10-12).

To live the life of prayer means to emerge from my drowse, to awaken to the communing, guiding, healing, clarifying, and transforming current of God's Holy Spirit in which I am immersed.

—Douglas V. Steere

DAILY EXERCISES

Read the chapter for Week 1 entitled "Prayer and the Character of God." Mark the parts that yield insight, challenge, or questions for you. In preparation, quiet yourself and reflect on the following words:

> Like the spiritual life itself, prayer is initiated by God. No matter what we think about the origin of our prayers, they are all a response to the hidden workings of the Spirit within.[1]

This week's daily exercises focus on the development of the practice of prayer in your life.

EXERCISE 1

Read 1 Samuel 3:1-14. This is a story about the boy Samuel and how Eli helps him recognize and respond to the voice of the Lord. What are your earliest experiences of prayer? What was your understanding of prayer as a child, and how has it changed? Who or what helped you recognize and respond to the presence of God in your life?

Devote at least five minutes of time to becoming present to God—the God who is with you now—and to focusing on God's love for you. Do so in whatever way helps you and seems authentic for you.

EXERCISE 2

Read Luke 11:1-4. One of Jesus' disciples asks him to teach them to pray. What do you feel this disciple really wanted? Put yourself in the his place and personalize the request to Jesus. What about you? What do you seek as you set out on this journey of "deepening your prayer"?

Devote at least five minutes of your time to becoming present to God—the God who is with you now. Do so in whatever way helps you and seems real. Take time to record your experience in your journal.

EXERCISE 3

Read Luke 11:1-4. Read the story with an eye and ear to the prayer Jesus taught his disciples to pray. On page 119, notice how the successive phrases of the Lord's Prayer invite you to assume several "postures" of prayer (adoration, surrender, etc.) in your relationship with God. Which phrase in the prayer represents your most common posture

before God? your least comfortable posture that challenges you to grow in your life with God?

Devote five minutes of your time to becoming present to God and responding to the fullness of God's call. Do so in whatever way you can. Take a moment to record your experience in your journal.

EXERCISE 4

Read Psalm 18:1-2, a psalm of adoration and praise to the Lord. Notice how in two verses the psalmist employs more than ten images to praise God and name who God is! Reflect on the adequacy of these images as expressions of your own praise and adoration for God. Personalize Psalm 18:1-2 by rewriting it and adding your own images for God.

Take five minutes to celebrate God's presence and express yourself to God in whatever way seems best (sitting, walking, dancing, singing). Record your experience in your journal.

EXERCISE 5

Read the following prayer (from Augustine's *Confessions*) slowly, out loud if possible. Let it penetrate your heart.

> I came to love you late, O Beauty, so ancient, so new.
> I came to love you late!
> Look! You were internal and I was external,
> running about in my ugly fashion,
>   seeking you in the beautiful things you made.
> You were with me, but I was not with you.
> Those things kept me far from you,
> even though if they were not in you, they would not be at all.
> You called and cried out and broke open my deafness.
> You gleamed and shone and chased away my blindness.
> I breathed in your fragrance and pant for more.
>   I tasted and now hunger and thirst.
>   You touched me and I burn for your presence.[2]

Devote five minutes to allowing Augustine's prayer to lead you into an awareness of God's presence. Take a moment to record your experience in your journal.

Review your week's journal entries to prepare for the group meeting.

Dealing with Impediments to Prayer

*R*ecently, I heard a woman talk about her prayer life with some friends in a faith-sharing group. She was frustrated, and her friends wanted to help. At their prompting she explained that for the past few weeks her prayer had been "dry," and she was not getting anything out of it. Since I had been invited to participate that night in their group, I asked the woman to tell us more about what she called dryness. She told how she had always been able to express her needs to the Lord and to feel comforted in her prayer times. "The words just flowed," she said, "and it was always such a beautiful experience! I sensed the Lord's presence so deeply, and I always felt inspired and uplifted. But now, I don't feel anything anymore, and words just do not come to my mind. When they do, they seem to fall flat, as if they were hitting a ceiling or bouncing around in my head. I just don't feel connected anymore!" Other members of the group confessed that at times they had experienced the same problem in their prayer.

This situation is not uncommon. Many Christians think that prayer should always be easy, natural, and spontaneous. We want to express ourselves in meaningful ways and to experience a sense of God's presence as we pray. We feel a sense of accomplishment when we can tell God clearly all that is in our hearts and minds. And certainly we experience comfort and inspiration in the feelings that can accompany our prayers. Could we be placing too much importance

on what we say and feel, and not enough on what God wants to communicate to us?

Praying is not always easy, natural, or spontaneous. If we take our prayer life seriously, we will likely experience times when praying becomes a challenge and a struggle. Many things such as fatigue, fear, doubt, illness, changing perceptions, and strong emotions can come between us and our prayer. It helps to look at these and see what we can learn from them about ourselves and our relationship with God. This week we will look at some common misunderstandings about prayer. We will also reflect on what we experience as obstacles to prayer and how we can deal with them.

Misunderstandings of Prayer

The First Letter of John reminds us, "In this is love, not that we loved God but that he loved us" (4:10). As I have said, prayer is always our response to the God who loves us and desires to be in communion with us. A meaningful prayer life is not something we achieve by pointing to our own merits or by becoming "spiritual gymnasts" who master a variety of techniques. While spiritual practices and methods facilitate our disposition to prayer, prayer itself remains a response of the heart to the free initiative of our loving God.

Many people doubt God's unconditional love and availability. Sometimes our life experiences make this truth hard to believe. We tend to compare God with people and to imagine God in human ways. If my father was not there for me as a child when I needed him, then I may well have believed that God, the Father, could not possibly be there either. If our parents were stern, rigid disciplinarians, always ready to judge and criticize, we may have difficulty accepting the idea that God's love is unconditional or that "divine judgment" serves the larger purpose of redemption and restoration. If we become frustrated in our attempts to pray, we may imagine that God is also tired of trying to connect with us. Because human love has limits, we tend to place limits on God's infinite love. But prayer invites us to ponder the mystery of God's utterly faithful way of loving.

Prayer is communion with God. It is a matter of making connections with the One who stands at the center of all life and joy, and of learning to live with those connections all the time.

—John Killinger

In the book of the prophet Hosea we find a particularly encouraging passage. Using some of the most touching images in prophetic literature, Hosea compares Israel to a wife to whom the Lord says, "I will take you for my wife in faithfulness; and you shall know the Lord" (Hos. 2:20). The prophet also compares God's love with that of a parent: "When Israel was a child, I loved him.… / It was I who taught Ephraim to walk, / I took them up in my arms.… / I led them with cords of human kindness, / with bands of love. / I was to them like those who lift infants to their cheeks" (Hos. 11:1, 3-4). But God also laments deeply the people's turning away and worshiping other gods. God struggles with a desire to give up on Israel in "fierce anger" (Hos. 11:9). In a beautiful soliloquy that has been preserved as a gem of the prophetic tradition, the Lord exclaims, "I will not again destroy Ephraim; for I am God and no mortal" (Hos. 11:9). This is the core truth that we find difficult to comprehend. God is not like us! When we enter prayer, we need not fear that God is too tired or irritated to be present to us. God is no mortal. God is faithful!

Because of this faithfulness, we can trust that in prayer we always meet God, whether our experience of prayer is easy or difficult. We can also trust that God's love and desire for us are greater than our ability to utter "good prayers" or even deeply felt prayers. We enter prayer as a response to God who already possesses us by love, not in an effort to reach One who is trying to elude us. For Christians, prayer is a sure encounter with God but not necessarily in the way we expect or desire. In our efforts to "succeed" with our personal agendas, we may fail to receive the unconditional love and intimacy that God freely offers in unexpected ways.

Christian prayer is always contextual; that is, it is affected by who we are, what we do, where we live, and how we feel. We are finite in the ways we respond to God. Often we experience certain elements of life as impediments to prayer. We are too tired, do not have enough time, do not have sufficient space in our crowded houses, or do not feel the way we think we should. Prayer can prompt one of the most poignant struggles of the Christian life and yet without a vital prayer life, genuine growth in faith is impeded.

Provided that we don't give up, the Lord will guide everything for our benefit, even though we may not find someone to teach us. There is no other remedy for this evil of giving up prayer than to begin again; otherwise the soul will gradually lose more each day.

—Teresa of Avila

Among the variety of obstacles to prayer, I have chosen to address three that surface most frequently in my life and ministry.

Time as an Obstacle

The first impediment is often expressed this way: "I don't have enough time! Between my job, family, and other commitments, twenty-four hours are never enough!" We live in a complicated, busy society, and our cares are many. Yet I am amazed at the many things we squeeze into our busy schedules when they seem important enough.

I remember one morning when I had decided I did not have time to pray. As I was preparing to leave for work, the doorbell rang. A service man from a local store was there to fix a recently installed appliance. He apologized for showing up unannounced but explained that he was in the neighborhood and had taken the opportunity to pay a call to my house. I welcomed him warmly and thanked him for thinking of us. Promptly, I called my office to say that I was going to be an hour or so late. I knew this would further cramp my day but could not pass up the opportunity to have my kitchen appliance serviced. Later, as I was driving to the office, a question popped into my head: Where did that hour come from? The bottom line was that I needed the repair and my decision was cost-effective! I was not sure I would have felt better if I had devoted the same hour to prayer on that hectic morning. With the repair man I got the results I wanted; maybe with God I would not have gotten my way.

Sometimes the time factor serves as an excuse to mask feelings of apathy or anxiety in prayer. While our feelings are important and God uses them to communicate with us, we must not allow them to determine our fidelity to the relationship. We pray not to "feel good" but to be faithful.

While few of us have much spare time, we often do not take advantage of time we have. Take, for example, the waiting room in a doctor's office. We check our watches frequently, hoping that time will move faster. We may read magazines, watch a little television, or observe people. Why not use these precious minutes or hours to connect intentionally with God? Last week a friend told me that her entire attitude about driving had changed dramatically when she started to pray in the car (not with her eyes closed!). She recounted how, when detained in heavy traffic, she used to become very frustrated and even violent. Now she thanks God for this slow time alone and feels that for the first time she is heeding Paul's advice to "pray without ceasing" (1 Thess. 5:17).

Giving time to prayer is a matter of priority and intention. We will make time for the relationship prayer expresses, if truly desired. Moreover, with hearts tuned in to God's presence in the midst of life, we will discover hidden calls to prayer in the daily round of activities.

Need for Control

A second key obstacle to a deeper, truer life of prayer is our need to control outcomes. In prayer we are called to let go, to surrender ourselves to God who loves us and knows us in ways we cannot even begin to imagine. Letting go is difficult, in part, because we do not trust that God's answers to our prayers, or even the experience of prayer itself, will be what we want them to be. As Christians, we sometimes claim that we trust completely in God's ways. Yet many of us try to tell God exactly what we want, as well as when and how we want it. When we pray, are we trusting in God or in our own intelligent opinions? I have heard people claim that we show great trust in God when we expect to get what we ask for. This is perhaps based on scripture passages reassuring us that "everyone who asks receives" (Matt. 7:8). However, many of us practice what I call selective listening to the Word of God. We fail to hear that whatever the specific hopes and desires of our prayers, God will give "good things to those who ask" (Matt. 7:11). Are we sure that in our prayer we are asking for these good things? God asks us to "strive first for the kingdom of God…and all these things will be given…as well" (Matt. 6:33). Is our prayer about seeking first the kingdom or about the things to be given us? In the Gospel of Luke, Jesus tells Martha that she is worried and distracted by many things (Luke 10:41). I wonder if our prayer is as honestly

We must in all our prayers carefully avoid wishing to confine God to certain circumstances, or prescribe to God the time, place, or mode of action.…For before we offer up any petition for ourselves, we ask that God's will may be done, and by so doing place our will in subordination to God's.

—John Calvin

127

trusting as Jesus': "Father…not what I want but what you want" (Matt. 26:39); "Our Father…your will be done, on earth as it is in heaven" (Matt. 6:10).

Mary questioned the angel who told of Jesus' birth; Joseph too had his doubts. Many times the disciples did not seem to understand when Jesus spoke of the kingdom of God. Yet, because of their yes, belief in Jesus is possible today. Is the attitude we take to prayer our own yes, a surrender to God's ways, trusting in God's mercy and love for us? Entering into prayer means taking a risk. We may not hear what we want to hear, or worse, we may not hear anything. A French spiritual writer of the seventeenth century, Jean-Pierre de Caussade, once wrote:

> The great and firm foundation of the spiritual life is the offering of ourselves to God and being subject to his will in all things.…Once we have this foundation, all we need to do is spend our lives rejoicing that God is God and being so wholly abandoned to his will that we are quite indifferent as to what we do and equally indifferent as to what use he makes of our activities. Our main duty is to abandon ourselves.[1]

Desiring to control the outcome of prayer may result from our fears and anxieties or lack of faith. An excessive need for control is founded either on secular values or on deep psychological needs rather than on the gospel message and the lifestyle of Christian disciples.

Fear of What We May Discover about Ourselves

A recent experience with a friend illustrates the final obstacle to prayer I want to address. A few weeks ago, this friend committed to spend one hour each day praying with scripture. When I saw her last week, she seemed eager to share her experience. After some initial hesitation, she confided that the past days had been very difficult for her. "Things that I thought were forgotten surfaced again," she exclaimed with dismay. As I listened, she continued, "There are areas in my life that I considered healed, but memories have come back to upset me. I don't like the way I am feeling. I was sure that I had left behind all anger and resentment, but they are still in me. I don't like myself when

I feel this way!" When I asked how she was dealing with her discomfort, she answered, "I don't think it was a good idea for me to pray so much at this time. Maybe I'll start this discipline again at a later time."

When we pray, we encounter not only God but also our own truth, the brokenness of our human condition. This is not a comfortable reality to face. It may help to remember Jesus' identification with everything that is deepest in our humanity, including strong emotions such as fear and anger. Jesus' prayers stand as evidence of his intimate relationship with God even as he confronted the challenges of his humanity. Christian prayer is neither therapy to obtain tranquility nor a relaxation technique. Encountering the living God sometimes shatters the surface peacefulness of our lives.

Prayer has been compared to a furnace of transformation. If we are willing to see clearly what is in our hearts and offer it to God, we gradually discover what it means to be conformed to the image of God. But staying open to the process is often painful and frustrating. If God seeks and loves us and we willingly respond, why all these difficulties? Again we turn to Jesus, God among us, taking on all aspects of our humanity, including our fatigue, frustration, and disappointment. His total surrender on the cross was not about understanding but about surrendering. We can bring our feelings of frustration, discomfort, and disappointment right into our prayer and wait in faith for God's response. We can express honestly our fears and discomfort and listen for the word God will speak to us. Alongside Jesus, we take prayer as a relationship between two friends, humbly accepting that the human condition limits one of the two. As we continue to journey in faithfulness, we join the blind men of the Gospel of Matthew: "Have mercy on us, Son of David!" (Matt. 9:27).

Begin where you are. Obey now. Use what little obedience you are capable of, even if it be like a grain of mustard seed. Begin where you are. Live this present moment, this present hour as you now sit in your seats, in utter, utter submission and openness toward [God].

—Thomas R. Kelly

DAILY EXERCISES

Read the chapter for Week 2, "Dealing with Impediments to Prayer." Keep a journal or blank book beside you to record your thoughts, questions, prayers, and images. Begin your exercises by thinking about the following quotation:

> In learning to pray, no laboratory is needed but a room, no apparatus but ourselves. The living God is the field of force into which we enter in prayer, and the only really fatal failure is to stop praying and not to begin again.[2]

These exercises will challenge you to identify the impediments to prayer in your life and to look carefully at your resistance to God's presence in your life.

EXERCISE 1

Read Isaiah 44:6-11. What are the common idols of our day? Identify a popular image of God with which you struggle or which makes prayer difficult for you (such as angry parent, distant creator, divine accountant, legalistic judge, chief executive of the universe, male God). Draw this image.

Now consider what image of God opens you to the divine presence and facilitates prayer (for example, shepherd, loving parent, creator, light)? Draw a symbol that expresses your truest image of God.

Devote several minutes to being present to God, who exceeds all our images and yet becomes real to us in Christ, "the image of the invisible God" (Col. 1:15). Record your experience in your journal.

EXERCISE 2

Read Matthew 26:36-46. In this passage, Jesus prays in the garden of Gethsemane, and the disciples cannot stay awake with him for even one hour. What do you think might have caused the disciples to have trouble staying awake and available to Jesus? Reflect on the three impediments to prayer described in this week's chapter. Which contributes most to your difficulty staying awake spiritually? Record your thoughts in your journal.

Devote at least five minutes to being present and available to Christ without falling asleep. Record your experience, insights, and challenges.

EXERCISE 3

Read Psalm 139:1-18. Explore how you feel about God's searching you and knowing you. Draw an image of your life as a house with rooms for each dimension of you (such as family, work, church, etc.). Invite the Lord to take an imaginary walk with you through the house. Notice your feelings about God and about yourself as you go from room to room. Also notice the Lord's response to each room. Reflect in your journal on how your feelings about your life or God may translate into either readiness or reluctance to pray.

Devote several minutes to opening afresh some part of your life to God's searching and knowing presence. Record your experience.

EXERCISE 4

Read Mark 9:2-9. In this story, Jesus leads his disciples "up a high mountain apart, by themselves" to experience him and themselves in God's transforming presence. Peter interrupts the experience with ideas about how to improve it, preserve it, or do something useful with it. What in you often interrupts your being present to God?

Devote at least ten minutes to being present to God, centering your attention on the voice that says, "This is my Son, the Beloved; listen to him!" Record your insights and experience.

EXERCISE 5

Read Matthew 11:28. Use your entire time to listen deeply to God. Leave your prayer time in God's hands. Do not work too hard. You might begin with Jesus' invitation: "Come to me, all you that are weary and are carrying heavy burdens, and I will give you rest." Rest in the Lord and release your heaviness to God. At the end of your time of silence, record your awareness, feelings, insights, surprises, or other responses in your journal.

Review your journal for the week in preparation for the group meeting.

Part 3, Week 3
Prayers of Petition and Intercession

Some time ago, my friend Sarah's father suffered a heart attack. Luckily Sarah was visiting him at the time. She administered CPR until the paramedics arrived and took him to a nearby hospital. After his condition improved, Sarah told a church group of her gratitude for the opportunity to have saved her father's life. She felt that God had guided her and protected her father. Many of her church friends gathered to offer prayers of thanksgiving for what Sarah considered her "little miracle." After a quick recovery, Sarah's father was released from the hospital and returned home to his family.

A few months later, Sarah called me. Her father had just been diagnosed with a malignant brain tumor. He was experiencing double vision and other symptoms. The tumor, the doctor said, was inoperable. His condition rapidly deteriorated. At the time of his death a few months later, he was unable to see, hear, or speak; he was a withered body lying on the bed, with no hope of recovery. My friend felt deeply anguished. Not only had her father died a painful and humiliating death, but she considered herself responsible for the catastrophe. "I should have let him die," she would cry. "At least he would have died in peace. Why did God allow this to happen?" I never found the right words to console her. I could only listen and hold her in prayer.

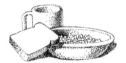

This story disturbs our deepest sensibilities, raising many natural and difficult questions. What happened here? Did God fail Sarah? Did Sarah "fail" her father by saving him in the first crisis? Did family and friends pray for the wrong thing?

Prayers of petition and intercession can be mystifying. Sometimes we feel that our prayers go unanswered, and we question the value of asking for anything at all. Other times, as in Sarah's case, we wonder if we have sought or asked for the wrong thing. If we cannot really know what is best for anyone at any given time, why ask at all? For centuries these questions have been the subject of debate and countless conversations in religious circles. Many books have been written on the topic, and Christians continue to wonder about them. We may not have clarity on all these issues, but we do know that Christ urges us to make our requests known to a God who loves us and cares for us. This week we will focus on prayers of petition and intercession, prayers for ourselves and prayers for others.

Prayer of Petition

In prayer we open ourselves to the chance that God will do something with us that we had not intended.

—Emilie Griffin

Petition means "to ask or to beseech." Petition is one of the fundamental stances of the human being before the mystery of God. Just as in adoration we recognize the wonder of God, in our prayers of petition we acknowledge our dependency on God. Because we believe in a relational God, we also believe that God desires a personal relationship with us. In this context we offer petitions for ourselves. Petition connects our human need with faith in a God who cares for us and desires our good. The problem arises when we think that we know what is best for ourselves and allow the conviction of our "knowing" to shape our petition. We earnestly pray for what we perceive to be the joy, healing, or goodness we need, forgetting that the prayer of petition is not a tool to manipulate God but a response to God out of our poverty and need. Humans cannot control the mystery of God's will. Yet often when we do not receive the desired answers to our requests, we feel resentful and hopeless.

I would like to suggest two necessary elements in our prayer of petition: (1) a willingness to ask, trusting the deep goodness and love in God's response, whether or not we can see it as such; and (2) a willingness to receive what comes as from the hand of God, surrendering to the divine will in an act of faith.

Asking. We present our needs to God, although God fully knows them already. "Even before a word is on my tongue, O Lord, you know it completely" (Ps. 139:4). The psalmist's awareness of God's omniscience does not prevent him from crying out to God: "You are my God; give ear, O Lord, to the voice of my supplications" (Ps. 140:6); "Incline your ear, O Lord, and answer me, for I am poor and needy" (Ps. 86:1). Like the psalmist, we do not pray to inform God of our needs; we pray because we depend on God and trust in God's love for us.

Often our prayers help us perceive our true needs more clearly. We may imagine that our need is for physical healing when the root need is for emotional or relational healing. We may begin by praying earnestly for a particular outcome and find over time that our prayers get "sifted" in God's presence. Self-centered, anxious, and superfluous aspects of our prayer simply fall away as the Spirit purifies our desires. This falling away is part of how God works to reshape our will so that it conforms more closely to God's perfect will. Jesus encourages us to seek, ask, and knock so that good gifts may be given by God and found by us (see Luke 11:9-10). More than anything, God wants to "give the Holy Spirit to those who ask him" (Luke 11:13). This is the greatest of gifts, the one that orders all else we could hope to seek because the Spirit discerns truly what is the will of God (see Rom. 8:27).

Petition, then, is not aimed at changing God's heart because God already desires the best for us. Instead, it unites our desires to those things that God already wishes to give us but that require our consent to be granted. Every time we ask God to come to our assistance, we open ourselves to the coming of God's kingdom within and among us. When we pray as Jesus taught us to pray, we ask for many things:

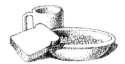

material sustenance, pardon, strength in our weakness, wisdom in our confusion, and comfort in our suffering. We come in faith to ask God, the giver of life, to sustain our spiritual, physical, and emotional life. We ask for the deep healing that may or may not include the cure of our illnesses. Above all, we ask for the grace of the Holy Spirit and the fulfillment of God's kingdom (Matt. 6:10).

Receiving. When we present our petitions to God, we yield to the one who knit us together in the womb (Ps. 139:13) and who knows us better than we know ourselves: "Before I formed you in the womb I knew you" (Jer. 1:5). My friend Sarah did not know what was best for her father. God is the only one who really knew. She thought it would have been better had he died "peacefully" of a heart attack. Others suggested that her father needed the extra time to prepare better for his final encounter with God. We can only guess what was in God's mind in this situation; but more important, we can trust what is in God's heart.

In prayers of petition and intercession, we exclaim with the psalmist, "I delight to do your will, O my God; your law is within my heart" (Ps. 40:8). Receptivity to God's response does not mean a resigned passivity to what God has already decided without our involvement. On the contrary, when we willingly yield ourselves to God, we become active collaborators in the divine plan, full-time participants in God's project for creation. By uniting our will to God's will, we join in Jesus' Gethsemane prayer. In fully accepting God's will, Jesus fulfilled his identity as God's Son, the Beloved, with whom God was well pleased (Luke 3:22). As we come to accept and desire God's will fully, we too fulfill the human identity we have been given as sons and daughters of the living God.

Prayer of Intercession

> *To pray for others means to offer others a hospitable place where I can really listen to their needs and pains.*
> —Henri J. M. Nouwen

Because we believe ourselves to be children of the one God, we express our solidarity and communion when we pray on behalf of others. In the Hebrew Scriptures we find great intercessors such as Abraham, Moses, and the prophets, who kept calling the people back to fidelity to the covenant and interceded for their sins. The Suffering Servant offers a biblical model of intercessory prayer: "He bore the sin of many, and made intercession for the transgressors" (Isa. 53:12). The author of the Letter to the Hebrews assigns this role to Jesus: Jesus as the great intercessor, the high priest, the mediator of the new covenant, offered once to bear the sins of many (Heb. 7:26; 9:15, 28). Paul offers Jesus' intercessory role as our hope in his Letter to the Romans, which presents Christ, not as the one who is to condemn, but as the one "who died, yes, who was raised, who is at the right hand of God, who indeed intercedes for us" (8:34). As Christians we maintain that God alone can grant us good things and that Christ is our true mediator or intercessor before God. When we offer prayers of intercession on behalf of others, we express our common need as children of the one God and join our intentions with the heart of Christ who purifies and presents our needs before God.

God is continually working out a redemptive process in this world, and God uses the faith of believing persons in the mysterious working of this process. Our prayers can and do make a difference. They are, as one writer puts it, "a cosmic fact, that…may tip the balance."[1] The tremendous dignity and privilege of being able to join God's saving, transforming intentions for this world should give us great courage in our prayers.

> *We do not have enough conviction about prayer. If we pray only a little, our prayers are answered only to that degree. If we pray much, we receive many answers. Christ's activity was founded on prayer. We must not make ourselves alone the center, but our prayers must show a sense of responsibility toward God…for the whole world.*
>
> —Toyohiko Kagawa

What to Pray For

Sarah and her friends questioned the legitimacy of their prayer. Like them, we really do not know what is best for anyone. What then do we pray for in our petitions and intercessions?

I have said that we pray because we trust God's promise to help us in our need. The question then is, "What do we really need?" In some situations, the need is most apparent, and we want to pray for those needs in a concrete fashion. Yet beyond the obvious needs, I would like to suggest three common human needs, necessary elements in our quest for healing, that we often overlook in our prayers of petition and intercession. They are our need for love, forgiveness, and peace.

Intercession is not only the best arbitrator of all differences, the best promoter of true friendship, the best cure and preservative against all unkind tempers, all angry and haughty passions, but is also of great use to discover to us the true state of our own hearts.

—William Law

When we stand before God, we realize how wounded we are, how sinful and limited our human response to God's love is. Like the tax collectors and sinners of Jesus' time, we come near to listen to him. Some would remind us that we do not deserve to be close to Jesus, that we are not good enough to enjoy his love. To those arguments Jesus responds with the parable of the prodigal son (Luke 15:11-32). Through this powerful story, Jesus reveals to us the unconditional love of a God who desires to welcome us back into the Father's house, not because of our deep contrition, but because of God's outrageous love. When we pray, we need to ask for openness to this love, to invite God's mercy into our lives. God's greatest desire is to be in communion with each one of us. This was Jesus' promise: "Those who love me will keep my word, and my Father will love them, and we will come to them and make our home with them" (John 14:23). Nothing could be more intimate. We need to ask for the grace to accept God's love for ourselves and for others, so that we in turn may love God and offer ourselves as the dwelling place of the eternal Lover!

We also need to ask for forgiveness for ourselves and for others, and for the grace to accept it. Many of us have difficulty letting go of the past. We cling to our guilt and our sin, even though God has already forgotten them. Recently I heard someone suggest that God throws our sins in a lake and then posts a "No Fishing" sign by it. To accept God's forgiveness and to forgive ourselves for being less than perfect are necessary conditions for our openness to forgive others. Our prayers of petition include asking for forgiveness and for the grace to extend that forgiveness to those who offend us.

Finally, when we pray we need to ask for peace. We can ask God to transform our lives into a gift of peace for others and ask that those for whom we pray receive it. A beautiful prayer attributed to Francis of Assisi, a thirteenth-century saint, begins with the request: "Lord, make me an instrument of thy peace; where there is hatred, let me sow love; where there is injury, pardon." When we pray like this, we open ourselves to the transforming power of the peace of the risen Christ. He gave this gift of *shalom* to a group of frightened disciples after his resurrection. "Peace be with you [*shalom*]" (John 20:19-21).

Prayer is personal but never private. When we pray we are always in communion with the body of Christ, the church, the community of all believers. In our prayers of petition and intercession, we ask for what we think we and others need but trust that God knows best. We ask openly and honestly out of our poverty, not as an attempt to control God. Moreover, when we ask for anything, we also make a deeper commitment to be faithful followers of Christ. As we present our petitions to God and ask for the coming of God's kingdom, we also commit ourselves to work for its realization to the best of our abilities.

Our prayers of petition and intercession are not a quiet activity but one full of energy and action. As we ask, we surrender; as we express our needs and hopes, we trust. There is nothing resigned about this form of prayer. It calls for faith, openness, and a deep commitment to work with God toward the coming of the kingdom for which we so earnestly pray.

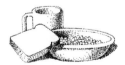

DAILY EXERCISES

Read "Prayers of Petition and Intercession" before you begin the exercises. Keep your journal beside you to record your thoughts, questions, prayers, and insights. Prepare yourself by considering the meaning of the following quotation:

> All your love, your stretching out, your hope, your thirst, God is creating in you so that [God] may fill you...[God] is on the inside of the longing.[2]

This week's exercises invite you to claim the yearnings of your heart in prayer and to join them with God's great yearning for you and for all people in Jesus Christ.

EXERCISE 1

Read Luke 11:9-13. For what do you typically pray? List some of your requests in your notebook or journal. Note your awareness of God's responses. What bearing do Jesus' words of guidance (*ask, search, knock*) have on your experience?

Devote at least ten minutes to your breath prayer. Record your experience in your notebook or journal. Continue using your breath prayer each day as often as you remember it.

EXERCISE 2

Read John 15:7. Note the conditions of this New Testament promise ("If you abide in me, and my words abide in you, ask...."). When you ask God for something, is your attitude one of willfulness ("I am determined to continue to ask for what I want, no matter what!") or willingness ("I present my needs to God but am willing to yield to the persuasions of God's wisdom and love.")? Apply the conditions of John 15:7 to something you are seeking, perhaps your breath prayer. How are you challenged? In what ways does your prayer change?

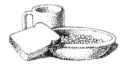

Devote at least ten minutes to your breath prayer. Record your experience in your notebook or journal. Continue to use your breath prayer frequently through each day.

EXERCISE 3

Read Matthew 6:31-33 several times. To reflect on what it means to focus on the kingdom of God, draw a large circle on a page in your notebook or journal. Around the circumference, name "all these things" about which you are anxious. Now consider what Jesus' words, "strive first for the kingdom of God," mean for you. As you gain clarity about what this priority means to you, write the priority in the center of the circle. Reflect on how this priority could change your life over time.

Devote at least a few minutes to your breath prayer. Note any insights about the relationship of your breath prayer to your reflection on priorities.

EXERCISE 4

Read Colossians 1:9-12. Focus on the expansiveness of Paul's hope and prayer for his fellow Christians. Now write a letter to persons in your family, Sunday school class, or workplace expressing your prayer for them. In doing so, give the love of Christ in you full rein to express your highest hopes and passion for their spiritual well-being.

Devote several minutes to your breath prayer. See if you can naturally incorporate your prayer for others as expressed in your letter. Continue your breath prayer throughout the day, remembering Paul's words, "We have not ceased praying for you."

EXERCISE 5

Read Ephesians 6:18-20. These words imply both spontaneity and intentionality in praying for others. "Pray in the Spirit at all times." As you pray your breath prayer, pay attention to people and situations that rise spontaneously in your awareness. Welcome them into your prayer with the love of Christ. Offer them to God in love, trusting the Spirit to work out the specifics. Be open to the appearance of enemies, difficult people, and unexpected faces from long ago. Trust the Spirit to make your prayer a means by which God's love touches these people today.

"Keep alert and always persevere in supplication for all the saints." Experiment by making a list of people you feel committed to pray for regularly, if not daily. Add to it others for whom you feel special responsibility or concern. If the list becomes quite long, break it into seven segments, one for each day of the week. Beginning today, spend a few minutes lifting several of these people to God.

Let your breath prayer adapt to the flow of God's love. Remember to pray it frequently each day.

Remember to review the insights recorded in your notebook or journal for the week in preparation for the group meeting.

Part 3, Week 4
Praying As We Are

Carol and George have been married for fifteen years. They have served as youth ministers in their church for several months. Recently the pastor invited them to attend a conference on the importance of prayer given by a guest speaker. The speaker's words deeply touched them, and they decided to visit a prayer group to which some friends belonged.

The first night the group gathered, George was very excited. He anticipated meeting new people and talking to others about his prayer life. Carol, on the other hand, was having second thoughts about their decision and wondered whether she belonged in a prayer meeting at all.

The prayer community met regularly in the home of one of the members. Upon arrival, Carol and George were warmly welcomed by all present. After brief introductions, songs were sung, and a passage from scripture was read. Immediately someone began to thank and praise God for the word just shared; soon all joined in a spontaneous chorus of praise and thanksgiving. After a brief pause, one of the participants was moved to share a testimony of the change wrought in his life through an encounter with Jesus the previous year. More expressions of praise and thanksgiving for God's goodness and mercy followed this moving story. Soon afterward, the leader invited those present to offer some simple prayers of petition. When the prayer time concluded, the host and hostess asked everyone to stay for

refreshments and informal sharing about the meeting. George felt delighted, full of energy and enthusiasm. Carol was drained, overwhelmed, and could not wait to get home. Once in the car listening to George, Carol felt miserable and thought that surely she was less holy and pious than George. George was empathetic, encouraging her to be patient and to give herself time to become comfortable praying in a group. Neither Carol nor George understood the dynamics of their conversation and arrived home confused and frustrated.

Such situations occur frequently in our congregations. People respond in different ways to the same stimulus and experience. We tend to assume that one party is right and the other wrong or at least that one is more advanced than the other. In this case, Carol feels "less open to prayer" than George. She apparently assumes that he is more receptive to prayer than she is. Yet the opposite could also occur. Carol could argue that this group was not able to be silent and reflective for one minute and that prayers were too emotional and superficial. Must Carol try to enjoy the spontaneous prayer group? Should we as Christians strive for uniformity in our responses to God?

We sometimes feel discouraged because we do not pray like someone we love and admire. However, spiritual writers and guides have consistently warned against casting people into one mold. Many great saints and mystics have cautioned Christians against forcing others to follow one's own spiritual path. One modern teacher, Urban T. Holmes, has provided a brief overview of the variety and richness of the Christian spiritual experience in his book *A History of Christian Spirituality*. He lists two intersecting scales that result in a typology of Christian spirituality. Several authors have used and adapted Holmes's ideas to help people identify their natural style of spirituality. Corinne Ware in her book *Discover Your Spiritual Type* has developed the "Spirituality Wheel Selector" as an instrument to help individuals and congregations explore their preferences.

During this week we will use these and other sources to reflect on the four types of spirituality that result when we use the two intersecting scales. My hope is that this study will help us gain a better understanding of Carol and George's predicament.

The Horizontal Scale: Mystery/Revelation

As Christians, we believe that the all-transcendent God is ineffable and incomprehensible. The book of the prophet Isaiah reminds us: "My thoughts are not your thoughts, nor are your ways my ways, says the LORD. For as the heavens are higher than the earth, so are my ways higher than your ways and my thoughts than your thoughts" (Isa. 55:8-9). Simultaneously, we believe that all created things provide ways of knowing God. Paul writes, "Ever since the creation of the world his eternal power and divine nature, invisible though they are, have been understood and seen through the things he has made" (Rom. 1:20).

At first glance, these statements may appear contradictory. However, they reflect the whole mystery of the Christian God: the God who is with us, Immanuel, yet who remains wholly Other. The Christian tradition has always reflected these two ways of speaking about and relating to God: the way of mystery and the way of revelation.

The way of mystery emphasizes the great dissimilarities between God and creature. It calls for humble seeking and self-emptying in imitation of Christ's love. As a mode of prayer, the way of mystery exhorts the seeker to "leave behind…everything perceived and understood…and…to strive…toward union with him who is beyond all being and knowledge."[1] This translates into a prayer that does not rely on reason, senses, images, or symbols. It is an expression of Christian tradition described by one writer as "that of naked faith, through which one is led in poverty and great longing beyond all concepts and images into a deep hidden knowledge of our union with God in Christ."[2]

In contrast, the way of revelation emphasizes the similarities between God and creation and emphasizes God's incarnation in the person of Jesus. As a mode of prayer, it uses created things, reason, imagining, and feeling as means to relate to God who is revealed and knowable. The renowned thirteenth-century Christian saint Francis of Assisi clearly represents this type of spirituality. Francis had a deep reverence for all God's creatures and viewed communion with them as an encounter with God. For him, all creation was transparent as a sacrament of God's presence. Francis saw God in everything: in the earth, sun, moon, stars, and fire, and in his own physical illnesses, blindness, and, ultimately, in his encounter with "sister death." In his beloved poem of praise, "The Canticle of Creatures," he expressed a fraternal relationship with all that is.

To know God is to know one's own true Self, the ground of one's being. So prayer is an intensely human experience in which our eyes are opened and we begin to see more clearly our own true nature.

—Kenneth Leech

The ways of mystery and revelation are not in competition with each other. They are to some degree complementary and could be placed at opposite ends of the same prayer spectrum. They are connected because the revelation of God is always linked to God's mystery and hiddenness. Moreover, one way is not more desirable than the other. Mystery emphasizes that nothing can fully capture or portray the reality of God, so it is acceptable to go to God in "nothingness." Revelation implies that every created thing shows something of the Divine, so it is acceptable to go to God through everything. Praying in the way of mystery aims to move us beyond sensory or mental awareness into a direct experience of union with God. Praying in the way of revelation looks for God in all things because all creatures are the expression of divine life and can therefore also lead to union with God. Both ways of prayer are solidly rooted in biblical spirituality and as such are valid options for the Christian spiritual seeker.

Where would we find Carol and George on this scale? From the little we know about them, it seems that George found God easily in the concrete testimonies of faith shared in the group. Perhaps Carol would have felt more comfortable if there had been some silent time that would have allowed her to enter into the mystery of God's presence in her preferred way. Is one better than the other?

The Vertical Scale: Mind/Heart

The second scale suggested by Urban T. Holmes[3] is the mind/heart scale. In our desire to know God, some Christians seek illumination of the mind, while others seek illumination of the heart. The former have a more rational or intellectual relationship with God. God to them is known through categories of thought such as goodness, love, truth. The latter seek more to have an affective or feeling relationship with God. The tension between mind and heart preferences is probably one more easily identified in our congregations. Have you ever heard members of your church strongly advocate the need for sermons with better content or the formation of Bible study groups? Do you find others who feel that the quality of fellowship or inspired singing in the church is more important than any sermon? Is one right and the other wrong? We know that both are needed to help a congregation grow. Since we will always find people at both ends of the scale, the challenge is to look at these poles as integral parts of one whole reality and not as opposites in competition. In my own ministry I spend considerable time helping people work through the tension caused by these two positions. For some, having an intellectual insight about God or an awareness of God's will is the central element of their faith. For others, feeling God's presence and loving care is the core of the religious experience. Again, is one better than the other?

I believe our emotions—all of them—belong in our prayers....Our prayers represent not just what we say but who we are, with all our complex longings and feelings.
—Timothy Jones

In the case presented in this chapter, could George's personality be more heart-centered and Carol's more mind-oriented? Might the emotions displayed in the group have made Carol uncomfortable?

Understanding our preferences enables us to recognize and revere the various ways each person reflects God's image. This understanding, in turn, suggests different approaches to prayer. What helps one person's prayer life may hinder another person's spiritual development. We need to be careful about casting people into one mold and assuming that one spiritual path or style of prayer, if helpful to us, must be helpful to everyone else. We need to remember that each person is a unique image of God, created with specific personality traits and preferences that are to be honored as we respond to God's initiative in prayer. Paul writes to the early Christians: "For as in one body we have many members, and not all the members have the same function, so we, who are many, are one body in Christ....We have gifts that differ according to the grace given to us" (Rom. 12:4-6).

If our gifts differ and we play different roles in the body, would it not make sense to surmise that we all relate to God in different ways?

Four Types of Spirituality

When we allow the lines represented by these two spectrums to intersect, we see the quadrants designated by Holmes as four types of spirituality. The following diagram comes from Corinne Ware's book in which she expands on Holmes's understandings of spiritual types.[4]

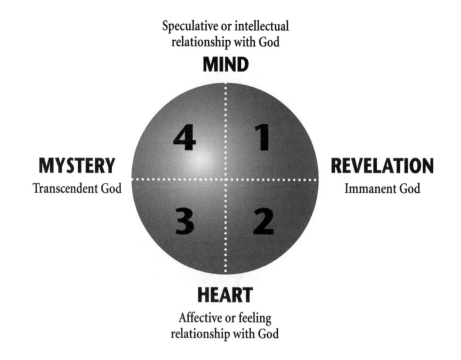

Speculative or intellectual
relationship with God

MIND

MYSTERY

Transcendent God

REVELATION

Immanent God

HEART

Affective or feeling
relationship with God

Type 1: Revelation/Mind. This type of spirituality favors theological reflection on concepts such as the Incarnation, God's love, or ethical issues. Christians in this group enjoy study groups and concrete ways of deepening the understanding of their faith. The gift of this type is theological reflection on the content of the Christian faith. The danger is what Holmes calls "rationalism" or the excessive intellectualization of the spiritual life.

Type 2: Revelation/Heart. The members of this group favor a more affective, charismatic spirituality. Their way to God is not the rational mind but the experience of the heart. Their gift includes warmth, enthusiasm, and energy in religious expression. The danger is becoming so convinced of the greater value of their felt experience that they tend to dismiss theological reflection as irrelevant.

Type 3: Mystery/Heart. Ware considers this type the most mystical. This group desires union with God, the Holy One. The gift of this type is an inspirational and uplifting spirituality that challenges others to be totally open to God. The danger is that this type of spirituality may become overly passive or retreat from reality.

Type 4: Mystery/Mind. Ware considers this the smallest group and, thus, the most difficult to describe. People who embody this type tend to be idealistic and radical in a desire to witness to God's reign. They have a passion for transforming society.[5] For them, prayer, theology, and action are one. They are intellectual visionaries, and their gift is precisely their vision of the ideal and their commitment to it. Their temptation is to an extreme moralistic vision. This group can dismiss those who do not support their "cause" with their same single-mindedness.

Identifying our spiritual type is not meant to box us into a given category. As Ware interprets Holmes, "once we have found where we fall within the total circle, we then have opportunity to grow by (1) acknowledging and strengthening our present gifts, (2) growing toward our opposite quadrant, and (3) appreciating more perceptively the quadrants on either side of our dominant type."[6] It is important to avoid stereotyping or oversimplifying the spiritual journey. No scales or schema can adequately explain the mystery of God and the mystery of the human response to God's initiative. The God of Jesus Christ remains beyond our ability to describe and eludes our feeble attempts to control, possess, or define. Paradoxically, in Jesus, the Otherness of God has joined creation. The late German theologian Karl Rahner expressed this eloquently:

> [Lord,] You must adapt Your word to my smallness, so that it can enter into the tiny dwelling of my finiteness.... You must make Your own

some human word, for that's the only kind I can comprehend....O Infinite God, You have actually willed to speak such a word to me!...You have come to me in a human word. For You, the Infinite, are the God of Our Lord Jesus Christ.[7]

This belief in the Incarnation encourages us to try to understand our humanity and to discover the richness of the various ways in which God wishes to be revealed to us.

When we look at Jesus as presented in the Gospels, we find that at various times in his life Jesus reflected different styles of prayer. He certainly emptied himself of everything in order to make his will one with God's will. He also saw God's presence in everyone and in everything: the children, the lilies of the field, the generosity of the poor widow, the faith of the centurion. Jesus knew the scriptures and used them to outline for his followers the radical demands of discipleship. But Jesus also wept when Lazarus died and was deeply moved over the city of Jerusalem. Jesus prayed alone, away from the disciples, and also encouraged them to pray with him. To be one with his Father was the deepest joy of Jesus' heart, and he desired this oneness for us all "that they may all be one. As you, Father, are in me and I am in you, may they also be in us" (John 17:21).

> *Breathe in the breath of the Spirit. Be free. Be simple. Prayer is a perfectly natural relationship between God, who loved you first, and you who try to love [God] back.*
>
> —Catherine de Hueck Doherty

As Christians, we believe that "where the Spirit of the Lord is, there is freedom" (2 Cor. 3:17). Jesus lived fully in such freedom. Each Gospel writer describes Jesus in a unique manner and helps us to see how Jesus revealed the various dimensions of God. By providing such a rich variety of images of God, the New Testament invites us to enter the mystery of the God who eludes all definition and yet has chosen to walk with us as a fellow pilgrim.

The gift given by Jesus after the resurrection is *shalom*: peace, harmony, unity, integrity within God's own being (John 20:19). Unity means not uniformity but oneness in the midst of diversity. There is diversity in the Trinity. There is diversity in Jesus. There is diversity in the Gospel writers. There were diverse languages at Pentecost, and yet the gift of the Spirit was unity in the diversity. "Indeed, the body does not consist of one member but of many" (1 Cor. 12:14). There are different prayer styles, various ways to become present to God's presence in our lives. The challenge is to understand one's individual style better and, in doing so, become free to appreciate and respect other approaches.

Carol may never understand why George liked the prayer group so much. George certainly does not comprehend why Carol did not enjoy such a wonderful experience. The hope is that as they develop spiritually, they will come to revere and appreciate the differences between them and the rich variety of gifts among members of the body of Christ.

DAILY EXERCISES

Read the chapter for Week 4 entitled "Praying As We Are." Be sure to note any questions or insights in your journal. Begin your exercises by reflecting on the following quotation:

> Pray as you can, not as you can't.[8]

With Exercises 1–4, you will experience prayer forms that are expressive of the four spiritual types discussed in this week's reading. We could characterize the types as head (revelation/mind), heart (revelation/heart), mystic (mystery/heart), and active (mystery/mind).

Exercise 1: "Head" Spirituality

Read John 3:16. Think about what this verse means. Paraphrase the verse in a sentence or two that capture the essence of its meaning for you. Then write a prayer to God that expresses your thoughts about what God has done for us and why we need what God has given to us.

Exercise 2: "Heart" Spirituality

Read John 3:16. List several people you love and those you have difficulty loving. Read the verse slowly for each person on your list, personalizing this verse as an expression of God's love for him or her: "For God so loved (name) that he gave his only Son, so that everyone who believes in him may not perish but may have eternal life." Include yourself. Pause to add your prayer for each person and to pray for what you need in order to love that person. Notice any changes in you as you affirm God's love for the person. Decide how you are going to express God's love and your love to the people on your list. Record your experience.

Exercise 3: "Mystic" Spirituality

Read John 3:16. Repeat this verse prayerfully as a way of focusing on God. Open your spirit to the loving attitude of Jesus Christ who allowed himself to be given for our salvation. Give yourself to the flow of God's boundless love for the whole world, a love that flows in and through you. As people and situations come to mind, bring them into the flow and allow them to be washed in God's bound-less love. Finally, carry some part of John 3:16 with you in your daily activities as a way of practicing openness to God's love. Record your experience.

EXERCISE 4: "ACTIVE" SPIRITUALITY

Read John 3:16. Today you will not be seeking to understand, feel, or contemplate the love described in this verse. Rather, be a living prayer today, an expression of God's sacrificial love. As you are able, take a walk through your house, your workplace, or your neighborhood. Bless everyone and everything you see with the words, "For God so loved the world…." Where do you see a need for God's love? Consider what Jesus would do in that situation, and choose a way to embody God's love in action. Record your experience.

EXERCISE 5

Read 1 Thessalonians 5:16-19. Take a moment to reflect on what these verses say about what it means to live prayerfully. Devote most of your time to the practice of being present to God and remaining in God's love. Use whatever approach helps you and seems most natural. During your last few minutes, reflect in your journal on these questions: (a) How am I experiencing God's presence and my presence to God these days? (b) What am I discovering about my way of praying and relating to God? (c) What helps me pray, and what gets in the way?

Review your journal entries for the week in preparation for the group meeting.

Part 3, Week 5
Psalms, the Prayer Book of the Bible

*W*hat feelings do you experience most frequently—gratitude, wonder, joy, boredom, anger, despair? Do you ever feel ashamed of your feelings of hatred or rage? What do you do with these strong emotions? How do you express them and how do you feel about them in relation to your faith?

Whatever our feelings, we will certainly find them expressed in the Psalms. This book, a collection of 150 prayers of the people of Israel, are meant to be sung accompanied by musical instruments. The Psalms are the poetry and music of the Jewish people at prayer and are deeply grounded in Hebrew spirituality.

The God of Israel is definitely interested in creation. The Hebrew scriptures tell of a God who breaks into history and is the Lord of history, a God who communicates with the people and pursues them. The Hebrew God is profoundly involved in human affairs. God appears to Abram and offers to make a covenant with him (Gen. 17:1-2). God heeds Rachel's prayer and opens her womb (Gen. 30:22). God speaks to Moses, assuring him that that the cries of the people have been heard, and they will be delivered from the Egyptians (Exod. 3:7-8). The God of the Israelites can also be convinced to change directions. When God threatens to destroy Sodom and Gomorrah, Abraham persuades God to spare the city of Sodom for the sake of ten righteous people living in it (Gen. 18:22-23).

The God of Israel desires an intimate relationship with the people. In spite of Israel's idolatry, God lures her and brings her into the wilderness to speak tenderly to her. God hopes that in the desert Israel will remember the days of her youth when she came out of the land of Egypt, and, there, once again return to God. Using powerful symbolic imagery, the prophet Hosea proclaims that God longs for the day when Israel will call God her husband, and God will take her for his wife forever (Hos. 2:14-20). The God of Israel is a gracious God who longs to enter into a passionate relationship of covenantal love with the people. In Hebrew spirituality God is the omnipotent creator and judge but also the companion in battle and the jealous lover.

People are driven to such poignant prayer and song as are found in the Psalter precisely by experiences of dislocation and relocation. It is experiences of being overwhelmed, nearly destroyed, and surprisingly given life which empower us to pray and sing.

—Walter Brueggemann

The Psalms emerge within the context of this personal relationship. Because of the deep conviction that God was among them, protecting, loving, rebuking, and guiding, Jewish people freely went to God with their feelings. They prayed in their anger, hatred, and frustration; they talked to their ever-present God of the pain of their exile, their powerlessness before the enemy, and the depth of their fears. They also went to God in their triumphs and with hearts full of gratitude for graces received. Every human emotion found expression in the Psalms.

This week we take a new look at this old collection of prayers and explore their role and significance in the prayer of contemporary Christians.

The Book of Psalms

The Book of Psalms covers a period of more than six hundred years in the history of the people of Israel. These 150 songs praise the God of creation and depict the struggles of God's people through the period of the patriarchs to the time after the Babylonian exile ended. The oldest psalms were prayed by the communities in which they originated, and they were later adapted and used in different situations the people faced. The psalms were set to the accompaniment of musical instruments, usually stringed instruments, such as a lyre or zither. They were gradually collected and initially remained unnamed, due to the large variety of material. Eventually, the Book of Psalms was written and became the foremost prayer book of the people of Israel. The original collection of the Psalms in Hebrew was completed by the third century B.C.E., though many of the individual psalms were much older. The Greek translation dates from the mid-third century B.C.E. (with later revisions) and is the version most used by the writers of the New Testament. Most modern translations come directly from the Hebrew text. When the first Christian communities used the Psalms as part of their prayer, they reinterpreted them in light of Jesus' life, death, and resurrection.

The Gospels present Jesus as the chief pray-er of the psalms. According to Matthew, Jesus spoke in parables to fulfill what had been spoken through the prophet: "I will open my mouth to speak in parables" (Matt. 13:35). In this instance he is quoting Psalm 78:2. In the same Gospel, Jesus uses Psalm 6:8 when he delivers his angry words against religious hypocrites who say, "Lord, Lord," but do not do the will of the Father: "Go away from me, you evildoers" (Matt. 7:23). The Gospels of Matthew, Mark, and Luke quote Psalm 110:1 to indicate that Jesus is the Lord of whom David spoke in the Book of Psalms (Matt. 22:44; 26:64; Mark 12:36; 14:62; Luke 20:42-43). According to Matthew, Jesus' final words from the cross are taken from Psalm 22:1: "My God, my God, why have you forsaken me?" (Matt. 27:46). In these words we hear the same sense of abandonment experienced by the psalmist of ancient Israel: "Why are you so far from helping me, from the words of my groaning? O my God, I cry by day, but you do not answer; and by night, but find no rest" (Psalm 22:1-2). The Gospel of Luke records other words spoken by Jesus from the cross: "Father, into your hands I commend my spirit" (Luke 23:46). These words parallel those of Psalm 31:5.

Today there are moments when we can identify with the psalmist just as Jesus did. We move from despair to surrender, from telling God how abandoned we feel to placing our lives in God's hands. The Gospels make other references to the psalms reflecting the significance of these ancient hymns in early Christian worship. As Christians, we are invited to let the psalms enrich our lives, to be our poems and

songs. These ancient hymns enable us to turn our strongest feelings and life experiences into prayers.

Division of the Psalms

Traditionally, the book has been divided into five parts, probably in imitation of the Pentateuch, the first five books of the Hebrew Scriptures:

Book I:	Psalms 1–41	Basic songs of worship
Book II:	Psalms 42–72	Songs of national concerns, emphasizing deliverance and redemption
Book III:	Psalms 73–89	Also hymns of national concerns, emphasizing worship and the sanctuary
Book IV:	Psalms 90–106	Songs of praise, with the themes of wilderness and wandering
Book V:	Psalms 107–150	Songs of praise

Within these main divisions we find subdivisions that make the psalms easier to understand for the contemporary reader. For example, there are Pilgrimage Psalms (such as 120–134) used in the annual journey to the Temple in Jerusalem during the high holy days; Individual Lament Psalms (such as 3–7; 12; 13; 22; 25–28; 35; 38–40; 42–43; 51; 54–57); and Communal Lament Psalms, in which the nation rather than an individual laments (such as 44; 60; 74; 79–80; 90; 123). There are also individual and communal Psalms of Thanksgiving, Psalms of Praise, Royal Psalms, and Wisdom Psalms. Contemporary scholars differ on methods of classification and on the exact name given to each subgroup. Nevertheless, the Book of Psalms remains a treasure of prayers that explores the full range of human emotions and experience and that places Yahweh, the God of the covenant, at the center of the human journey.

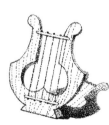

Difficulties Praying the Psalms Today

Often the psalms play a marginal role in the prayer of contemporary Christians. I have identified three difficulties encountered when approaching the Book of Psalms:

1. Resistance to praying with our feelings.
2. Images of God that seem to contradict the God revealed by Jesus.
3. Harsh language and attitudes that appear at odds with the Gospel message.

Resistance to praying with our feelings. We live in a culture that applauds self-control and is suspicious of the expression of strong emotion. There is a covert assumption that one must especially avoid any expression of powerful, negative feelings. In mainline U.S. culture, this is particularly true when it comes to men showing deep sadness, grief, or fear, and women expressing anger or hatred. It is widely accepted that "men do not cry," and women are expected to be "nice and sweet." Even for people who have no trouble with sadness or fear, the psalms of rage and anger present a serious problem. This prevailing attitude attains new depths among many Christians who mistakenly believe that in their time of prayer they should be composed and calm. Yet several psalms demonstrate the acceptability of praying with our grief and anger, even when directed to God (Psalms 35; 109; and 137), as in Jesus' cries from the cross (Matt. 27:46).

Praying with the psalms can be a liberating and healing experience for many of us. Expressing our brokenness, fears, joys, and anger when we pray, far from being an obstacle and a cause for anxiety, can become transforming moments when our deepest and strongest emotions become prayers. What better place to express our deepest feelings than in the presence of our loving God!

Images of God that seem to contradict the God revealed by Jesus. Frequently, Christians complain that in the psalms they encounter a God of fear, a God who loves only some and wishes the destruction of all enemies. This God resembles a crusader out to exterminate evildoers

> *The wide range of expression in the Psalter—the anger and pain of lament, the anguished self-probing of confession, the grateful fervor of thanksgiving, the ecstatic joy of praise—allows us to bring our whole lives before God.*
> —Kathleen Norris

who oppose God's plan. Such an attitude seems to contradict Jesus' words, "Do not resist an evildoer....Love your enemies and pray for those who persecute you" (Matt. 5:39, 44). The God of Jesus "makes his sun rise on the evil and on the good, and sends rain on the righteous and on the unrighteous" (Matt. 5:45). How do we reconcile the vengeful God of the psalms with the compassionate father in the parable of the prodigal son (Luke 15:11-32)? How can we imagine the Christian God taking sides in a war and destroying one group so that the other may win?

To understand the psalmist's prayer, we attempt to place ourselves in the historical and theological context in which the psalms were written. The concept of "chosen people" is integral to Hebrew spirituality. Yahweh, the God of gods, the God of creation and of all that is, was specifically the God of Abraham, Isaac, and Jacob. Jews believed that they were special and that God was guiding them and preserving their life as a tiny, vulnerable nation. As the different psalms were written over a long period of time, they not only portrayed the struggle of the people of Israel but also reflected varied and evolving human understandings of who God was.

Is this pattern so different from today? As Christians in relationship with the living God, we perceive our God in many different ways throughout our lives. For some, God is a just judge; for others, God is always loving and compassionate. Many see God as distantly omnipotent and omniscient. Others see God as walking hand in hand with them in the midst of their daily routines. At moments in our lives we experience God as friend and companion. We often see God as our protector, defender, and deliverer. But God may also seem mysteriously absent in our crises. The question of who God is has been part of the human quest from ancient times. The Book of Psalms offers us the Jewish understanding of the Israelites' God and invites us to approach this God with the entire gamut of human emotions, just as Jesus and the early Christians did.

Harsh language and attitudes that appear at odds with the Gospel message. When Christians today read Psalm 137, they frequently feel revulsion; something turns inside and cries, "This is wrong!" How can we possibly pray, as the psalmist does, for a blessing upon those who will dash babies against a rock (v. 9)? How can we call this kind of writing the Word of God?

The psalms frequently reflect the emotional state of a people suffering dehumanizing experiences. The people, in their pain, call for divine justice but refrain from human vengeance: "Repay them… according to the evil of their deeds.…Because they do not regard the works of the LORD, or the work of his hands, he will break them down and build them up no more" (Ps. 28:4-5). The psalmist prays for divine justice on those whom he considers evil in the eyes of God. This evil is frequently defined as a direct injustice or attack on the people the Lord has chosen to be God's own. Thus, the psalmist considers any attack on the Israelites an attack against God. The hatred, pain, and bitterness of the Israelites' suffering under the Babylonians and others find expression in the "harsh" psalms. These are sometimes referred to as the Imprecatory Psalms, which call down God's curses on the enemy. Over the centuries, many Christians have identified the "enemies" referred to in the psalms as forces and powers that try to pull us away from God and attack us when we resist. This understanding may open up new insights as we pray with the psalms.

Finding a Home in the Psalms

The psalms encourage contemporary Christians to allow their feelings to find a home in prayer. God does not expect us to approach prayer only when we feel calm and collected. We approach our God as we are, with raw feelings and emotions, and allow God's embrace to touch, heal, or affirm them. In prayer we express the resentment we feel against someone who has hurt us: "In my distress I cry to the LORD.…: Deliver me, O LORD, from lying lips, from a deceitful tongue" (Ps. 120:1-2). In moments of depression and despair we exclaim, "Out of the depths I cry to you, O LORD…hear my voice!" (Ps. 130:1-2). When feelings of gratitude well up inside our hearts, we say, "I love the LORD, because he has heard my voice and my supplications" (Ps. 116:1).

> *But the continuing appeal of the psalms is not only that they help us articulate the full range of our experiences and emotions; they offer us that help in the context of prayer. The psalms are primarily human speech to God. They arose out of the life of a praying community, Israel, responding to its experiences in the context of relationship to God.…It is not merely life itself, but life lived in relationship to, and in conversation with, God that permeates the psalms.*
>
> —Larry R. Kalajainen

In moments when we feel abandoned and when God seems silent, we pray, "Incline your ear to my cry. For my soul is full of troubles.…O LORD, why do you cast me off? Why do you hide your face from me?" (Ps. 88:2-3, 14). As we bring our feelings to God in prayer, we acknowledge God's presence in them, and we open up to hear what God may be trying to say through them. Feelings become our companions on the journey, and we stop seeing them as enemies. In the safe space created by prayer, we welcome our feelings, accept them, and then, with childlike trust, turn them over to our loving God.

DAILY EXERCISES

Read the chapter for Week 5 entitled "Psalms, the Prayer Book of the Bible." Record your questions and comments in your journal. Reflect on the following quotation as you begin your daily exercises:

> Jesus understood who he was and what he was called to become by praying the psalms....The psalms, infused with this presence of Christ, make accessible and actual for us the full range of Jesus' experience. In praying the psalms, we enter into that world of meaning and find our own wilderness sojourn illuminated and clarified. In praying the psalms we pass through our own hearts to the heart of God as revealed in Jesus' inner life.[1]

In these exercises, you will find a challenge to pray the Psalms with candor and, in so doing, to enter more fully into the vitality of Jesus' life with God.

EXERCISE 1

Read Psalm 8. Join with Jesus Christ in praying this psalm. Let each verse lead you to celebrate who you are before God, the magnificence of creation, and the human calling. What verses do you imagine spoke to Jesus as he prayed this psalm? What verses connect most deeply with you? Commit a few special verses to memory. Repeat them as you go about your daily tasks as a way to praise God.

EXERCISE 2

Read Psalm 10 aloud. Reflect on what circumstances might have inspired someone to write this psalm. Remember that "the poor" might refer to anyone who feels powerless or disregarded by those who have power. Try to pray this psalm as Jesus may have prayed it. Imagine the persons with whom Jesus may have identified as he prayed these words. Do you have any difficulty in praying this psalm? Identify with "the poor" in your own community as you pray the psalm again. Offer your prayer in the spirit of Jesus. Record your insights and experience.

EXERCISE 3

Read Psalm 22:1-11 and meditate on it verse by verse. As you read verses 1-5, identify the parts of your life in which you feel God's absence (vv. 1-2). Discover also the parts of yourself that want to trust God nevertheless (vv. 3-5). Express both feelings to God. Listen to God in the silence.

Meditate on verses 1-11, remembering that Jesus prayed this psalm as he hung on the cross. Sit before a picture of Jesus, a cross, or an icon. Imagine Jesus' human feelings and questions. How does the psalm illumine your ability to identify with Jesus and his humanness? What does the psalm suggest about Jesus' experience of having faith in the extreme moments of suffering and aloneness? Write your thoughts in your journal.

EXERCISE 4

Read Psalm 46. Imagine praying this psalm in the company of Jesus and all the saints who lived such faith, especially in times of trouble. Personalize verses 2-3. Bring to mind the things that can and do shake your faith as you pray the words, "Therefore we will not fear." Record your insights and experience.

EXERCISE 5

Find a psalm that gives voice to how you feel at this time about your life and your relationship with God. Write a paraphrase of the psalm that captures the prayer of your heart. What do you imagine was happening to the psalmist when he wrote the original words of the psalm? Read the psalm and your paraphrase, and pray the words once more, united in spirit with the psalmist.

Remember to review your journal entries for the week in preparation for the group meeting.

Exploring Contemplative Prayer

*O*ne of the most colorful stories in the New Testament is without a doubt the story of Martha and Mary (Luke 10:38-42). Luke tells us of the day when a woman named Martha welcomed Jesus into her home. Martha had a sister named Mary who sat at the Lord's feet and listened to what he was saying. Meanwhile her sister, Martha, kept busy with many household tasks, which distracted her. Finally Martha came to Jesus and complained that her sister, Mary, had left her to do all the work by herself. Would he tell her to offer some help? According to Luke, Jesus answered with the familiar words: "Martha, Martha, you are worried and distracted by many things; there is need of only one thing. Mary has chosen the better part, which will not be taken away from her."

The Gospel story does not explain what this "better part" is; consequently, it has become the subject of countless sermons and reflections. One of the most common interpretations of this passage declares Martha a "busybody" activist and Mary a contemplative example in her attentiveness to Jesus. Those who explain the story in this fashion frequently maintain that Jesus clearly exalted being over doing, prayer over service, contemplation over action. Anyone intentionally walking the Christian path knows of the ever-present tension between these two polarities. Throughout twenty centuries of

Christianity, various schools of spirituality have emphasized one or the other while maintaining that both contemplation and action are integral components of the Christian journey.

This week we focus on contemplation and contemplative prayer and their significance in the lives of Christians today.

Contemplation

If contemplation is the "better part" to which Jesus referred in the Martha and Mary story, he was certainly not speaking of Mary's sitting in contrast to Martha's movement. Martha's problem was not her work in the kitchen or her desire to be a gracious hostess. Rather, Jesus pointed out that she was worried and distracted by many things, not the least of which was her resentment toward her sister. Martha missed the point, not because she was serving, but because she lost sight of the "better part": Jesus' presence in her home. I do not think that Jesus meant for Martha to stop preparing the meal; instead, he meant for her to open the eyes and the ears of her heart to be present to him. Upon Jesus' arrival, Mary gave him her total attention. In contrast, Martha engaged in many tasks in a self-preoccupied manner that took her awareness away from Jesus' presence.

In this context, we may define contemplation as an awareness of God's presence and action. It means seeing reality as God sees it. It means being able to see God in everything and everything in God. When we live in a contemplative way, the whole creation becomes a sacrament of God's presence, an icon through which we encounter the divine. Most of us have experienced such moments of total transparency. At times a sunset over the ocean or the song of a bird or the laughter of a child takes us beyond what our senses perceive into the very mystery of God.

In truth, all Christians are called to contemplation, as evidenced in the Fourth Gospel. John, more than any other New Testament writer, underlines the oneness of Jesus with God, especially in chapters 14–17. Before his arrest, Jesus prays that the disciples might be one as the Father and he are one (John 17:22). This union with God is

> *Only when we are able to "let go" of everything within us, all desire to see, to know, to taste and to experience the presence of God, do we truly become able to experience that presence with the overwhelming conviction and reality that revolutionize our entire inner life.*
>
> —Thomas Merton

the deepest expression of contemplation—Jesus' prayer for everyone! Therefore, every person must have the capacity to be contemplative. Why, then, do some Christians believe that contemplation is beyond them, reserved for only a few?

One answer to this dilemma may lie in the various ways in which Christians understand contemplative prayer.

Contemplative Prayer

In popular circles, persons often use the words *contemplation, meditation*, and *mysticism* interchangeably. Consequently, many persons are unclear about the meaning of contemplative prayer. To confuse matters further, there is a subtle belief that to pray contemplatively, one has to be an otherworldly eccentric who experiences visions and other mystical phenomena. If you consider contemplative prayer as out of reach, it is time to look again at your understanding of this way of prayer.

In simple terms, contemplative prayer is "a way of making oneself aware of the presence of God who is always there."[1] It differs from meditation, which involves reasoning, words, and images. In true contemplative prayer, one abides in mystery, open to being taken by God in love along a way one cannot know. Throughout the history of Christianity, spiritual guides have regarded contemplative prayer as an encounter with the "unknowing." Because intuition and awareness rather than thinking are central to this experience, such prayer tends to be unitive: we find ourselves—our true selves—in God.

One of the obstacles blocking our contemplation is the inclination to displace the deepest longing of our hearts onto external possessions. Our culture lures us with promises of fulfillment and personal realization; all we have to do is drive a certain model of car or wear designer clothes. If our investments are solid and we manage to be debt free, we will have peace. Advertising and conventional wisdom promise satisfaction if we submit to the gods of the market economy. Surely our society makes it hard to live from one's center! But external things cannot satisfy the soul. As Augustine wrote, a prominent quality of the

The most fundamental step I believe we can take toward opening our spiritual heart is to open our longing for God: our yearning for God's fullness in us and the world, through and beyond every desire we may have. That longing is placed deep in us as a reflection of God's wondrous, loving desire to be full in us.
—Tilden H. Edwards

human spirit is its restlessness: "You have formed us for yourself, and our hearts are restless till they find rest in you."[2]

Another cultural value that forms an obstacle to contemplation is the rugged individualism of those "brave" enough to try to make it on their own. This attitude makes contemplative prayer sound like a foreign concept. Contemplative prayer acknowledges that we cannot make it on our own; we cannot force an experience of God's presence dwelling within us, no matter how hard we try. Rather, we pray by believing that we are God's beloved and that God dwells within us, already united with us if we only open up to that awareness. Moreover, we believe that God freely loves us and that our baptism and faith have equipped us to experience this mystery of undeserved and unearned love. In contemplative prayer we listen to and see reality through the Spirit who dwells within us (Rom. 8:9; 1 Cor. 2:6-13).

Teresa of Avila, a Spanish mystic of the sixteenth century, saw that the journey of the soul to God began with the soul's remembrance of its true identity. She wrote, "I don't find anything comparable to the magnificent beauty of a soul and its marvelous capacity. Indeed, our intellects, however keen, can hardly comprehend it, just as they cannot comprehend God; but He Himself says that He created us in His own image and likeness."[3] We often forget this deepest identity when we pay attention to the many voices of our culture, but in prayer we are able to recover the sense of our identity as children of God.

In chapters 11–22 of the book of her *Life* (*Vida*), Teresa explains the soul's friendship with God by using the allegory of a garden. In the soul's garden, we do not need to plant seeds or pull up weeds because God has already done that. We simply need to water it, and the water is prayer. She insists that it is only with God's help that we "strive like good gardeners to get the plants to grow."[4] Our task may appear simple, but it is not always easy. The many cares of our lives, Martha's "worries and distractions," often become obstacles to our oneness with God.

During Week 4 of this unit on prayer, we reflected on two of the ways we speak about and relate to God: the way of mystery and the way of revelation. In more ancient terms, the way of mystery is called *apophatic* and the way of revelation is called *kataphatic*. This week we call again upon the wisdom of our tradition in order to gain a deeper understanding of contemplative prayer.

Approaches to Contemplative Prayer

Both ways of knowing God can help us understand contemplative prayer. *Apophatic* and *kataphatic* are Greek terms that describe two ways of entering contemplative prayer: One employs thoughts and images and is called the way of revelation (kataphatic way); the other is the way of mystery (apophatic way), which transcends ideas, thoughts, and symbols and enters, through love, into God's mystery.

Ignatius of Loyola (described in Part 2, page 96) was a man of deep contemplative prayer and a strong proponent of the kataphatic way. In his *Spiritual Exercises*, he encourages the use of imagination, feelings, senses, reason, will, and memory to enter the experience on which we meditate. He suggests that we place ourselves imaginatively in the scripture passage ("composition of place") in order to see, hear, smell, taste, and touch the people and places described there. Ignatius also suggests that we use the imagination to become active participants in the Bible story. This switch from rational to imaginative activity can make us more receptive to a deeper personal knowledge of Christ. At the end of the *Exercises*, Ignatius continues to offer ways to experience being at one with Christ in his passion and glory. He describes a contemplative prayer in which one moves beyond imagining Jesus' thoughts or feelings in the Gospel story to developing a sense of personal union with him. The Ignatian method's strength is its ability to immerse the entire person—body and soul—in profound Christian truths. Through prayer experiences based on Christ's life, Ignatius reveals how images and symbols become transparent to the mystery of God's self-giving love.

The apophatic approach emphasizes that no idea, thought, or symbol can fully reach God as God is. Several significant writers, including the anonymous author of *The Cloud of Unknowing* (fourteenth-century England), John of the Cross (sixteenth-century Spain),

and Thomas Merton (twentieth-century United States) have interpreted this way. *The Cloud*, a clear, concise book on the nature of apophatic prayer, urges its readers to enter into the kind of prayer where one is at home in a "dark cloud" beyond all thoughts and images. This author, along with many others in the Christian tradition, warns that no technique can bring about this experience and that contemplation is ultimately God's gift. He suggests a method that is now called "centering prayer." Those who choose this prayer style use a meaningful word (such as *Jesus, God, Love*) and then release any distracting thoughts or images in order to center attention on the reality behind the word. In centering prayer, as in any other apophatic method, one seeks to go beyond all words, thoughts, and images and to enter the center of one's being, awaiting the gift of total awareness of God's presence within.

These approaches to prayer offer two different ways to grow in the soul's friendship with God of which Teresa of Avila spoke. A practical woman and also a gifted contemplative, Teresa wrote extensively, presenting primarily the way of revelation. Yet one can see both approaches in her work. Regardless of one's preferred approach, contemplation in the Christian tradition is understood as an awareness of God's presence beyond thoughts and images. This experience is the product not of our efforts or merits, but of our faithful response to God's grace. In the kataphatic tradition such awareness comes through the transparency of everything; in the apophatic approach it comes through forgetting and "unknowing." Both approaches aim to free us from the false self in order to find the true self in God.

My secret is very simple: I pray. Through prayer I become one in love with Christ. I realize that praying to him is loving him.... The poor who live in the slums of the world are the suffering Christ...and through them God shows me his true face. For me, prayer means being united to the will of God twenty-four hours a day, to live for him, through him, and with him.

—Mother Teresa

The Fruits of Contemplative Prayer

We have seen that contemplation is the work of love—not our love for God but God's love for us. The Christian God is a relational God who desires all to share in that love: "If we love one another, God lives in us, and his love is perfected in us" (1 John 4:12). Jesus experienced this union to the fullest and desired it for us all. Yet he further promised, "Those who abide in me and I in them bear much fruit" (John

15:5). True contemplation leads not to self-absorption but to the emptying of oneself on behalf of others. Teresa of Avila wisely taught her nuns: "You may think that as a result [of the union with God] the soul will be outside itself and so absorbed that it will be unable to be occupied with anything else. On the contrary, the soul is much more occupied than before with everything pertaining to the service of God." [5] It is necessary that Christians honestly examine the fruits of their contemplative prayer. The following list may assist in this reflection.

True contemplative prayer leads to

- the experience of God within, which silences other voices that deny our human dignity.
- the awareness of God's infinite love for us through no merit of our own.
- self-knowledge that leads to humility; that is, to walk in truth.
- compassion and works of mercy.
- peace.
- freedom.

Martha and Mary live within each one of us. Yes, we would love to sit close to Jesus and put aside all distractions and cares simply to be with him. Yet the Martha within worries and gets distracted by many needless anxieties. The purpose of contemplative prayer is to take us deep within to the place where God is, in order to rest in God and become more aware of God's radical transforming love for us. When we allow time and space for this gift to be revealed, our various tasks become acts of love, and our suffering becomes redemptive. We will have chosen to dwell with Jesus in the heart of God. We will have chosen the "better part," and it will not be taken away from us.

The spiritual life can be lived in as many ways as there are people. What is new is that we have moved from the many things to the kingdom of God. What is new is that we are set free from the compulsions of our world and have set our hearts on the only necessary thing.

—Henri J. M. Nouwen

DAILY EXERCISES

Read the chapter for Week 6, "Exploring Contemplative Prayer," and note in your journal your insights, learnings, and questions.

One characteristic of progress in the spiritual life is an increasing reliance on God in our daily living and our praying. An increasing reliance on God is sometimes accompanied by a preference or even a sense of call toward a simpler form of prayer that emphasizes our words and thoughts less and God's communication with us and presence in us more. "I have given up all my non-obligatory devotions and prayers," wrote Brother Lawrence, "and concentrate on being always in [God's] holy presence; I keep myself in [God's] presence by simple attentiveness and a loving gaze upon God."[6]

These exercises will invite you to practice some traditional forms of contemplative prayer—of turning your eyes to God in simplicity of faith and love. These forms may be unfamiliar to you but enter them with an openness that God may speak to you in new ways. Also you will receive the opportunity to assess where you are at this point in your journey of deepening prayer. Exercise 5 will serve as the basis of the sharing during this week's meeting.

EXERCISE 1: PRAYING WITH A PRAYER OF REPETITION

Read Philippians 2:12-13, where Paul identifies two parts of the spiritual life: our part (v. 12) and God's part (v. 13). Reflect on your role and God's role in your ongoing transformation in Christ. What is your awareness of the active presence of "God who is at work in you"? What is the quality of your cooperation with God "enabling you"?

Devote several minutes to praying the phrase "for it is God who is at work in you." Give your total attention to discerning the presence of God who is at work in you. Record expressions of your awareness in your journal.

EXERCISE 2: PRAYING WITH THE JESUS PRAYER

Read Luke 18:13, giving particular attention to the publican's prayer. Long ago, the publican's prayer became the basis for a contemplative prayer method called the Jesus Prayer, widely used in the Eastern

Orthodox Christian tradition. The most common form of the Jesus Prayer is "Lord Jesus Christ, Son of God, have mercy on me, a sinner." Sometimes persons abbreviate it to "Lord Jesus Christ, have mercy on me" or simply to "Lord Jesus, have mercy."

Spend some time praying the Jesus Prayer. Repeat it gently, letting the words focus your attention on God while expressing your need for grace. When you find your mind wandering, return to the prayer. Try developing an inner rhythm that suits you. For example, say the first half ("Lord Jesus Christ, Son of God") as you inhale and the second half ("have mercy on me, a sinner") as you exhale. Let the prayer move from the mind to the lips, until it gradually enters the heart. Allow it to foster an interior openness to God in the background of your daily activities.

EXERCISE 3: PRAYING WITH A VISUAL FOCUS

Read 2 Corinthians 3:18. In contemplative prayer, we are "seeing the glory" of God with "unveiled faces." Many Christians practice spiritual seeing by praying with a visual focus. Western Christians have commonly used the cross, a crucifix, or other works of art (including images in stained glass windows) to fix their inner eyes on Christ. Eastern Orthodox Christians commonly use icons (Greek for "image"), which are images of Christ and other saints that serve as windows onto spiritual reality.

Devote some time to "praying with your eyes," using a visual focus. Choose a cross, a favorite picture of Jesus, an icon, or a piece of art that draws you into the mystery of God. Inwardly express your desire to meet God. Gaze upon the visual focus without analyzing or evaluating what you see. Reach for God through your eyes, and let God reach for you through the "eyes" of the visual focus. Rather than seeking insights about God, seek to be seen and known by God. When distracted, calmly return your attention to the visual focus. After some minutes in this form of prayer, close your eyes, keeping your image in mind. Record your experience in your journal. As you move through the day, remember that you can also see the image of God in *people.*

EXERCISE 4: CENTERING PRAYER

What special words have power to lift your eyes to God and your heart to the Spirit? In centering prayer, we use a single word to focus on God and prepare ourselves for the gift of God's presence. The contemporary form of centering prayer, as presented by Thomas Keating, Basil Pennington, and others, is based on the teachings in a fourteenth-century classic called *The Cloud of Unknowing*.

Devote your daily exercise time to the practice of centering prayer. Choose a sacred word that represents your desire for God or God's yearning for you. A simple word is best, such as *love, God, Jesus, light, peace,* or *beloved*. Sit comfortably and close your eyes. Take several slow breaths to help you relax. Silently offer your sacred word to God as a sign of your desire for and consent to God's presence and action within. As you become aware of other thoughts, memories, feelings, or images, instead of fighting them, gently return to your sacred word. Remain in this state of rest and receptivity to God for approximately ten minutes. End with the Lord's Prayer or some other prayer. Remain quiet for a few more minutes. Write a few words in your journal about your experience.

EXERCISE 5: SCRIPTURAL CONTEMPLATION

Read Luke 10:38-42. The story of Martha and Mary illustrates the centrality of listening to God as a priority in the Christian life. During this final exercise, let the story of Martha and Mary guide you in discovering where you are in the journey of deepening prayer.

Reflect on the passage one verse at a time.

"[Jesus] entered a certain village, where a woman named Martha welcomed him into her home."

In what ways does Christ enter your awareness and life? How are you welcoming Christ in daily life, and what practices do you find most helpful?

"[Martha] had a sister named Mary, who sat at the Lord's feet and listened to what he was saying."

What obstacles did Mary have to overcome in deciding to leave the kitchen and sit at the Lord's feet? How have you grown and what challenges do you still face in learning to sit at the Lord's feet and listen?

"But Martha was distracted by her many tasks."

What continues to interrupt your presence to God in prayer or in daily life? Do as Martha did: Tell Jesus your trouble and what you think you need (v. 40). What is his response?

"There is need of only one thing."

What is the one thing you need in order to progress in prayer and love? What would Jesus say?

Now listen to the Lord. Imagine yourself sitting with Mary at the Lord's feet, listening to his teaching over the course of this study. Gaze into his face. What are you seeing in Jesus? What is Jesus seeing in you? What is he saying to you? After several minutes of loving attention to Jesus Christ, write notes in your journal from this time of communion.

Review your journal entries for the week in preparation for the group meeting.

Part 4

Responding to Our Call:
The Work of Christ

Gerrit Scott Dawson

Part 4, Week 1
Radical Availability

So, what am I supposed to do now? This question arises for many of us after we accept Christ's invitation to follow him in the journey of the spiritual life. After we have read the scriptures, meditated on them, and prayed, the new day stretches out before us. What do Christians do?

In Part 4 of *Companions in Christ*, we will consider the idea of vocation—what God calls us to be and do in the world. Each of us has a unique combination of personality traits and gifts. When we are able to put into practice the design that God has put within us, we find high levels of energy, fulfillment, and purpose. Ideally, what we are to do as Christians is to live in loving service to God in the world, according to the way we were created. We share in the ministry of Jesus who gave himself completely to us.

As this theme unfolds, we will explore what it means that God has given each of us a spiritual gift to use in our work with Christ. Ultimately, I hope each of us will discover a joyful, invigorating role in the church through which we may exercise our gifts in concert with others to the praise of God. That is where we want to go; but to get there, we have to do some essential work first.

In our society, questions concerning vocation seem natural. We live in a culture that greatly values self-fulfillment. I believe that living in alignment with God's purposes for us is the surest path to such

satisfaction. But discovering our call and exercising our gifts are not of first importance in the Christian life. They cannot be, because most Christians have not had the freedom or power to make many choices about the circumstances of their lives. The slaves, the women, and the working poor who comprised so much of the early church had little say in their vocational choices. The primary call of God to us, then, must be audible in all stages, conditions, and seasons of life. This call is profoundly simple, yet, as T. S. Eliot wrote in *Four Quartets*, answering it costs "not less than everything." Moreover, the successful discovery of our gifts and particular calling depends upon our acceptance of this primal summons from God.

Many stories in the Bible describe how people are called to particular service. In each case, there is a basic call around which all the other details of life swirl like harmony around a strong melody. Persons are called to abandon their lives completely into God's hands. There is just no way around this. A test precedes any consideration of what you are to do in the world: Have you let go of everything to give yourself to God? Again and again, the people we encounter in the Bible are called to a radical availability. God shakes them free of every other constraint so that they trust only in their Lord. Then the vision of a particular service and the power to do it can be given.

> *At every moment we practice a surrender that has no limits, a surrender that includes all possible methods and degrees of service to God....Our sole duty is to submit ourselves to all that God sends us and to stand ready to do [God's] will at all times.*
> —Jean-Pierre de Caussade

Oswald Chambers in his book *My Utmost for His Highest* has written of the "gracious uncertainty" that "marks the spiritual life":

> To be certain of God means that we are uncertain in all our ways, we do not know what a day may bring forth. This is generally said with a sigh of sadness; it should be rather an expression of breathless expectation. We are uncertain of the next step, but we are certain of God. Immediately we abandon to God, and do the duty that lies nearest. [God] packs our life with surprises all the time.[1]

We are called to love the Lord our God with all our heart, soul, and mind. Our certainty rests only in God. The priority of God can entertain no division between spiritual life and work life, family time and recreation time. God commands; God calls for first place in every aspect. From such basic commitment and truth arises every other consideration of vocation.

This week we will consider several stories of biblical characters and how they followed the first call of committing all to God. We will see that sometimes this primal vocation involves literal abandonment of all we have. At times it means willingness to put our present positions at risk. And at times we continue in the same life but for a whole new reason. In every case, our first call involves embracing the "gracious uncertainty" that follows saying yes to God.

Abram and Sarai

The story of Abram and Sarai marks the beginning of a new phase in God's expression of love for a wayward humanity. These two were to begin a lineage of people called apart from the world in order to be a blessing to the world. At first, the call came to Abram alone:

> Now the LORD said to Abram, "Go from your country and your kindred and your father's house to the land that I will show you. I will make of you a great nation, and I will bless you, and make your name great, so that you will be a blessing....In you all the families of the earth shall be blessed." So Abram went, as the LORD had told him (Gen. 12:1-4).

The first call was to leave familiar and beloved territory—his country, his extended family, and his father's house. He was not required to give up everything, for he traveled with his wife Sarai, his nephew Lot, and all his servants and possessions. And with the call, God made great promises: Abram's family would grow into a populous nation, and the entire earth would be blessed through him. But to reach the goal, he had to set out for a destination known only as "the land that I will show you." At age seventy-five, Abram had to uproot his personal household and journey blindly to "God knows where." Everything familiar was shaken loose. He was certain only of God.

Esther

Esther, a Jewish woman, became queen of Persia during the reign of Xerxes (486–465 B.C.E.). During those days, a large number of God's people who had been scattered during the Exile a century earlier still

lived in foreign lands. No one in the Persian court knew of Esther's faith or heritage. She had been discovered during a royal search for a new queen after the old one had enraged the king by daring to defy him. Esther's beauty and graciousness overwhelmed Xerxes.

Meanwhile, one of the king's officials, in a personal fury at Esther's cousin Mordecai, convinced the king to sign an order to exterminate all the Hebrews in the land. Mordecai sent a message to Esther, urging her to intercede with the king on behalf of her people. But Esther understood the ways of the court and the temper of the king. She sent word back to Mordecai reminding him that the penalty for approaching the king unbidden was death. Mordecai replied with a message that surely was no less than a call from God:

> Do not think that in the king's palace you will escape any more than all the other Jews. For if you keep silence at such a time as this, relief and deliverance will rise for the Jews from another quarter, but you and your father's family will perish. Who knows? Perhaps you have come to royal dignity for just such a time as this (Esth. 4:13-14).

This prophetic word identifies several important aspects of God's call. First, Mordecai reminded Esther of her deepest identity as one of God's own people. Then he boldly asserted how dangerous this moment of call was for her. He did not veil the threat. In the critical hour of opportunity, if she sought to save her life, she would surely lose it. Third, Mordecai asserted the fulfillment of God's purposes even without her cooperation. God would be faithful to the Hebrews, passing over Esther and using another means to save them. Finally, Mordecai asked Esther to consider that her new, elevated station in life had been given to her for precisely this moment. She was given a royal position not to preserve it at all costs but to risk it in response to God's call.

Esther was not only beautiful in appearance. She was a woman of extraordinary strength and courage. She heard God's call in Mordecai's words and sent this reply: "Go, gather all the Jews to be found in Susa, and hold a fast on my behalf....I and my maids will also fast as you do. After that I will go to the king, though it is against the law; and if I perish, I perish" (Esth. 4:16). She called for prayer and support from all of God's people. But Esther also resolved to do what she alone could do. Her courage was built on a complete abandonment to the care of God. "If I perish, I perish." She held back nothing, risking not only wealth and comfort but also her very life. And she succeeded. The king received her favorably, lifted the edict, and ultimately elevated the status of all the Jews in Persia.

Jesus' Answer to God's Call

Jesus' ministry was characterized by radical availability, both to his Father in heaven and to those around him. He began his public life by submitting to John's baptism of repentance, though he himself was without sin. Interestingly, such an act of availability led immediately to a sign of confirmation. The Gospels tell us that as he came out of the water, the Holy Spirit descended upon him in the form of a dove, and a voice from heaven spoke, "This is my Son, the Beloved, with whom I am well pleased" (Matt. 3:17). God the Father affirmed the nature and work of the Son as his public ministry began.

In a succinct but profound way, this story reveals the reality that God is triune; such knowledge will deeply inform our explorations throughout the coming weeks. The voice from heaven, that of God the Father, announces to the world that Jesus is the Father's beloved Son. From all eternity, the Father and the Son have existed in a relationship of love so intimate that they could be called one. Throughout his life with us, Jesus constantly prayed to his Father, revealing that though he had become human, his oneness in communion with God remained. The Holy Spirit who descended upon Jesus is also one with God and has been known as the very bond of the Trinity. That Jesus should teach us to begin our prayers with "Our Father…" is nothing less than an invitation to all humanity to join in the wonderful fellowship of love that defines God!

Throughout the three years of his ministry, Jesus was constantly accessible to God's call, spending large amounts of time in prayer. Mark recalls the time when, "in the morning, while it was still very dark, [Jesus] got up and went out to a deserted place, and there he prayed" (1:35). And Luke tells us, "Now during those days he went out

to the mountain to pray; and he spent the night in prayer to God" (6:12). Such devotion formed the basis for Jesus to say, "I have come..., not to do my own will, but the will of him who sent me" (John 6:38).

Jesus' intimate relationship with God flowed forth from prayer into his works of compassion. His life of healing can be summarized in his simple words to the centurion whose servant lay near death, "I will come and cure him" (Matt. 8:7). It was his will to be interrupted by the needs of others and to meet those needs with his healing, forgiving love. Constantly welcoming outcasts, Jesus declared, "I have come to call not the righteous but sinners" (Matt. 9:13).

Such obedience to God led Jesus into conflict. He said of the laws of Moses, "I have come not to abolish but to fulfill [them]" (Matt. 5:17). Yet Jesus' healing on the Sabbath and overturning the money tables in the Temple scandalized the religious leaders. Although they sought his life, Jesus continued his ministry of love.

Jesus' willing obedience continued even though betrayal and death lay ahead. Several times, we read that he predicted his death. And praying in the garden of Gethsemane, Jesus acknowledged the end he was facing. In his true humanity, he hoped to avoid the suffering; but as Immanuel, God with us in radical availability, he gave himself to God: "My Father, if it is possible, let this cup pass from me; yet not what I want, but what you want" (Matt. 26:39). The essence of abandonment followed as Jesus gave his life on the cross.

Jesus came to the "far country" because he was sent. Being sent remained uppermost in his consciousness. He never claimed anything for himself. He was the obedient servant who said and did nothing, absolutely nothing, unless it was said and done in complete obedience to the one who sent him.
—Douglas P. McNeill, Douglas A. Morrison, Henri J. M. Nouwen

Jesus' Call to the Disciples

Jesus called his followers to a similar life of obedience as part of their intimate relationship with him. The Gospels record Jesus calling one person after another to this radical availability. "Follow me," he said to Simon Peter and Andrew, "and I will make you fish for people" (Mark 1:17). They immediately left their nets to follow Jesus. Shortly thereafter, Jesus called James and John. They left not only their nets but also their father sitting in the boat! "Follow me," Jesus said to Levi the tax collector; Levi got up and left his coins in the tax booth (Mark 2:14). Like Abram, these early disciples were called to an unknown destination. All they knew was the person Jesus, and he provided their only certainty. This bond with Jesus, forged in radical availability, brought closer ties than those of family: "Here are my mother and my brothers! For whoever does the will of my Father in heaven is my brother and sister and mother" (Matt. 12:49-50).

A rich young man came to Jesus inquiring about eternal life. Mark records Jesus' call that paid little respect to the man's wealth:

> Jesus, looking at him, loved him and said, "You lack one thing; go, sell what you own, and give the money to the poor, and you will have treasure in heaven; then come, follow me." When he heard this, he was shocked and went away grieving, for he had many possessions (10:21-22).

The demands on the young man felt overwhelming. Jesus made it clear to his disciples, in words that echo Mordecai's to Esther, "If any want to become my followers, let them deny themselves and take up their cross and follow me. For those who want to save their life will lose it, and those who lose their life for my sake, and for the sake of the gospel, will save it" (Mark 8:34-35).

Only out of this total yes to his call can Jesus' followers begin to share his work. We may hold nothing back. Everything is subject to forfeit. And the essence of this call and response is the Great Commandment, "Love the Lord your God with all your heart, and with all your soul, and with all your mind, and with all your strength" (Mark 12:30).

Lydia

Those of us who find such demands from Jesus daunting may find solace in the story of Lydia. A merchant who heard the call of Christ and heeded it obediently, Lydia did not leave home or change profession:

> A certain woman named Lydia, a worshiper of God, was listening to us; she was from the city of Thyatira and a dealer in purple cloth. The Lord opened her heart to listen eagerly to what was said by Paul. When she and her household were baptized, she urged us, saying, "If you have judged me to be faithful to the Lord, come and stay at my home" (Acts 16:14-15).

You aspire to live dangerously for the sake of Christ. Each day you will ask yourself the meaning of his word, "Whoever wants to save their life will lose it." And one day you will understand what this absolute means.

How will you come to understand? Search. Seek and you will find.

—Brother Roger of Taizé

Lydia abandoned herself to God in her baptism, yet continued in her prosperous profession. Now, however, she uses her resources to become the host for the church in Thyatira. At the end of Acts 16, we read that Paul and Silas leave prison and accept Lydia's invitation of hospitality. There they find a flourishing fellowship of brothers and sisters in the Lord (Acts 16:40). Everything changed for Lydia, but her external circumstances remained the same. She followed a deeper vocation while maintaining the same professional duties.

So we see that heeding God's call can mean leaving home and all that is familiar. It can demand our accumulated wealth and security or dare us to place our blessings, even our lives, at risk. It can also mean simply living where we are but with an entirely new set of priorities. In every case, our particular vocation in God's service arises from our response to the basic call to radical availability.

DAILY EXERCISES

Be sure to read the chapter "Radical Availability" before you begin these exercises. Keep a journal or blank book beside you to record your thoughts, questions, prayers, and images.

This week's exercises will give you an opportunity to begin reflecting on your calling or vocation in life.

EXERCISE 1

This week's chapter considered several stories of biblical characters (Abram and Sarai, Esther, Jesus, Jesus' disciples, and Lydia) and how they followed the first call of committing all to God. Which of their stories is more like your story, and in what ways? Meditate on the scripture passage related to the character of your choice. Identify connections with your experience and your own God-given opportunities. Pray to the Lord to open your heart and to give you courage for the next step in your journey.

EXERCISE 2

Read Luke 10:25-37. This story reveals the quality of life and love that God wants to give us. What kind of life do you want to inherit? Spend time in prayer with the phrase "Do this, and you will live." What specifically is the Lord calling you to do?

EXERCISE 3

Read Isaiah 6:1-13. Isaiah experienced God's presence and call in the course of Temple worship. Do as Isaiah did here: Outline in your journal the story of your first sense of God's calling and your response ("Here am I; send me"). Drawing on your experience, describe what "God's call" means for you.

EXERCISE 4

Read Mark 10:17-22. Meditate on Jesus' words to the rich man as words to you. What area of your life have you closed off to God's call and, as good as it seems by all external standards, may prevent you from

receiving the life God wants to give you? In prayer, risk placing your whole life, including all of your achievements, in God's hands. Rest in the assurance that Jesus loves you and knows you as you are. Record your insights.

EXERCISE 5

Read Psalm 103. Meditate on God's nature as expressed in this psalm, and bless God's holy name with your own affirmations. Identify the verses that touch your spirit and resonate most deeply with the work and call of God in you. How do these verses about God speak to you of your vocation in God? Pray through the psalm verses that especially draw you, blessing God's holy name with all that is in you. Receive and rest in the blessing of God's presence.

Review your journal for the week in preparation for the group meeting.

Part 4, Week 2
Living Reliance

*L*ast week I may have set you up for failure or at least created some anxiety about what God calls you to do. We looked at stories of people who risked everything for God. Perhaps you felt, as I did, that the faithfulness of Abram, Esther, Jesus, and the disciples differs greatly from our own. I realized that quite often I make myself unavailable to God. I may say that I offer myself but then proceed to do just what I want anyway. Rarely do I live in obedience to God's call for any sustained length of time. Radical availability seems like radical impossibility! Trying to work together with Christ becomes one more heavy stone on my pile of guilt. But what if God has anticipated this very sense of failure, which serves in fact as an expected beginning to joyful participation in the life and work of Jesus?

Last week we saw that when Jesus called the rich young ruler to radical availability, the man "was shocked and went away grieving, for he had many possessions" (Mark 10:22). Jesus went on to comment, "Children, how hard it is to enter the kingdom of God!" His words astounded the disciples. If the rich and successful were not in God's favor, then who was? They asked, "Then who can be saved?"

Jesus replied, "For mortals it is impossible, but not for God; for God, all things are possible." Jesus understood that we cannot of our own power generate or sustain our radical availability to God. Consistently working with Christ to enter the kingdom of God is not

humanly attainable. God calls us then to more than we can do on our own.

We stand at the threshold of a paradoxical truth in the spiritual life: At precisely the point where we abandon ourselves to God, we realize we have done nothing by our own power. When we feel we have accomplished the Herculean task of giving over everything—all control, all claim, all ambition—we discover that God gets all the credit. God enables our will, quickens our belief, empowers our service. Our availability, while crucial, is but the tiniest step; even that step is not taken without divine prompting and enabling.

Last week we noted Jesus' perfect availability to God. Out of his life of prayerful communion with God, Jesus taught with wisdom and healed with power. He also summoned others to follow him in abandonment to God. We are called to be like him. Yet we know that we cannot be like him. "For mortals it is impossible." Jesus, while mortal, also was and is much more. He is Immanuel, God with us. Jesus is God incarnate, come in the flesh. So while fully human, he is also fully divine, the "exact imprint of God's very being" (Heb. 1:3). And "for God, all things are possible." Only Jesus, who bears the titles Son of Man and Son of God, can empower us to share in the life of radical availability that he lived as a human being.

To share in the work of Christ means not so much our working for Christ but our inviting him to work in and through us. We cease trying to be in ourselves what he is and agree to his living in us all that he is as both human being and God. We grow toward that spiritual reality named by Paul in his letter to the Galatians, "It is no longer I who live, but it is Christ who lives in me" (2:20).

Thus, we may not frame the whole subject of what we are to do in the world, what our mission is, in terms of ourselves. Rather, we consider our life's task in terms of Jesus Christ. The issue is not my spiritual journey and my quest for God. That's backward. What matters is God's quest for me, indeed, God's quest for the whole world. The Son of God came down from heaven seeking us. That's what counts. Who Jesus is then becomes the most important consideration in determining what you and I are to do.

I am depending too utterly on my own strength. I act as if my knowledge were complete and my own power sufficient. I forget to remember that God is my strength and the source of the power without which no thing is possible.… There is strength in God sufficient for my needs, whatever they may be.

—Howard Thurman

We would be wise not to get ahead of this understanding. Even mighty works in the name of Christ will come to nothing if they are not grounded in this essential order: not I, but Christ; not me for God, but God for and through me. When we make this connection, then even the smallest actions by the most limited of people become great contributions to the kingdom.

The Vine and the Branches

Jesus gave us a powerful symbol in John 15 for this relationship of participating in the work of God. The image is that of a grapevine. The thick, long vine grows along the ground or attaches itself by tendrils to another tree or a frame. From the vine, little branches shoot out, intertwining as they climb. From these branches the clusters of grapes come forth. A cultivated grapevine may grow very long and high, with many bunches of fruit hanging down.

The grapevine had long been a symbol for Israel, God's people. Commentator Ray Summers notes that on the temple in Jerusalem, a huge grapevine was carved into the stone of the entrance.[1] Its trunk rose higher than a person, and its branches spread out farther above, adorned with rich gold leaves and bunches of gilded grapes. Moreover, during the brief time of Israel's revolt against Rome, the coins minted bore the grapevine as the symbol of the nation. The grapevine served as an image of hope that the people could be something fruitful for their God.

But in reality, the grapevine became a reminder of failure. The Hebrew prophets often employed this figure of speech in terms of judgment (see Isaiah 5:1-10): Israel, the vine that had not produced the fruit God expected. Instead of choice fruit, wild grapes had sprung forth, worthless either for wine or food. God's people, by their own efforts, could not fulfill their task in the world.

Jesus, however, employed the symbol in a new way. Summers suggests that the conversation recorded in John 15, on the night before the crucifixion, may have taken place near the Temple, under the light of the Passover moon, with its beams shining upon the engraved vine

on the temple entrance. Here Jesus said, "I am the vine, you are the branches" (John 15:5). This understanding is crucial. Jesus took Israel's place. He stood in for God's people as the one who is expected to produce the fruit of obedience, worship, and faithfulness. In effect, Jesus said, "I am that vine on the Temple. I have come to be the source, the very plant that produces fruit for God. Now you are the branches that grow from me, the vine. You are the tiny shoots that come forth and in due season bear the grapes. So stay connected to me."

Jesus' image was stunningly obvious. Branches don't try to live apart from the vine. They are just there, effortlessly letting the vine produce its life through them, resulting in a harvest of grapes. No branch leaps off the tree. No branch tries to do anything. Branches simply remain, held by the vine, yielding fruit. We are to do the same.

Not remaining in the vine has predictable consequences: "Abide in me as I abide in you. Just as the branch cannot bear fruit by itself unless it abides in the vine, neither can you unless you abide in me.…Those who abide in me and I in them bear much fruit, because apart from me you can do nothing" (John 15:4–5). Cut off from the vine, the branches might as well be thrown away. Apart from Christ, we can do nothing.

Living Reliance

As we seek to find out what we are to be doing with our lives in the world to fulfill the call of God, we discover that we are called to do nothing on our own. We require a living reliance upon Jesus Christ, the vine. He alone has done what we cannot do: He offered the perfect response of humanity to God.

This discovery, on the one hand, brings tremendous relief, for we are not expected to do what we are unable to do. We are not thrown back on ourselves and left to our own failings. Christ Jesus has lived the life of obedience on our behalf. He will fulfill in us now the life we were meant to live.

On the other hand, this discovery delivers a dire blow, a kind of death, for it signifies the end of pride and independence from God.

In an age of self-preoccupation, Christ calls us to living reliance and utter dependence. Of course, the secret lies in being connected to Jesus; in losing our self-will to him, we gain our whole lives. We become what we were meant to be, and we find fulfillment beyond measure. Our ability truly to choose and will what is good for us and for the world is restored. We thereby discover that we were meant not for isolated rugged independence but for communion with God and one another.

So the focus of life turns from self to Jesus Christ. We gaze upon his faithfulness. Here in the likeness of our own sinful flesh, he healed our humanity from within. For though tempted, he was obedient. Jesus lived in constant communication with the one he called "Abba." He embraced the broken ones and challenged the self-important ones. He remained faithful even to death on the cross. We concentrate then, not on ourselves and our inability, but on Jesus' life of obedience, which he offers to us.

Living reliance means our counting on what John Calvin called "the wonderful exchange." Jesus touched sinners like us and, far from being defiled, cleansed them. He touched the ill and, far from catching their disease, healed them. He welcomed the outcast and brought them within the fold of his care without condoning any sin or cruelly leaving people as they were. Rather, he restored them to the humanity they had lost. He embraced the world even unto death; and dying, far from being destroyed, he rose with eternal life for the world.

The one who prayed for us in the garden in his agony, prays for us even now at the right hand of God. He offers, as a human being, his worship on our behalf. He offers his obedience in our stead. He has become the Vine so that we might be branches. His life in us produces fruit. We do nothing but abide. He acts through us.

Lesslie Newbigin has written eloquently of this passage in his commentary on John, *The Light Has Come*: "This fruit is not an artifact of the disciples; it is the fruit of the vine. It is the life of Jesus himself reproduced in the lives of the disciples in the midst of the life of the world…the fruit is…love and obedience."[2]

Jesus' own love and obedience becomes ours as we are connected to the vine. The fruit of our lives is his humanity expressed through ours. We simply agree to stay connected. Newbigin continues,

> But it is necessary to "abide" in Jesus, and this means a continually renewed action of the will. It is the continually renewed decision that what has been done once for all by the action of Jesus shall be the basis, the starting point, the context of all my thinking and deciding and doing....but "the loyalty demanded is not primarily a continual being *for*, but a being *from*; not the holding of a position but an allowing oneself to be held." (Bultmann)[3]

We consent to be in Jesus' care, to be where he has put us: restored, forgiven, included in his perfect humanity and obedience. We agree to be from him and to be held by him. We invite him to reproduce his life in us.

What are we supposed to do in the world for God? We begin by abiding in the vine. Moment by moment as life happens around us, we say, "Jesus, produce your life in me. I will go where you send me. I offer my life in your service to those around me—not because I am even able to be available to you but because you have grafted me into the vine. You produce fruit through me." Living reliance on the vine makes radical availability possible.

Let us focus on Jesus and on living reliance upon him. Professor Thomas F. Torrance has written,

> It is Christ the object of faith who holds on to us and saves us even when our faith is so weak. The Christ in whom we believe far exceeds the small measure of our faith, and so the believer finds...security not in [a] poor believing grasp of Christ but in the gift of grace....It is not therefore upon the strength of our faith that we rely but upon the faithfulness of Christ.[4]

This reliance runs counter to our usual thinking. We chastise ourselves: I must do *more* for God. It seems impossible that doing nothing for God of our own will accomplishes far more. It feels as if we'll just be sitting around singing while the world dies. But as we begin to abide in the vine, inviting Jesus to produce his life in us and getting ourselves out of the way, our lives will become fruitful beyond imagination.

On one hand, [God] demands our love and service and on the other, [God] is the actual source and originator of our ability to love and serve. We can only fully respond to the demand by fully accepting the gift; and to do this is the whole secret of the saints.

—Evelyn Underhill

Jesus asks for radical availability, and we cannot offer it. He asks us if we love him more than anything; and we turn away our eyes, for we are full of self. He asks us to let go, and we walk away in shame, for we have many possessions. We can't do it.

But Jesus has already done it. He gave up all, as a mortal, for God. He loved God with all his heart, soul, mind, and body. He established the new vine. And he says, I did this for you. I am doing it for you. Will you agree to it? Will you let me do in you what you cannot? Will you let my faithfulness be the measure of your life? Will you let me hold you? Will you let me be life in you?

We blow off steam trying to control life rather than letting God's energy pass through us to enrich our lives and our world. We are so full of our own need to accomplish and to act that we have no room to receive the power God waits to bestow. If we approached life with open hands, in poverty of spirit, we could receive the resources we need for effective living.... Jesus did not make things happen. He allowed things to happen through him, through his openness and receptivity.

—Thomas R. Hawkins

DAILY EXERCISES

Read the chapter for Week 2, "Living Reliance." Keep a journal or blank book beside you to record your thoughts, questions, prayers, and images.

This week, use your daily exercise time to explore the meaning and promise of responding to God's call out of a "living reliance" on Christ. For example, as you seek to respond to God's calling, how are you encountering the limits of your self-reliance and hearing the invitation to a greater reliance on Christ? Remember the shift and promise contained in the words of the chapter:

> To share in the work of Christ, then, means not so much our working for Christ but our inviting him to work in and through us.…We grow toward that spiritual reality named by Paul in his Letter to the Galatians, "It is no longer I who live, but it is Christ who lives in me" (Gal. 2:20).

EXERCISE 1

Read John 15:1-5. Draw an image of a vine and its branches that illustrates what "living reliance" on Christ means to you. How would you interpret your image as a picture of the life you seek or the life that Christ seeks to live in you? (Draw on a sheet of paper, not in your journal. Bring your drawing to the group meeting where you may choose to display it on the center table for the opening worship. It need not be beautiful or artistic, simply expressive of the vine and branches.)

Bring to mind the primary activities that fill your life right now. In what ways do you feel that the activities of your life are connected or disconnected from the Lord? Spend the remainder of your time abiding in Christ and opening yourself to the flow of divine love in and through you.

EXERCISE 2

Read Acts 9:10-19. Ananias's vision of the Lord and the Lord's instructions concerning Saul remind us that the Lord sometimes nudges us to do things that we neither understand nor appreciate. Often we are tempted to discount or ignore such promptings. What inner nudging, dreams, or persistent thoughts seem to be urging you to reach out to certain persons or to act on certain concerns? What relationship do you sense between paying attention to these inner promptings and staying connected with Christ? Record your thoughts in your journal.

EXERCISE 3

Read Romans 7:14-25. Reflect on Paul's inner struggle and his deep frustration over his inability to live up to the expectations of God's law. Find places in your life where you identify with Paul's struggle and describe them in your own words. To what extent have these kinds of struggles brought you to greater reliance on Christ? What does it mean at these places of inner weakness to rely on Christ rather than on yourself to resolve the dilemma? In prayer, offer your weaknesses to Christ. Record what you experience and learn.

EXERCISE 4

Read 2 Corinthians 12:1-10. Paul's "thorn in the flesh" represents a weakness with which he struggled mightily, but precisely what it was remains a mystery. The significance comes in Paul's interpretation of it. He sees this thorn as God's way of deflating his inclination to boast so that God can work through him.

Meditate on Paul's living reliance, especially in the phrase, "My grace is sufficient for you, for power is made perfect in weakness." Is some aspect of who you are—some "thorn in the flesh" that will not go away—urging you to rely more on God in order to fulfill your calling? With what limitation do you struggle? What weakness embarrasses you? Perhaps God is calling you to see this thorn in a new way. In prayer, begin to make this area of weakness available to God and see what happens.

EXERCISE 5

Read 2 Corinthians 1:3-7. These verses remind us of another way we rely on God for the resources to respond to our call. God comforts

us in our affliction, Paul writes, so that we may be able to comfort others. Think of a past wound or hurt that has enabled you to feel compassion for persons who face similar challenges. What were the circumstances, and how did you experience God's consolation or call in the midst of your affliction (v. 3)? How is God calling you to use your suffering for the sake of others? In prayer, begin to offer your wounds to the God who heals and redeems.

Remember to review your journal for the week in preparation for the group meeting.

Part 4, Week 3
Bearing the Fruit of the Vine

*D*o you feel as if we have been bouncing back and forth between extremes? The question has been, "What am I supposed to be doing for God?" The answers have seemed contradictory: everything and nothing. God lays claim to everything, absolutely every corner and crevice of our beings. Yet at the same time, we realize that we can do nothing on our own. Apart from Christ Jesus, "our striving would be losing" as Martin Luther said.

So what are we supposed to be doing? Answers to the question that are just slightly off the mark can send us barreling down terribly defeating paths. If we try too hard to be constantly available, we may end up becoming Christian perfectionists. We may hate ourselves for our failures. We may start trying to do more (and trying to get everyone else to do more), always striving to measure up to what God requires and never making it. We may become mean, legalistic, guilt-slinging Christians. On the other hand, we may become so enamored of grace, counting on God to do everything, that we get lazy. We may wait so passively for God to work through us that we end up with no prayer life, no service life, no discipline, and no hope. In such a state, we can hardly be distinguished from much of the culture.

The balance lies in the image of the branch remaining in the vine that we began considering last week. We look at a vine or a tree and

How do we discover which part of God's vision is ours? Insight comes when we reflect on what evokes our most passionate criticism, our deepest grief, or energizes us to new possibilities…. When we pay attention…we begin to get glimmers of the aspects of God's vision that may be ours to carry out.

—Jacqueline McMakin
with Rhoda Nary

rarely give a second thought as to how the branches remain connected to the larger trunk. A branch is held by the tree even as the branch holds to the tree. The bark joins the two so that we cannot really tell where one begins and the other ends. The branch is a conduit for the vine and receives water and nutrients from its trunk. In this way the tree or vine grows up through its branches. And those branches produce fruit according to their design.

No branch lives without connection to the source. It does not try to leap off and become an independent tree. Neither does it resist the design of the vine, trying to block its natural growth. A branch on a grapevine allows grapes to come forth without effort.

When we translate this image to the relationship between Christ and us, we readily see that we are called to dwell in him. We do not try to live apart from Jesus Christ. We consent to be in the position he has given us. He has declared us to be branches in him, the Vine. Our position is a result of the work he has done.

The fruit we produce will be Jesus' life coming forth through us. This consideration of what we are to do in the world continually returns to who Jesus is, what he has done and is doing in the world.

The Fruit of Love

Lesslie Newbigin notes that in Jesus' life on earth, he did not enter each day with a fixed agenda or an inflexible, planned course. Rather, he lived to be interrupted. The changing, unexpected occurrences of daily life produced the opportunities for love. Jesus expressed his love for God through availability to love whoever came before him in whatever way was required. He obeyed the demands of such love for the world even to the point of dying a criminal's death upon the cross as an innocent man:

> Jesus had no program of his own. He planned no career for himself....He simply responded in loving obedience to the will of his Father as it was presented to him in all the accidents, contingencies, and interruptions of daily life, among all the personal and public ambitions and fears and jealousies of that little province of the Roman empire.[1]

Jesus' life provides the pattern for us. Dwelling in his great love, held in his grace even as the vine holds the branches, we welcome the reproduction of such love through us. Jesus told his disciples, "As the Father has loved me, so I have loved you; abide in my love. If you keep my commandments, you will abide in my love, just as I have kept my Father's commandments and abide in his love…love one another as I have loved you" (John 15:9-10, 12). Being companions in Christ means loving in the way Jesus did. Newbigin continues,

> So the disciple.…will not be concerned to create a character or career for himself. He will leave that to the wise husbandry of the Gardener who alone knows what pruning, what watering and feeding, what sunshine or rain, warmth or cold is needed to produce the fruit he desires. The disciple will "learn obedience" by following Jesus in the same kind of moment-by-moment obedience to the will of the Father as it is disclosed in the contingent happenings of daily life in the place and time where God has put him.[2]

The bonds that connect us are the bonds of love, God's love for us, which draws us, but also our love for God and neighbor, which can never be separated from each other.… We cannot love God and hate or even be indifferent to our neighbor.

—Roberta C. Bondi

The measure of our lives will not be in career and the name or place we make for ourselves. These things may come. But the deeper measure is the love and obedience we show in the midst of life that sometimes sends us rising to the stars and other times sends us crashing to the depths. We honor God in our daily tasks and work. But even more important than what we do is how we do it. Is the legacy of my labor one of love? Can I see an interruption as a call of God? Do I understand that my life is not really my work or status or success but my life in Christ Jesus expressing itself in love for those around me?

The Apostle Paul summarized all we have been considering: "The only thing that counts is faith working through love" (Gal. 5:6). What matters in life is the faith by which we say yes to Christ Jesus and the way we express such faith toward others in love. That's the essence of our Christian call, whether we are functioning at full capacity in an extremely demanding job or lying paralyzed from the neck down on a hospital bed. Whether we are overextended in a plethora of relationships or lonely from leave-takings, the call of God is the same: faith expressing itself through love. Faith takes the position of receiving grace in Christ Jesus. Love enacts that grace toward others.

The Role of the Holy Spirit

What is required of us is quite simple. Yet the balance of radical availability, living reliance, and fruitful love is hard to maintain. We keep getting in the way of what God in Christ wants to do through us. The reality of sin defeats our impulse toward love with old grudges, present lusts, or anxieties about the future. Abiding in Christ is supposed to be as effortless as being branches on the tree, but our lives reveal that it is not that easy.

At this point we must recall the person of God the Holy Spirit. Shortly before his crucifixion, Jesus promised his disciples that though he would be leaving them, he would send the Holy Spirit to dwell within and among them. The Spirit would bring to mind the words of Jesus and teach the disciples the true meaning of his life, death, and resurrection. Jesus said that it is the work of the Spirit to take what is of Jesus—his faithfulness, his love, his obedience, his forgiveness—and give it to us (John 16:14-15). So the presence of the Holy Spirit within us is the key to our continual abiding in Christ Jesus, which leads to a fruitful life.

Paul tells us that "God's love has been poured into our hearts through the Holy Spirit that has been given to us" (Rom. 5:5). By that Spirit, we are adopted in Christ as God's sons and daughters. Therefore, when we cry out to God in prayer, "it is that very Spirit bearing witness with our spirit that we are children of God" (Rom. 8:16). The Holy Spirit is God consenting to live within us, ever urging us from the inside out toward a deeper relationship with Christ. Here is the source of our believing and our acting. Paul states, "Through the Spirit, by faith, we eagerly wait for the hope of righteousness" (Gal. 5:5), which Jesus has accomplished for us.

And the Spirit is the source of power for winning the struggle against the old nature and sustaining growth even amidst difficult circumstances. Paul prays that his readers will "be strengthened in [their] inner being with power through [God's] Spirit" (Eph. 3:16). This mighty strength enables us to deny sin and live for God. By the Spirit, we "put to death the deeds" (Rom. 8:13) of the sinful self and live vigorously for God.

Andrew Murray has written eloquently of the role of the Holy Spirit in connecting us to Christ: "All the fulness is in Jesus; the fulness of grace and truth, out of which we receive grace for grace. The Holy Spirit is the appointed conveyancer, whose special work it is to make Jesus and all there is in Him for us ours in personal appropriation, in blessed experience. He is the Spirit of life in Christ Jesus."[3]

The Spirit is the conveyer of Jesus Christ and all his graces to us and through us. Abiding in Christ then is the work of the Holy Spirit within us. By the creative, life-giving power of God the Spirit, fruit is grown though us.

Our part, though small, is crucial. We are to ask the Spirit to work in us and to consent consciously and deliberately to being branches in the vine that is Jesus Christ. Each moment requires such openness of us. We renew our consent to let the Spirit flow through us day by day and hour by hour. Murray continues, "Just as the branch, already filled with the sap of the vine, is ever crying for the continued and increasing flow of that sap, that it may bring its fruit to perfection, so the believer, rejoicing in the possession of the Spirit, ever thirsts and cries for more."[4]

As the union of the branch with the vine is one of growth, never-ceasing growth and increase, so our abiding in Christ is a life process in which the divine life takes ever fuller and more complete possession of us.

—Andrew Murray

We may thus pray continually, "God, I cannot. But you can. By your grace I am connected to Jesus Christ. I agree to what you have done! And I know that even my agreeing is a gift. Nevertheless, you desire this act of my will. So by the power of the Holy Spirit, whom you have caused to dwell in me, grow the fruit of love in my daily life."

The scriptures employ many images for this action of living reliance that leads to the fruit of the vine. The archetypal example is Mary's response to Gabriel, when the angel announces that she will conceive the Son of God. She replies, "Here I am, the servant of the Lord; let it be with me according to your word" (Luke 1:38). Gabriel has revealed what God will do. Mary does not have to create the plan or muster the power of God. She simply agrees. Based on a devoted, loving relationship as the servant and handmaiden of God, she invites God to go ahead and act in accordance with the promise made. This kind of active consent to what God desires to do in and through us is the way to become fruitful branches of the Vine. We do not try to manufacture the fruit in our own strength; we actively choose to invite God to grow the fruit through us.

Fruit and Gifts

Fruit is expected of every Christian, regardless of stage or condition of life. In John 15, Jesus defined this fruit in terms of love and obedience. Paul expanded the image when he wrote, "The fruit of the Spirit is love, joy, peace, patience, kindness, generosity, faithfulness, gentleness, and self-control" (Gal. 5:22-23). These attitudes and actions characterize the life lived in obedience to God and reliance on the Holy Spirit. We cannot make ourselves produce such fruit. But we can ask God to grow such love through us. And we can focus our minds toward exhibiting such qualities.

> *There is simply no way we can be obedient to the command to love without grafting ourselves onto the vine of Christ: "Whoever remains in me, with me in him, / bears fruit in plenty; / for cut off from me you can do nothing"(John 15:5). The choice set before us is therefore the choice of enlargement or withering.*
>
> —Robin Maas

To use another scriptural image for this process, we dress ourselves in the clothing of the Spirit (Col. 3:12-17). This is not done in the sense of covering up our true nature with the appearance of Christian values. Rather, based on our identity in Christ, we consciously adorn ourselves with the clothes appropriate to our position. Since we are branches in the vine that is Christ Jesus, we may deliberately cultivate what suits our station in life. We want to look the part that has been given to us. Again without trying to do it in our own strength, we set our imaginations, focus our minds, and direct our actions in accord with what Christ Jesus has said he wants to do in us.

With this necessary foundation laid, we may begin to consider what specific work in the world God wants to do through us. We may now ponder how God has given each of us a particular gift for service that makes our place in the whole vineyard splendidly unique. Every Christian has been so gifted for service that the universal church of Christ renders a marvelous diversity of ministry within the unity of the Spirit. Fruit takes precedence over gifts. But the gifts give zest to our living reliance and continual obedience. In the next section, we will consider more closely the nature of spiritual gifts and their place as we join in the work of Christ.

DAILY EXERCISES

Read the chapter for Week 3, "Bearing the Fruit of the Vine," before you begin the exercises. Keep your journal beside you to record your thoughts, questions, prayers, and insights.

This week use your daily exercise time to explore the fruitfulness of your response to God's call, not in terms of how much you are doing but in terms of who you are becoming through the spirit of Jesus Christ. You might review the fruit of your participation in *Companions in Christ* thus far. Drawing on Jesus' image of the vine and branches in John 15, think about whether there have been any new buds of life in you. What fruit is the Vine already producing in and through you?

EXERCISE 1

Read Romans 1:7. Meditate on what it means that you are "God's beloved…, who are called to be saints." List three to five persons, living or dead, who embody this meaning for you. Do not include biblical characters. Under each name, note the qualities of humanness and holiness that draw you to that person, and why. Pray with the affirmation, "We are God's beloved…, who are called to be saints."

EXERCISE 2

Read Galatians 5:13-26. Meditate on the fruit of the Spirit listed and on evidence of the fruit in your life in community. What do you see? What fruit would others say they see in you?

Identify an area of your life where you feel you are not bearing the fruit of the Spirit. What would it mean for you to let yourself be guided by the Spirit who already lives in you? Spend some time in prayer asking the Spirit to help you with these challenges. Jot down any insights that may come.

EXERCISE 3

Read Philippians 3:2-11. Paul uses strong words to warn the Philippians of the temptation among religious people to mistake adherence

to a set of religious practices or conformity to a moral code for the fruit of life in Christ. How do you distinguish between the two in your life—your own efforts to create a good life and the fruit that comes from abiding in Christ?

Draw a circle. Around the boundary, write all of the commitments and efforts you make to live a good life, including achievements that make you proud. Within the circle, write words or images that represent the full fruit of life in Christ for which you long. Reflect on the relationship you see between what is around and what is within the circle. In prayer, open your heart to the goodness God gives us through faith in Christ.

EXERCISE 4

Read Acts 2:42-47. Reflect on the close relationship between the abundant fruit of the early church and the root practices of that community. Make a list (or draw a picture) of the fruits and roots that you see in the description.

Now turn your attention to your congregation. What fruit do you experience in your church? What fruit does the surrounding community see and experience? What are the root practices of your congregation that nourish those fruits? In prayer, ask God to show you the underlying condition of your spiritual roots as a church. Note your responses.

EXERCISE 5

Read Romans 8:18-28. Where in your community are creation's inhabitants "subjected to futility" and yearning to be set free from "bondage to decay"? Pray for renewal there, offering yourself to the renewing influence of the Spirit in those places. Record your thoughts and experience.

Review your journal for the week in preparation for the group meeting.

Part 4, Week 4
Gifts of the Spirit

*W*e have been considering what God wants us to do in the world. We know that God asks for our complete availability, and we know that apart from the grace of Jesus Christ, we can do nothing. On our own, we are unable even to believe in God's love or offer our lives in service. But by the power of the Holy Spirit, we may live for God. Abiding in Christ as branches remain in the vine, we give our consent for God to produce fruit through us. That fruit includes love, joy, peace, patience, kindness, goodness—the very life of Christ Jesus reproduced through us.

The fruit of the Spirit may grow in the dullest, slowest, and weakest, as well as in the brightest, fastest, and strongest. Astonishingly, God chooses to work through available vessels, no matter how broken or worn we seem to be, in whatever circumstances we happen to be. Royalty and servants, bosses and workers, able-bodied and infirm—all have one basic vocation. All are called to consent to the work of Christ in their life; all are called to show the love of Jesus to others by the same Spirit.

Our common grace and task being clear, we may now celebrate the wonderful variety in God's creative work. Every Christian has been given a spiritual gift. Simply defined, spiritual gifts are particular abilities given by Christ through the Holy Spirit for the good of the whole church so it may do Christ's work in the world.

There are many different gifts. Scholars list anywhere from a minimum of nineteen up to thirty-one, with some saying there is no end to the variety of gifts God bestows. Each one of us has at least one spiritual gift that complements our God-given personality and character. Our gift or gifts cry out for expression and use. And using our gifts brings a great release of energy coupled with joy. We feel as if we are doing easily just what we have always wanted to do.

Over the next two weeks, you will have the opportunity to help others in your group discern their particular gifts, while allowing them to help you discern your own. How you may develop and use these gifts in Christ's service will be a matter of continuing discernment. This reading prepares you for that work as we consider the basic scriptural texts on spiritual gifts.

The Holy Spirit, Giver of All Gifts

Paul begins, "Now concerning spiritual gifts, brothers and sisters, I do not want you to be uninformed" (1 Cor. 12:1). Right away, we may realize that spiritual gifts can cause confusion in a church, and their healthy use requires accurate knowledge about these gifts. Before going further, Paul sets spiritual gifts in their context. He reminds his readers of the foundational importance of the Holy Spirit: "No one can say 'Jesus is Lord' except by the Holy Spirit" (1 Cor. 12:3). Paul credits our most basic confession to God the Holy Spirit. Here we may take his cue and consider the Spirit more deeply before proceeding.

The great Swiss Reformer, John Calvin, writes convincingly of our need for the Spirit's work:

> First, we must understand that as long as Christ remains outside of us, and we are separated from him, all that he has suffered and done for the salvation of the human race remains useless and of no value to us....It is true that we obtain this by faith....
>
> But faith is the principal work of the Holy Spirit. [It is] a supernatural gift that those who would otherwise remain in unbelief receive Christ by faith....
>
> [Christ] unites himself to us by the Spirit alone. By the grace and power of the same Spirit we are made his members....To sum up, the Holy Spirit is the bond by which Christ effectually unites us to himself.[1]

Beloved young Christian, take time to understand and to become filled with the truth: the Holy Spirit is in you. Review all the assurances of God's word that this is so....Pray, think not for a moment of living as a Christian without the indwelling of the Spirit. Take pains to have your heart filled with the faith that the Spirit dwells in you, and will do...mighty work, for through faith the Spirit comes and works.

—Andrew Murray

God the Holy Spirit creates faith in us so that we may see and believe who Jesus is. Then the Spirit unites all the love and obedience of Jesus Christ to us. The bond or spiritual glue of the Spirit joins us to Christ. On our own, all the love of Jesus is outside us. By the Spirit's uniting, knitting, and weaving, Jesus comes to dwell within us.

This work is the very power of God, but it is not violent to creatures as fragile as we. The Spirit, in divine humility, works gently with us, inviting our cooperation and enduring patiently our storms of willfulness. Professor Thomas F. Torrance writes, "If it is only the Almighty who can be infinitely gentle, the Holy Spirit may well be characterized as the gentleness of God the Father Almighty."[2] The Spirit woos rather than overwhelms and whispers more than shouts. Torrance quotes the ancient writings of Cyril: "His coming is gentle. Our perception of him is fragrant; his burden is very easy to bear; beams of light shine out with his coming. He comes with the compassion of a true Guardian, for he comes to save and to heal, to teach, to admonish, to strengthen, to exhort, to enlighten the mind."[3]

As light falls upon the world silently, invisibly, doing its work of sustaining all life, so the Spirit falls upon us and shines within us in a quiet, steady way. All the while, the Holy Spirit humbly illumines Jesus Christ, giving him the glory and prominence and directing our attention to rely upon him alone.

While bringing the gift of faith, the Spirit also labors to make us more and more like Jesus. Calvin writes, "By his secret watering, the Spirit makes us fruitful to bring forth the bud of righteousness....For by the inspiration of his power he so breathes divine life into us that we are no longer actuated by ourselves, but are ruled by his action and prompting."[4]

The Holy Spirit, though gentle, does work in power, "persistently boiling away and burning up our vicious and inordinate desires, he enflames our hearts with the love of God." In summary, Calvin tells us that "whatever good things are in us are the fruits of [the Spirit's] grace."[5] This is the sweet, mighty Spirit at work in the church who, in addition to faith and fruit, bestows gifts upon us.

From this foundation, Paul can say that the same Spirit who

Have a great reverence for the work of the Spirit in you. Seek [the Spirit] every day to believe, to obey, to trust, and [the Spirit] will take and make known to you all that there is in Jesus. [The Holy Spirit] will make Jesus very glorious to you and in you.

—Andrew Murray

enables a similar basic faith in every Christian also dispenses a wide variety of spiritual gifts. Each one of us is "given the manifestation of the Spirit" (1 Cor. 12:7). In other words, the spirit of Jesus Christ is made known through believers in wonderfully diverse ways. Every believer is different, yet each one is gifted. No one is passed over. God delights to give gifts to us since we are dearly loved children. And God is infinite in creativity, so we do not all come out exactly the same. God rejoices in the variety.

The grace of God in Christ Jesus is poured out like a great wave over the church. But that metaphor goes only so far. The wave of God's grace does not wash everything into a bland sameness. Rather, grace polishes each one to a unique brilliance. None is expendable. We are not better when some are absent. The church is at its best with all present and the unique combinations of gifts flourishing.

Every single one of us has been made to shine. There is a particular gift in you. You have a part to play that no one else can. You add a nuance to the story of God's love in Christ that makes it more wonderful. You add a color to the palate of grace. Without your gift the hues are not as vivid. As Paul says, all the gifts "are activated by one and the same Spirit, who allots to each one individually just as the Spirit chooses" (1 Cor. 12:11).

These individually tailored gifts, however, are not only for our personal enjoyment. Paul finishes the sentence, "To each is given the manifestation of the Spirit for the common good." Here we may switch from the image of the vine and its branches to the image of the body of Christ: "For just as the body is one and has many members, and all the members of the body, though many, are one body, so it is with Christ. For in the one Spirit, we were all baptized into one body....Now you are the body of Christ and individually members of it" (1 Cor. 12:12-13, 27). Paul describes how all the parts of the body must work together in order for the whole to function. Next week we will consider more closely the different expressions of the body of Christ manifested in various churches, and how, like bodies, each has a particular shape, character, and temperament. For now, we realize that the gifts are meant to benefit the whole.

The gifts [of the Spirit] are a means of transmitting the powerful and purposeful divine presence into the flesh and blood of humanity. It is an intimacy with God that sheds light on the active presence of the resurrected Christ. It is an inner power that makes the whole person receptive and obedient to a new way of living abundantly and effectively in service to God's kingdom.

—Charles V. Bryant

First Corinthians 12 names gifts that may seem splashier than other lists in the New Testament: working of miracles, discernment of spirits, various kinds of tongues, interpretation of those tongues, gifts of healing. With these are included gifts more readily understood, such as faith, wisdom, forms of assistance, and leadership. We realize that the Spirit comes to us in power, and the community of Christ's people may expect to see many wondrous sights. Yet these more demonstrative gifts are to be balanced with wise and discerning minds.

Gifts That Unify the Body

In Ephesians 4:1-16, Paul concentrates on the importance of our unity as one body of Jesus Christ. The gifts discussion is again placed in its context. Paul begins by reminding us of our most basic calling to follow Jesus and urges us "to lead a life worthy of the calling to which you have been called" (v. 1). The common expression of our call is the fruit of the Spirit, here described as living "with all humility and gentleness, with patience, bearing with one another in love, making every effort to maintain the unity of the Spirit in the bond of peace" (vv. 2-3).

Then Paul goes on to describe our common foundation of "one Lord, one faith, one baptism, one God and Father of all" (vv. 5-6). From that shared core, God's diversity arises: "But each of us was given grace according to the measure of Christ's gift" (v. 7). Jesus who dwelt among us also ascended to heaven, and from his place at the right hand of God he poured forth the Holy Spirit onto the disciples. With the Spirit come gifts: "The gifts he gave were that some would be apostles, some prophets, some evangelists, some pastors and teachers, to equip the saints for the work of ministry, for building up the body of Christ, until all of us come to the unity of the faith and of the knowledge of the Son of God, to maturity, to the measure of the full stature of Christ" (vv. 11-13).

The gifts listed in Ephesians are for leadership. Gifted leaders equip the rest of the believers, the saints, for the ministry of the whole church. Leadership builds up the body so that as one, we grow to be more and more like Christ. Joining in the work of Christ means becoming like him, and that forming process occurs through the exercise of spiritual gifts. The apostles were eyewitnesses to the resurrected Jesus and laid the foundation for the church through the ages by bearing witness to all that Jesus said and did. Prophets build on that base, calling the church out from the world to be a people dedicated first to God. Evangelists can then lead the church back into the world with the message of the gospel. Pastors nurture members of the body through the stresses of life, while teachers continually link daily living with the stories and truths of scripture. Together, such leadership equips a body that both gathers together and is sent into the world. The gifts employed make the body healthy and strong as it expresses the work of Christ.

One Body, Gifted for Service

Romans 12:1-8 focuses on less spectacular gifts that are no less important than the apparent gifts in First Corinthians or the strong leadership gifts in Ephesians. As ever, Paul sets the context before speaking of the gifts themselves. Here he urges his readers toward radical availability. His appeal is based, however, not on an individual's effort to please God but on the mercies first given by God in Christ. Realizing these, we may present our bodies "as a living sacrifice." Such consecration is continual, and its fruit is being "transformed by the renewing of your minds." This is an organic change, created by God but consented to and chosen by us day by day.

From here, Paul employs the image of the body to express how each of us is important yet all of us are interrelated: "For as in one body we have many members, and not all the members have the same function, so we, who are many, are one body in Christ, and individually we are members one of another" (vv. 4-5). The organically connected communion of believers is yet individually gifted for service to one another: "We have gifts that differ according to the grace given to us" (v. 6). Paul encourages believers to act in love in accordance

with our unique gifts, to use who we are and what we have, not trying to be anyone else but vigorously being who God has made us to be: "prophecy, in proportion to faith; ministry, in ministering; the teacher, in teaching; the exhorter, in exhortation; the giver, in generosity; the leader, in diligence; the compassionate, in cheerfulness" (vv. 6-8).

This passage echoes Ecclesiastes 9:10: "Whatever your hand finds to do, do with your might." We are called to kindle the gifts by using them in service. The more we employ our gifts, the more they blossom. By contrast, stifling or hiding our gifts can lead to spiritual diminishment.

So, what are your gifts, and what are the gifts of those with whom you have been traveling as companions in Christ these past several months? Where are you and your group friends already using your gifts? Where do you feel led to be using them? The exercises this week and your meeting time will help you discern your unique spiritual gifts and those of your companions.

> *We develop our gifts…when we use them for the good of others….Our gifts are to be given away so that the whole human community is richer for our having been here.*
>
> —Joan D. Chittister

DAILY EXERCISES

Read the chapter for Week 4, "Gifts of the Spirit." Keep a journal or blank book beside you to record your thoughts and insights.

Your primary assignment for each daily exercise time is to begin to name the gifts that you have observed in each person in your small group. You will be given some scripture for reflection but direct the majority of your time toward this preparing for the group meeting. Each day select one to three group members for prayer and naming of gifts. Focus on one person at a time, and ask God for an awareness to see and celebrate the gifts God has given him or her.

- First, think about each person's unique contribution as a group member since the beginning of your time together.
- Second, recall what he or she has communicated during the past three sessions about the things most enjoyed, the dreams for a better world, and the potentials for love latent in wounds and weaknesses.
- Then record your insights and affirmations in your journal.

When you have gathered your affirmations and insights about a person, read over the list of New Testament gifts printed at the end of the exercises for this week (pages 217–21), and search for gifts you associate with what you have seen. Interpret the gifts broadly and creatively. Although you should not feel overly constrained by the list (there are other gifts), try to stay within the list as far as you are able before you name others.

Finally, write a card to each group member identifying and affirming gifts. In the cards you will describe

1. Gifts you clearly see in each person. Beside or beneath each gift, add a few words describing how and where you have seen these gifts.
2. Gifts you see as potentials in each person. Describe briefly how or where you have seen these potentials.

Important: Before the meeting, compare your cards to a group roster to make sure you have cards for everyone. Your group leader will inform you if this process will require one or two meetings (depending on the size of your group) and which members will wait until the second meeting to receive their cards if two meetings are needed. Bring the cards to the next group meeting.

EXERCISE 1

Read Ephesians 4:7-13. Meditate on the hope of growing together "to maturity, to the measure of the full stature of Christ." Think about that in light of this week's work of affirming one another's gifts for Christ's ministry. Follow the guidelines for completing gift cards, and begin the process of writing a card for each group member.

Consider what it would mean for these persons to grow to maturity according to the measure of the full stature of Christ. Pray for their maturity in using the gifts God has given them. Pray for your ability to speak the truth in love concerning their gifts so that they may see their gifts with new clarity.

EXERCISE 2

Read 1 Corinthians 12:1-27. Meditate on the mystery of our relationship in Christ and our dependence on one another for building up the full ministry of Christ. Follow the guidelines for completing a gift card for each group member.

Use any remaining time to reflect on your own gifts. Draw an image of a physical body. Figuratively speaking, where would you locate yourself and your gifts if this were a picture of the body of Christ in your congregation? Name the gifts that are implied by locating yourself there.

EXERCISE 3

Read Matthew 25:14-30. Meditate on the good news that God has given gifts to each group member for the increase of God's kingdom on earth. Offer a prayer that each may discover his or her gifts and use

them well rather than bury or hide them. Follow the guidelines for completing a gift card for each group member.

Use any remaining time to reflect on the two kinds of persons Jesus describes in the parable of the talents. In what ways do you see yourself in both characters?

EXERCISE 4

Read Romans 12:1-8. Meditate on Paul's counsel that we think about our gifts with "sober judgment, each according to the measure of faith that God has assigned." Follow the guidelines for completing a gift card for each member of the group.

Use any remaining time to identify attitudes that limit your ability to appreciate others' gifts or to value your own gifts. Offer these attitudes to God in all honesty. Ask God to free you to appreciate your friends the way you want them to appreciate you.

EXERCISE 5

Read 2 Timothy 1:2-7. Ponder the powerful and confirming role that we play in recognizing and naming one another's gifts. Follow the guidelines for completing a gift card for each group member.

Use any remaining time to reflect on persons who have kindled "the gift of God" in you and called forth your gifts. What qualities in them helped you to be yourself? Pray for the grace to be such a faithful friend for the members of your group.

Please review your journal entries for the week in preparation for the group meeting.

A List of Spiritual Gifts

Dan R. Dick wrote the following list; it is used by permission. (See footnote on page 221.)

These gifts are derived from Paul's listings of spiritual gifts in Romans 12:6-8; 1 Corinthians 12:4-11; 12:27-31; Ephesians 4:11-12.

Administration—The gift of organizing human and material resources for the work of Christ, including the ability to plan and work with people to delegate responsibilities, track progress, and evaluate the effectiveness of procedures. Administrators attend to details, communicate effectively, and take as much pleasure in working behind the scenes as they do in standing in the spotlight.

Apostleship—The gift of spreading the gospel of Jesus Christ to other cultures and foreign lands. This is the missionary zeal that moves us from the familiar into uncharted territory to share the good news. Apostles embrace opportunities to learn foreign languages, visit other cultures, and go where people are who have not heard the Christian message….It is no longer necessary to cross an ocean to enter the mission field. Even across generations, we may find that we need to "speak other languages" just to communicate. Our mission field might be no further than our own backyard.

Compassion—This gift is exceptional empathy with those in need that moves us to action. More than just concern, compassion demands that we share the suffering of others in order to connect the gospel truth with other realities of life. Compassion moves us beyond our comfort zones to offer practical, tangible aid to all God's children, regardless of the worthiness of the recipients or the response we receive for our service.

Discernment—This is the ability to separate truth from erroneous teachings and to rely on spiritual intuition to know what God is calling us to do. Discernment allows us to focus on what is truly important and to ignore that which deflects us from faithful obe-

dience to God. Discernment aids us in knowing whom to listen to and whom to avoid.

Evangelism—This is the ability to share the gospel of Jesus Christ with those who have not heard it before or with those who have not yet made a decision for Christ. This gift is manifested in both one-on-one situations and in group settings, both large and small. It is an intimate relationship with another person or persons that requires the sharing of personal faith and a call for a response of faith to God.

Exhortation—This is the gift of exceptional encouragement. Exhorters see the silver lining in every cloud, offer deep and inspiring hope to the fellowship, and look for and commend the best in everyone. Exhorters empower the community of faith to feel good about itself and to feel hopeful for the future. Exhorters are not concerned by appearances; they hold fast to what they know to be true and right and good.

Faith—More than just belief, faith is a gift that empowers an individual or a group to hold fast to its identity in Christ in the face of any challenge. The gift of faith enables believers to rise above pressures and problems that might otherwise cripple them. Faith is characterized by an unshakable trust in God to deliver on God's promises, no matter what. The gift of faith inspires those who might be tempted to give up to hold on.

Giving—Beyond the regular response of gratitude to God that all believers make, giving as a gift is the ability to use the resource of money to support the work of the body of Christ. Giving is the ability to manage money to the honor and glory of God. Givers can discern the best ways to put money to work, can understand the validity and practicality of appeals for funds, and can guide [church leaders] in the most faithful methods for managing [the congregation's] financial concerns.

Healing—This is the gift of channeling God's healing powers into the lives of God's people. Physical, emotional, spiritual, and psychological healing are all ways that healers manifest this gift. Healers are prayerful, and they help people understand that healing is in the hands of God, that healing is often more than just erasing negative symptoms. Some of the most powerful healers display some of the most heartbreaking afflictions.

Helping—This is the gift of making sure that everything is ready for the work of Christ to occur. Helpers assist others to accomplish the mission and ministry of the church. These "unsung heroes" work behind the scenes and attend to details that others would rather not be bothered with. Helpers function faithfully, regardless of the credit or attention they receive. Helpers provide the framework upon which the ministry of the church is built.

Interpretation of Tongues (see Tongues)—This gift has two very different understandings: (1) the ability to interpret *foreign languages* without the necessity of formal study to communicate with those who have not heard the Christian message or (2) the ability to interpret the gift of tongues as a *secret prayer language* that communicates with God at a deep spiritual level. Both understandings are communal in nature: the first extends the good news into the world; the second strengthens the faith within the fellowship.

Knowledge—This is the gift of knowing the truth through faithful study of the Scripture and the human situation. Knowledge provides the information necessary for the transformation of the world and formation of the body of Christ. Those possessing this gift challenge the fellowship to improve itself through study, reading of the Scripture, discussions, and prayer.

Leadership—This is the gift of orchestrating the gifts and resources of others to achieve the mission and ministry of the church. Leaders move the community of faith toward a God-given vision of service, and they enable others to use their gifts to the very best of their abilities. Leaders are capable of creating synergy, whereby the community of faith accomplishes much more than its individual members could achieve on their own.

Miracle working—This gift enables the church to operate at a spiritual level that recognizes the miraculous work of God in the world. Miracle workers invoke God's power to accomplish that which appears impossible by worldly standards. Miracle workers remind the fellowship of the extraordinary nature of the ordinary world, thereby increasing faithfulness and trust in God. Miracle workers pray for God to work in the lives of others, and they feel no sense of surprise when their prayers are answered.

Prophecy—This is the gift of speaking the Word of God clearly and faithfully. Prophets allow God to speak through them to communicate the message that people most need to hear. While often unpopular, prophets are able to say what needs to be said because of the spiritual empowerment they receive. Prophets do not foretell the future, but proclaim God's future by revealing God's perspective on our current reality.

Servanthood—This is the gift of serving the spiritual and material needs of other people....Servants understand their place in the body of Christ as giving comfort and aid to all who are in need. Servants look to the needs of others rather than focus on their own needs. To serve is to put faith into action; it is to treat others as if they were indeed Jesus Christ himself. The gift of service extends our Christian love into the world.

Shepherding—This is the gift of guidance. Shepherds nurture other Christians in the faith and provide a mentoring relationship to those who are new to the faith. Displaying an unusual spiritual maturity, shepherds share from their experience and learning to facilitate the spiritual growth and development of others. Shepherds take individuals under their care and walk with them on their spiritual journeys. Many shepherds provide spiritual direction and guidance to a wide variety of believers.

Teaching—This is the gift of bringing scriptural and spiritual truths to others. More than just teaching church school, teachers witness to the truth of Jesus Christ in a variety of ways, and they help others to understand the complex realities of the Christian faith. Teachers are revealers. They shine the light of understanding into the darkness of doubt and ignorance. They open people to new truths, and they challenge people to be more in the future than they have been in the past.

Tongues (see Interpretation of Tongues)—This gift has two popular interpretations: (1) the ability to communicate the gospel to other people in a *foreign language* without the benefit of having studied said language (see Acts 2:4) or (2) the ability to speak to God in a secret, unknown *prayer language* that can only be understood by a person possessing the gift of interpretation. The gift of speaking in the language of another culture makes the gift of tongues valuable for spreading the gospel throughout the world, while the gift of speaking a secret prayer language offers the opportunity to build faithfulness within a community of faith.

Wisdom—This is the gift of translating life experience into spiritual truth and of seeing the application of scriptural truth to daily living. The wise in our fellowships offer balance and understanding that transcend reason. Wisdom applies a God-given common sense to our understanding of God's plan for the church. Wisdom helps the community of faith remain focused on the important work of the church, and it enables younger, less mature Christians to benefit from those who have been blessed by God to share deep truths.

From *Revolutionizing Christian Stewardship for the 21st Century: Lessons from Copernicus* by Dan R. Dick (Nashville, Tenn.: Discipleship Resources, 1997), 97–101. Used by permission.

The Body of Christ Given for the World

*T*he Holy Spirit has poured out gifts for service upon every believer. When we employ our gifts in the church, we discover a marvelous sense of energy and fulfillment. The gifts are meant to draw us ever more deeply into community with the other members of Christ's body. And that body is meant to grow: Our arms are continually open to welcome new members with their unique gifts. A living body maintains a steady state and shape, yet is simultaneously always changing and constantly replenishing itself. So the church remains always centered on Jesus Christ but is nevertheless not static but dynamic, not closed but open in its communion. Through the healthy use of spiritual gifts, the church grows and adapts in ever new ways, even while maintaining its basic form as the body of Christ.

Our spiritual gifts are not necessarily connected to our talents or education or what we do for a living. Our place in the body of Christ may differ greatly from our place in the workaday world. Thus in the church we may have a new identity. In the church, world leaders may become recipients and humble servers, while the meek of the world may become celebrated leaders. The CEO who bears so many expectations at work is free in the body of Christ to get on the floor and cuddle children in the nursery. A homemaking mother who converses with children all week may be a wise elder in the body of Christ. The

church of Jesus Christ grounds us in a life more real than the daily world and provides us with a deep sense of purpose and belonging.

Sending and Gathering

At the same time, the open circle of the church sends its members out into the world. We engage in mission work wherever we are, in whatever we do. We exercise our gifts, not only in the company of the church, but also through the church to the world. Though we may be absent physically from our fellowship during the week, we remain spiritually connected. The life of the body constantly influences us. In countless situations, each of us enacts the mission of the church wherever we are. We bring a taste of life in the body of Christ to a world that may know only fragmentation and loneliness. We bring coherence to the chaos, generosity in place of greed to situations, compassion to the forsaken.

And the world partakes of Christ's servants as fruit that satisfies spiritual hunger. Others may be starving for the hope within us, and in their need they may gobble up our time and attention. That is what we live for. Our fruit, the life of Jesus reproduced through us, is meant to feed a hungry world. Out in daily life we give and give; we may find ourselves, as Jesus predicted, used and taken advantage of. Without God's help, we will be exhausted at the end of the week, which comes as no surprise. We need to return to the fellowship of the body to replenish our spirits through community, worship, and study. And we need to turn daily to God for renewal through prayer, meditation on scripture, and spiritual friendship.

Particular Mission

Of course, no single church, and certainly no individual, can meet all the demands of this yearning world. God has not given the whole task to any of us! Rather, different parts of the body of Christ have different functions in the universal church. Communities of Christians have different personalities and different priorities for service, just as individuals do. Some churches feel called primarily to ministries of

When Jesus first drew his followers together, he did not turn them in upon themselves. Immediately he sent them to treat massive hurts of spirit and body that festered in the world around them.... When he spoke of the community that would abide eternally in God's presence, it clearly would be the community of those who fed the hungry, welcomed the stranger, clothed the naked, cared for the sick, visited the prisoner.

—Stephen V. Doughty

Part 4 • Responding to Our Call: The Work of Christ

224

evangelism, while others concentrate on works of concrete service. God directs some communities consistently toward global mission and others toward the local community. One church may find its identity in housing the poor while another is home to the highest art of worship in that area. Individual members naturally find themselves drawn to churches that are compatible with their gifts and sense of call.

Gustav Nelson has studied models for the church of the twenty-first century that will be both faithful to our calling and adaptable to our situation. He writes,

> The mission of the church…is the sum total of the life and work of each member. When a person joins a church, a congregation increases its mission; when a person leaves a church, a congregation decreases its mission. The church's mission can be defined as what church members do during the week in their life and work—in their families and in their occupations…[and] in their volunteer work.…
>
> A lean church structure sets church members free to live out their lives in the world. Active members will not spend a lot of time in the church building. They are to take up their residency in the world.[1]

The church's mission is the total of the life and work of each member. We gather together and remember who we are. We gather in worship and prayer around Jesus, our Lord and Redeemer. Then we are sent out until we meet again. And wherever we go, whatever we do, we are God's radically available people who consent to be in living reliance on Jesus Christ so that the fruit of the Spirit may be grown through us for the nurture not only of the church but also of the world. We find that the spiritual gifts we have been given for aiding this portion of the body of Christ spill over into life in the world. Though the personality and particular emphasis in every church will differ, all are called to be communities who enter the rhythm of gathering and sending, nurturing the body while always opening it to expansion. Every one of us is engaged in mission.

For example, a woman who loves dogs may discover that her passion can be a deeply meaningful ministry. She trains long hours with her faithful charges to develop dogs who can be companions for persons with AIDS, guardians of those at risk for heart attack, or visitors in nursing homes. Teachers, counselors, and lawyers enact the

Paul tells us that the gifts we operate really work because God works them (see Phil. 2:13). Because of this spiritual energy or divine grace, faithful use of our gifts is nothing short of miraculous. It goes beyond mere human abilities. The results are manifold and inestimable simply because they become the very energy of God flowing with purpose and freedom.
—Charles V. Bryant

compassion of Christ whenever they sit patiently and listen to the complicated, sad stories of persons whose lives have been heavy with neglect. The time they take and the care they administer are the very mission of the church.

Less directly, but not less important, all who engage their work with integrity and skill share in the work of Christ. The accountant's numbers that can be reconciled with the truth show forth the praise of God in their precision. But more, they enact the work of God who upholds the world in justice. The straight cut of wood planed in the factory echoes our Creator's delight in form and shares the church's witness that God's people trade in excellence and vigor.

In the world, we may carry groceries to the car for an older person, write letters of thanks, clean house, study botany, pray all night on our beds, drive a bus, or deliver mail. We may do all these activities as part of the mission of the body of Christ in the power of the Spirit. We may use our imaginations to consider how what we do participates in the love, goodness, beauty, and truth of God. Our attitude toward what we do can transform even drudgery into opportunity for service and praise. Everything done in the name of Jesus (even if we do not name him aloud) is part of the life of the body. But we need one another in our regular gatherings to help us remember how we are engaged in mission everywhere.

Gifts and Community

Our life together is essential for nourishing our life in Christ and enabling us to see our lives in mission. In First Peter, we read instructions for the communal life of God's people and the exercise of gifts:

> Above all, maintain constant love for one another, for love covers a multitude of sins. Be hospitable to one another without complaining. Like good stewards of the manifold grace of God, serve one another with whatever gift each of you has received. Whoever speaks must do so as one speaking the very words of God; whoever serves must do so with the strength that God supplies, so that God may be glorified in all things through Jesus Christ. To him belong the glory and the power forever and ever. Amen (4:8-11).

This brief passage highlights several concepts related to gifts:

1. As ever, love is the greater context for a consideration of gifts. Love characterizes our communion. The love of Jesus Christ for his body, the church, undergirds all that we are and do. The measure of our lives is the way we allow the love of God made known to us to flow through our lives to one another. This passage identified hospitality as a particular expression of love needed for the common life of God's people. This spiritual gift is part of Christian character. We recognize that we belong to one another and abide in one another as fellow branches in the Vine, so what we have may be freely shared.

2. As recipients of grace and gifts, we are stewards whose task is to serve one another. The Greek word *oikonomoi*, translated as "stewards," offers a rich illustration of our life together. The root of the word means "house." Stewards were servants entrusted with administering the affairs of a large household on behalf of its owner. Then as now, households required a steady inflow of goods and services to keep running. Provisions had to be secured for the members of the household, and regular maintenance and repairs made on its property. In due season, the land of the estate yielded the fruit of their labors. Good stewards managed the economy of the household with skillful efficiency so that people's needs were met and the harvest was robust.

   In Ephesians, we see this comparison between Christ's people and a household affirmed: "So then you are no longer strangers and aliens, but you are citizens with the saints and also *members of the household of God*" (Eph. 2:19, emphasis added). Being stewards of the house calls us to the realization of the grace and gifts God has given and in turn to offer them to the other members of the household. We may not minimize the resources God has given us. Through the Holy Spirit, we have access to a limitless supply of grace in Christ. Of course, we frail stewards have limits that we must respect. But

We will grow in grace not when we isolate ourselves from others and pay only a passing compliment to the community of Christian faith. We will grow in grace when we place ourselves regularly and faithfully in that mixed multitude of saints and sinners, of strangers and spiritual friends that we find in the average Christian congregation.

—Thomas R. Hawkins

I imagine that many of us have a far greater capacity to be conduits of grace than we have yet known. The Spirit waits for the invitation of the stewards to pour out God's love through the expression of our spiritual gifts.

As good stewards, we make an honest assessment of our resources. We acknowledge our gifts and our limits even as we rely on the boundless energy of God's love. From such a posture, we may look after the interests of the whole house, the church, and consider where and how we are called to contribute. Serving one another out of the bounty of God's love, the entire household may thrive. In this way, a needy world will receive its share of our plentiful harvest.

3. The gifts are given to each of us for the sake of one another. This is a nuance on the last point. We cannot exercise our spiritual gifts in isolation. They are not given to be hidden. Spiritual gifts are not bestowed for satellite use. The church is a communion, an organically connected body. We are not a civic organization, a political party, or a charity. We are called to be together as Christ's body on earth.

When we have discovered, by grace, our need for a constant, living reliance upon Christ Jesus the vine, our whole lives will orient around that truth. Jesus becomes the very organizing principle for all of life. He is, as the hymn says, "the heart of our own heart." Thus gathering together as the body of Christ is not optional. Worship is vital. It is the very first activity God asks of us. Praying for brothers and sisters in Christ Jesus becomes as important as taking care of our own bodies. Meeting together for study and prayer is as necessary as eating and exercising are for the body. And serving the world in the name of Christ is not optional but foundational. You and I are accountable for doing these activities.

Early in the church's life, there was only one congregation in each location, only one group of believers in a town. Today we may choose what portion of the body of Christ to join but

When we describe "Church" we like to say that it is a gift-evoking, gift-bearing community....No community develops the potential of its corporate life unless the gifts of each of its members are evoked and exercised on behalf of the whole community.

—Elizabeth O'Connor

not whether we will be part of the body itself. The principle remains constant: Believers are connected organically to the body. If the church we attend is not a place where God speaks to us, if it does not provide the primary bond of fellowship in our lives, then we must overcome inertia and habit and go where we are called to be. In that portion of the body of Christ to which we are called, we may heartily, vigorously realize how necessary this community is and commit ourselves fully to its life.

We serve one another only by being connected. Of course, that happens in many places throughout the week. We exercise our gifts in the home, at work, at play, and in service. We connect with one another over the phone, around the water cooler, and on the streets. But the body must gather at least weekly in order to know its identity, to serve one another, to worship and plan and live together.

4. God calls us to exercise our gifts with a zestful, robust reliance on the Holy Spirit. The gifts are given to be used with abandon. Peter tells us that the one who speaks should do so with all urgency, passion, confidence, and joy, knowing that the words are blessed by God—not because we think we are so great, but because we trust that God will speak through us as we serve others in love through our words. If it is a word of encouragement, we may say it with confidence in God's grace. If it is a word of teaching, we may speak with the enthusiasm of trusting that God is making the divine self known. If it is a call to commitment and action, we may be bold with conviction that God has a plan for us. If it is a word of prayer, we may pray with faith that God hears and answers. If it is a tender whisper of mercy, then we say it with all the consolation of the shepherd who carries his lambs in his arms.

And Peter tells us that if our gifts are in the area of service, we should serve with all the strength God supplies. We may pick up pencils and bulletins in the sanctuary as if we

We do not have to worry about the results, since they belong to God. Our calling is to discover the spiritual ability and use it for its intended purpose. Nothing in the scheme of God's salvation is more demonstrative of obedient discipleship than our grateful reception of the gifts of the Spirit and our proper use of them.
—Charles V. Bryant

were cleaning the throne room of God. We may take a casserole to someone as if we were feeding the Lord Christ. We may make copies as if we were multiplying loaves and fish for the masses. Whether we clean a house, wash a wound, make a call, write a check, listen to a person's story, or give someone a ride to the doctor, we may do so as if Jesus himself were the recipient—because he is! And we rely on his strength to accomplish the task.

5. The ultimate purpose of the gifts is to serve one another so the church can bring the love of God to the world in such a way that glorifies God in all things through Jesus Christ. The gifts are given to be used robustly in connection to one another so that the church might be a witness to the world God loves. Spiritual gifts employed with love bring glory to God.

The point of receiving gifts is not just that we might be personally fulfilled, though we will be. It is not that our spiritual journeys will be more complete, though they will be. Discerning our call to follow Christ is not merely so we will get more out of our church experience. Gifts are given so that we might lose ourselves in service to God by serving one another and so that Jesus Christ is known and glorified throughout the world. As a by-product, all we ever yearned for will be ours. But that comes only when we lose ourselves in service to Christ.

What we are to do for God in the world and how we are to live our very lives as Christians begin and end with Jesus Christ. He calls us to himself, to a radical availability we cannot sustain on our own. But Jesus also stands in for us, giving us not only his forgiveness but also his obedience. He reproduces his life through us as we consent to his loving presence. Jesus sends the Holy Spirit to us, who comes bearing gifts for service. Employing these gifts, we grow in our oneness as Christ's body as a deeper and deeper community is created. We live, then, for "the praise of his glorious grace that he freely bestowed on us in the Beloved" (Eph. 1:6).

DAILY EXERCISES

Read the chapter for Week 5, "The Body of Christ Given for the World"; note in your journal your insights, learnings, and questions.

Listen afresh this week for the call of God to you and your church. Use this week as a time to gather up the insights, gifts, and guidance you have received from God and your small-group friends. You might want to review your notes from the previous four sessions. Articulate the call and spiritual gifts from God you celebrate for your vocation as a member of Christ's body. Remember that Christ's ministry happens in and through all that you are and do in the world, not only through organized church activities. Remember to pray for the other members of your small group as you listen together to the Lord's call to your church.

EXERCISE 1

Read 1 Corinthians 1:26-31. In light of Paul's encouragement to "consider your own call," reflect on the affirmation of gifts that you received in the last group meeting. Make a list of the gifts that the group named. Reflect on the gifts that confirm what you already knew about yourself, the gifts that surprised you, and the gifts that most challenge you. "Consider your own call" in light of these gifts.

EXERCISE 2

Read Mark 11:15-19. Meditate on this picture of Jesus in the Temple in his day. Now picture Jesus in your church today. What would Jesus see, hear, feel, affirm, and question? What would he recognize and not recognize as an expression of his life and mission? Write a dialogue with Jesus about his vision for your church and what it means to be "a house of prayer for all the nations." Listen in prayer for ways you can use your gifts to help that happen.

EXERCISE 3

Read Acts 13:1-3. The Holy Spirit who guided the church at Antioch to "set apart for me Barnabas and Saul for the work to which I have

called them" sometimes leads us to unite with others who are called to a common work. With whom (in your group or your church) are you sensing a shared mission? Toward whom is the Holy Spirit leading you for the purpose of responding to a need? Pray about your call with openness to the Holy Spirit's enabling guidance.

EXERCISE 4

Read Matthew 9:9-13. Meditate on Jesus' relationship with Matthew, the tax collector, and the way in which Matthew brought Jesus into his circle of friends. Turn your attention to your circle of friends and colleagues. How does Jesus want to participate in your relationships? In prayer, bring to mind the people you interact with daily. Sit quietly in anticipation of what Jesus might call you to do and say.

EXERCISE 5

Read Matthew 25:31-46. Meditate on the call to the church to see and respond to "the least of these" with whom Christ has united himself. What prevents you from seeing the people that Jesus names? What practices would enable you to see them? What would help you and your church to see those Jesus saw, be present to those for whom Jesus was present? Pray for eyes to see and the heart to respond.

Review your journal entries for the week in preparation for the group meeting.

Exploring Spiritual Guidance: The Spirit of Christ

Wendy M. Wright

Part 5, Week 1
How Do I Know God's Will for My Life?

*I*n Part 4 we explored what it means to hear and respond to God's call in our lives. We looked at the importance of relying on God and recognizing our gifts as we seek to live faithful lives. But a growing clarity about vocation or call still does not make it easy to follow Christ. Every day we face decisions, opportunities, and challenges in the living out of our discipleship.

While still in graduate school, I was asked to give a retreat to a group of women on the theme "Women of Wisdom." In the arrogance of my youth and inexperience, I tended to see myself as the leader, come to share my learning with women who, because of their backgrounds, knew little about the historic spiritual wisdom of the Christian tradition. But during the course of this retreat, a woman approached me who turned out to be my teacher more than I hers. "For years I've been asking people wherever I go, how do I know God's will for my life?" she said excitedly. "No one ever gave me a good answer until recently, and I want to share that answer with you." I found myself intrigued because her question was not only a crucial one in the history of Christian spirituality but also a common and troubling question for many people today. What does God want of me? How do I live the Christian life? What is God's word to me in the various decisions I must make? Have I chosen the path God intends for me? In short, how do I know the will of God?

> *While call requires response and obedience, we will not be given a road map....We are given building blocks to see what can be done with them, using for the task all of our intelligence, creativity, sensitivity, and love.*
>
> —Farnham, Gill, McLean, and Ward

235

My retreatant leaned closer to me and smiled. "If you think you can see God's will laid out neatly before you for the next five, ten, or twenty years as a clearly defined path, this is emphatically not the will of God. But if you sense that the next hesitant step you are about to make into an uncertain future is somehow directed by God, that is most probably God's will for you."

This woman's words have stuck with me over the years, both because she surprised me into listening for wisdom in unexpected places and because there is deep understanding in the words she passed on. Living into the Christian life in a serious and personal way is not an easy business. It is not a matter of simply following the rules or doing what we should. Sometimes it is a murky undertaking. It forces our childhood faith to change and grow. Life becomes more complex than we had planned. We may find ourselves at an impasse we never could have imagined. And while the living word of the gospel offers guidance, we discover that its application to our daily lives is not always clear. How do we "walk in God's ways"?

Discerning God's Will

A commonly held idea we need to abandon is that the "will of God" is some rigid, predetermined scheme we are expected to figure out, as if God had a great computerized master plan. In this view, our task (or rather our test) is to figure out how to "download" the plan and mechanically follow its instructions. A more helpful understanding of God's will might be described as "God's longing for our lives" or "the direction in which Love draws us." This divine longing is not merely private, although it is deeply personal. Love is drawing all of us. We respond to Love communally, as well as individually. Our response comes in the midst of family, work, our faith communities, and our larger communities. Perhaps it helps most to think about our response to God's will as our yes to the spirit of God that moves and lives among us, prompting, enlivening, and drawing us more deeply into the loving reality that God intends the world to be.

It would be naive to imagine that any of us could respond unfail-

> *When people seek God's will, their quest leads them to yearn for the will of God, even as God, in love, yearns for them.*
>
> Danny E. Morris and
> Charles M. Olsen

ingly to the Spirit's promptings. Indeed, from the time of the early church, Christians have been aware that our ability to respond faithfully to God is compromised in countless ways. Sometimes we are so self-preoccupied, fearful, or swayed by other voices that we cannot even sense God's call to us. Our minds and hearts are full of confusing and conflicting messages, from both within and around us.

Perhaps if we look back to our adolescence, we can see this complex reality with stark clarity. In our teen years, the questions "Who am I?" and "What am I to do?" tended to be paramount. The culture said one thing and the church another; our parents and our peer groups pulled us in different directions; our childhood selves and our emerging adult selves likely added confusion. After making it through the struggles of adolescent identity, we probably discovered that our sense of identity continues to evolve. Indeed, God invites us throughout our lives to unlearn and relearn our most fundamental identity.

The Christian spiritual tradition refers to the process of sorting out the "voice" of God's spirit from other conflicting voices as the art of "discernment." Both tradition and experience confirm that discernment is truly a spiritual challenge.

For this reason, discernment is not typically a solitary practice in the church. Responding authentically to God's spirit happens best within the context of community, with the guidance of scripture, tradition, and other believers—all of which are means of grace. Discernment requires particular attention. We need to guide one another in discernment. Such guidance can take a number of forms that we will explore the next few weeks. For example, discernment can be practiced between two people in a form traditionally called spiritual direction. It is not direction in the usual meaning of that word. Rather, two people listen to understand and respond to the leading (the direction) of the Holy Spirit. Sometimes discernment has been practiced in small intentional communities such as faith-sharing or covenant groups. It has been the specific focus of certain practices such as the Quaker Clearness Committee, a small-group practice in which an individual or couple may gain clarity about a major concern or decision. Occasionally, the principles of discernment have been analyzed

Discernment often depends on gifts that we do not have. We need one another's insights, resources, and prayer.

—Jeannette A. Bakke

and a clear process outlined. Ignatius of Loyola did this in the sixteenth century with his *Spiritual Exercises*, an intense and structured program of guided prayer designed to realign the heart, mind, and will of the participant with the spirit of Christ.

Throughout its history, the church has been concerned about following the guidance of the Spirit and has affirmed that Christians can aid one another in this guidance. We all need the leading of the Spirit, so it may help us to consider the many ways we can open ourselves to this guidance within the community of Christ's disciples. Before enumerating these, however, it is important to distinguish spiritual guidance from other forms of guidance common to our experience.

Understanding Spiritual Guidance

First of all, spiritual guidance is not primarily about problem solving or about finding definitive answers to questions. It is more about living gratefully and gracefully into the rich, beautiful, painful texture of life and finding God there; more about sensing God's life-giving invitations in the midst of stagnation; more about living into the unfolding mystery of life of which we are a part. Thus spiritual guidance is not primarily counseling or therapy, although they are related fields. Spiritual guidance is not theological instruction or the giving of advice. Nor is it simply the friendly, commiserating listening that one neighbor might give to another. When we seek the guidance of the Spirit, we focus on the dynamic, living presence of God's spirit working in the life of an individual or community. Spiritual guidance can never simply apply generic principles to particular situations. It requires informed attention to the often surprising movement of God's spirit in concrete circumstances.

Why might you choose to seek out spiritual guidance, either as an individual or as a member of a group? Perhaps because you are haunted by the same unrelenting question that haunted my retreatant years ago: How do I know God's will for my life? Perhaps because even though your life is full of many things, it is somehow still empty, and God is the only "more" that can fill the gaping hole. Maybe the God you always thought you could count on has "disappeared" in the midst of death, divorce, or illness. Maybe you suddenly find yourself on fire with a new vision of the world, compelled to offer yourself generously in service. Or perhaps going to church once a week, and even to Bible study, is not meeting the urgent hunger you feel for prayer, the hunger to become more intimate with God.

Spiritual guidance is concerned with a person's entire life lived in response to God's leading, not only with the inner devotional world. Still it is not meant to take the place of other necessary forms of guidance offered within the faith community. A Twelve Step or similar program is essential for someone struggling with addiction. Marital difficulties, depression, career planning, or questions about what the church teaches are appropriately guided by trained counselors, therapists, and Christian educators. So spiritual guidance may help a person suffering from addiction, relational problems, work issues, or theological questions; but such guidance should not be expected to solve these issues. Rather, spiritual guidance assists a person in discovering the presence and guidance of God's spirit in the midst of all life's experiences.

Learning to Be Attentive

To be authentic and helpful in leading others toward knowledge of God's will, spiritual guidance needs to be carried out in a manner that differs somewhat from other helping professions. Attentiveness to God's spirit requires deeply receptive, prayerful listening. Practicing the art of attending to the Spirit involves us in contemplative listening. Such listening is quite distinct from the various ways in which we generally listen to one another. Think about it. In our common experience, we usually listen in self-referential ways. At a social gathering, we may appear to be listening to a guest but are really focused on what we will say in response to make an impression or keep the conversation going. We may listen primarily to form judgments, since we are often tempted to categorize people and events according to

> *We define Christian spiritual direction, then, as help given by one Christian to another which enables that person to pay attention to God's personal communication to him or her, to respond to this personally communicating God, to grow in intimacy with this God, and to live out the consequences of the relationship.*
>
> —William A. Barry and William J. Connolly

Focused stillness creates an empty space in which to test the rough edges of experience and to discover wider perspectives....
Without cultivating times of silence and solitude, we cannot create an environment of obedient listening in which to hearken to God's voice.

—Thomas R. Hawkins

our norms of acceptability. We may listen for information, as we do in a classroom. Sometimes we listen carefully to another's argument in order to respond effectively to the argument. We may listen in order to sympathize and relieve someone's discomfort or to help solve the person's difficulties.

The kind of listening involved in spiritual guidance differs from these common ways of listening to one another. It is holy listening, rooted in silence. It seeks emptiness in order to be filled with the Spirit. It is permeated by humility. Such listening assumes that the Spirit is active among us and works through us. So it makes space for that movement. It is primarily receptive, patient, watchful, and waiting. Yet it does not fear action when action is called for. Such listening is generously flexible, hospitable, and warm. It embraces the widest possible spectrum of life's beauty and pain. It acknowledges the creation of all people in the image and likeness of God. It approaches life as a mystery into which we joyously and generously live. While in one sense a gift, such listening is generally cultivated over the years as we prayerfully attend to the Spirit in our own lives and as others listen to us in the same grace-filled way.

The focus in spiritual guidance is on a person's relationship with God and the responses that relationship calls forth. Since we are whole people and cannot separate our inner and outer lives, conversations in spiritual guidance may range over many topics—our families of origin, our ethnic or cultural roots, troubles with a spouse or children, the meaning of our work, the moral stands we take, the way we allocate our resources, the manner in which we schedule our time, the content and methods of our prayer, the spiritual disciplines we undertake, or the devotional exercises in which we engage. Any facet of life may come into consideration. But in spiritual guidance it will be considered in relation to the discerned movement of the Spirit. "How is God connected to this matter?" Here lies the root issue of spiritual guidance. When we pay attention in an open and discerning way, the God-connection in every aspect of our lives can become clear.

The following excerpt helps us understand what happens in a spiritual guidance relationship:

Spiritual direction is basically the guidance one Christian offers another to help that person "grow up in every way…into Christ (Eph. 4:15)." A spiritual guide is someone who can help us see and name our own experience of God.…

1. *A spiritual guide listens to us.* When we need someone to hear our life story in terms of faith, a spiritual guide offers hospitable space for us to speak and be heard. Often we do not fully know our thoughts or experiences, our questions or unresolved issues. We do not know until we have had a chance to put them into words before an attentive and receptive ear. A spiritual director can "listen us into clarity," helping us articulate our thoughts, feelings, questions, and experiences in relation to God.

2. *A spiritual guide helps us to notice things.* God's presence and the ways of the Spirit are not generally self-evident to us. They are subtle and unobtrusive, often hidden in the midst of ordinary events and interactions. It takes practice to see the grace of God in everyday life. A spiritual mentor can help us pay attention to signs of grace, to listen for "God's still small voice" in our daily encounters and experiences. A guide can also direct our attention to the dynamics of our heart, so that we can become more aware of how God speaks to us through it.

3. *A spiritual guide helps us to respond to God with greater freedom.* When we begin to notice God's presence, guidance, provision, and challenge in our daily lives, we are faced with choices. How shall we respond? The choice is not always easy. God's presence and provision are comforting, naturally eliciting gratitude and praise. But God also faces us with the darker realities in our lives, calling us to genuine change. It is hard to let go of old habits and ways of being. Out of this encounter, God calls us to a new sense of purpose and mission in life. A spiritual director can encourage us toward a fuller freedom to respond to God in loving obedience.

4. *A spiritual guide points us to practical disciplines of spiritual growth.* Without the help of particular practices it is difficult to become more aware of, and responsive to, God's activity in our lives. Most of us could use guidance on ways of prayer that attune us to God's presence. We may need suggestions for spiritual reading, tips on keeping a journal, or reminders about the nature of authentic humility in self-examination. Perhaps we need someone who has practiced fasting to help us stay on track with our efforts. A spiritual companion can suggest various practices to us as they seem

appropriate and help us to discern when and whether to change them. A guide can also help keep us accountable for the disciplines we commit ourselves to.

5. *A spiritual guide will love us and pray for us.* This is probably the most important function of a companion in Christian faith. The love of a spiritual director for the one directed is always mediated by the love of Christ. It is agape love. The ongoing expression of that love is faithful prayer, both within and beyond meeting times. If this is in effect, many inadequacies in a guide can be covered by grace. If it is not present, even virtuoso technique can scarcely make up for it![1]

DAILY EXERCISES

Margaret Guenther writes the following:

> So what does the spiritual director teach? In the simplest and also most profound terms, the spiritual director is simultaneously a learner and a teacher of discernment. What is happening? Where is God in this person's life? What is the story? Where does this person's story fit in our common Christian story?[2]

This week's daily exercises invite us to explore the gift of holy listening to God's presence in one another's lives. Use your time to reflect with the exercises and to commune with God in prayer.

EXERCISE 1

Read 1 Samuel 3:1-18 with an eye toward Eli's role as a spiritual guide with Samuel. How did Eli respond to Samuel, and what did Eli do that helped Samuel recognize God's call in his experience? How would you have responded to Samuel's persistence? Identify the "Elis" in your life who have listened to you with patience and helped you name your experience of God.

Review the five points of what happens in a spiritual guidance relationship printed on pages 241–42. Reflect on where you see any of these dynamics at work in the story of Samuel or in your own relationships.

EXERCISE 2

Read Acts 8:26-40. The story of Philip with the Ethiopian eunuch reveals dimensions of evangelism and faith sharing but also of a spiritual guidance relationship. List the features of spiritual guidance that you see illustrated here. Have you had relationships that shared such features? What made those experiences good or difficult?

EXERCISE 3

Read Acts 8:26-40 again. Write a first-person account of the Ethiopian eunuch sharing with Philip some aspect of his search for wholeness. Pay close attention to clues the story gives about the man's situation:

where he is going, where he is coming from, and whether he finds what he was looking for (see Deut. 23:1). Use your imagination to identify with the eunuch. Why might he feel separated from his own creative vitality? What might draw him to the passage from Isaiah? Take a moment to reflect on where you can actually identify with the eunuch's situation in your current life.

EXERCISE 4

Read Acts 8:26-40 a third time. Write a first-person account of Philip's journey with the Ethiopian eunuch. Use your imagination to identify with Philip. Describe how your relationship with the eunuch unfolded. Explore how you received the Spirit's guidance even as you were offering guidance—from start to finish in this relationship.

In closing, bring to mind someone you will be seeing soon. Lift this person to God in prayer and, when you do meet, follow the lead of Christ's spirit. Later, record your experience and insights.

EXERCISE 5

A particularly helpful spiritual exercise in discerning God's movement in your life is called "the examen," a structured and regular review of daily life that emphasizes either assessment of your faithfulness (examination of conscience) or awareness of God's presence (examination of consciousness). In this final part of *Companions in Christ*, the last of each week's daily exercises is an invitation to various forms of daily examen. Typically, the examen is practiced on a daily basis, but we will be using it as a weekly exercise.

The following examen is adapted from Ben Campbell Johnson's process for "integrating the life of prayer into the ordinary events and decisions of everyday life." Keep your journal handy to make notes.

Gather the week. Identify the ten or twelve major events of your week, including prayer, particular conversations, meetings, meals, work, and planned or unplanned occurrences. List them.

Review the week. Reflect upon each occurrence listed. Recall what was happening within you, what you were feeling, and how you were reacting or responding. This is the actual substance of your daily life.

Give thanks for the week. Thank God for each part of your week, for your life, for the lives of others who were part of your week, and for God's presence in your week. Celebrate the particular gifts you received in the expected and unexpected occurrences that enriched your week.

Confess your sin. Acknowledge your faults in thought, word, and deed toward God, neighbor, creation, and yourself. Name the times when you feel you may have ignored subtle promptings or warnings of the Spirit.

Seek the meaning of the events. Reflect on the underlying significance of each event. Ask yourself such questions as, What is the theme of the week's events, gifts, and challenges? Where did Jesus experience something similar and how did he respond? What is God saying to me or inviting me to learn? What am I being called to do? Write down what comes to mind.[3]

Remember to review your journal entries for the week in preparation for the group meeting.

Part 5, Week 2

Spiritual Companions

*I*deally, the entire church should be a community of spiritual discernment. In a sense, that is what the church is meant to be—a community focused on discerning and doing the will of God. Unfortunately too few people experience the church this way. Church activities tend to focus on evangelism, church growth, fund-raising, teaching and learning groups, programs for children and youth, or crisis intervention for families and individuals in need. These are all significant and necessary functions. Yet they leave many people empty, departing from classrooms, fellowship halls, or sanctuaries with their spiritual hunger unmet. As Christians, we may draw on a rich heritage of well-tested models and promising experiments in spiritual guidance to feed that hunger.

The Gospel of Luke (24:13-35) tells a story that reveals something important to us about spiritual guidance. After the crucifixion, two disappointed and distraught disciples were walking down the road that led to Emmaus. They met a stranger with whom they shared news about the terrible events of the last few days. Inviting him to stay with them as the day drew to a close, the disciples recognized the stranger as Jesus when he broke bread with them. After his departure, the disciples could scarcely contain their excitement! "Didn't our hearts burn within us when he spoke to us on the road?" they asked.

> *Conversion [is] a lifelong process of letting God remove the scales from our eyes so that we can more and more embrace the reality of God's overwhelming love for us. In this lifelong process of withdrawal and return we need one another to help us to overcome our resistance to the light.*
> —William A. Barry

Six centuries after this Gospel story was written down, Gregory the Great commented on this passage. God, he said, is experienced among us in just the same way as on the road to Emmaus. God is known by the burning of our hearts, known in our shared love of God, known as existing between us. Indeed, God is known precisely when we journey with one another, talking of the questions dearest to our hearts and finding there both companionship and God's living presence.

The Christian spiritual life, although intimate and personal, can never be isolated or privatized if it is to remain authentic. We share this life together. From the earliest centuries, Christians have affirmed that spiritual discernment is best done with at least one, if not several other believers. From the past we get a glimpse into the variety of ways spiritual companionship has been practiced.

One-on-One Spiritual Guidance

Perhaps the most classic form of one-on-one spiritual companionship is found in the deserts of Egypt, Palestine, and Syria during the fourth through sixth centuries. The church had passed through a period of intense persecution when martyrdom had been the height of Christian witness. Now a different kind of martyrdom became a witness to new life in Christ. Many embraced the "white martyrdom" of the ascetic life (rather than the "red martyrdom" of physical death). Through practices of prayer, self-discipline, and mortification, the ascetic martyr "died" to his or her "false self"—the proud, greedy, grandiose self admired by the general culture—and was reborn to the "true self" in Christ—the charitable, humble, other-centered self of a pure heart. Such radical transformation was understood to be a real struggle with the "demons" that disfigure the human heart.

Those who sought this new life went to the deserts looking for spiritual mentors who had been through the forge of transformation and had emerged reborn. Charismatic figures, such as Anthony of Egypt, were legendary. They had authority because of their gift of discernment. They were gifted to see into the hearts of those who came to them and to perceive what particular demons had gripped them. Out of their own hard-won experience they could offer guidance in the process of opening one's heart to the transfiguring grace of God. In the silence and solitude of the desert, a deep capacity for listening could be cultivated, a listening for the word of God, a listening for the brush of the Spirit.[1]

The one-on-one mentoring relationship between a seeker and a spiritual abba (father) or amma (mother) was one of intense trust, obedience, and spiritual intimacy. The seeker unguardedly opened his or her heart before the elder, revealing all its thoughts and movements; and the elder could then discern what was needed. From that tradition we have collections of "Sayings" that give us a glimpse into the wisdom these masters passed on to their disciples. Here are two examples of writing from these collections:

> A brother asked one of the elders: What good thing shall I do, and have life thereby? The old man replied: God alone knows what is good. However, I have heard it said that someone inquired of Father Abbot Nisteros the great, the friend of Abbot Anthony, asking: What good work shall I do? And that he replied: Not all works are alike. For Scripture says that Abraham was hospitable and God was with him. Elias loved solitary prayer, and God was with him. And David was humble, and God was with him. Therefore, whatever you see your soul to desire according to God, do that thing, and you shall keep your heart safe.[2]

> Amma Syncletica said: It is good not to get angry. But if it should happen, do not allow your day to go by affected by it. For it is said: Do not let the sun go down. Otherwise, the rest of your life may be affected by it. Why hate a person who hurts you, for it is not that person who is injust, but the devil. Hate the sickness, but not the sick person.[3]

This early desert model of spiritual guidance has persisted over the centuries with some variations. Holy Christian men and women, authenticated by their gifts, the fruits of their works, and the holiness of their lives, have always gathered disciples around themselves. In the church of the Middle Ages many holy women, some of them visionaries or prophets, functioned as spiritual guides in their communities. In fourteenth-century England, a woman named Julian lived in a hermitlike cell in the city of Norwich and listened to the spiritual concerns of people in all walks of life who came to the window of her cell.

There is the clear call to perfection, to holiness, to fullness of life in Christ. The call to be perfect (teleios) (Phil. 3.15) is variously translated as a call to spiritual maturity (RSV and NEB) and to spiritual adulthood (J. B. Phillips). It is this process of spiritual maturing which is the purpose of spiritual direction.

—Kenneth Leech

Another holy woman of the same century named Catherine, from the Italian city of Siena, was called "mother" by her band of spiritual disciples. Her urgent, scolding letters to public figures, including the pope, were heeded because of her reputation as a trustworthy guide in discerning God's spirit.

This one-on-one model of guidance has historically taken other forms, some linked to other institutional roles within the church. In the Middle Ages, the practice of one-on-one spiritual direction became more a function of the clergy who often advised people in approved methods of prayer and formal principles of the spiritual life.

Today, one-on-one spiritual guidance has returned more to the early model. We can see clear examples of this in Jesus' gracious relationship to his band of disciples and in the caring companionship of the early church. Discernment is a gift given to the church for the good of the church, exercised by certain people regardless of whether they are men, women, laity, clergy, or officeholders in the church. The focus is on the individual's growing relationship with God. The spiritual director or guide facilitates the growth and development of that relationship. The individual's experience of God is the starting point and is always to be revered. Contemporary spiritual guides do not see themselves primarily as "answer people" or "fix-it people." They are not gurus or master teachers who tell others what to do. They do not foster dependence or assume inordinate importance in the lives of those they seek to guide. Rather, they are in the service of God and the person who comes to them.[4] A spiritual guide offers a safe, confidential space to look at one's life in the light of God's presence and purposes. Because the spiritual guidance relationship focuses entirely on the person and his or her relationship with God, the spiritual guide enables the seeker to name what is happening in life's struggles, surprises, and challenges. By going beneath the surface of life's events, the person seeking guidance can make connections with scripture and insights from spiritual tradition, listening and responding to God's call.

Howard Rice has written a simple description of the nature of one-on-one spiritual guidance:

In a one-on-one relationship, the spiritual guide's responsibilities are these:

1. to listen carefully to what people say about themselves and their spiritual lives,
2. to encourage their desire (expressed or hinted at) to recognize and respond to God's presence in their lives,
3. to suggest the practice of certain disciplines that will enable spiritual growth and open them to the Holy Spirit's presence,
4. to challenge them to examine their lives honestly in the light of God's forgiving love, and
5. to pray with and for them.[5]

Spiritual Friendship

A variation of one-on-one spiritual guidance is spiritual friendship. Spiritual direction and spiritual friendship are not equivalent. In a relationship between a spiritual guide and the person seeking guidance, there is a certain asymmetry. The focus is upon the relationship between God and the person seeking guidance, upon that person's life and prayer rather than the life of the guide. On occasion the spiritual guide's personal experience might explicitly enter in but only if it could be of help in some way to the individual seeker.

Spiritual friendship, on the other hand, is an utterly mutual and equal relationship. The sharing between two such friends goes both ways, eliciting mutual self-disclosure. Friends see themselves as peers. Neither sees the other as more experienced or authoritative. A healthy interdependency grows between them.

The church's history provides wonderful examples of spiritual friendships. The Celtic church honored the tradition of the "anmchara" or soul-friend, a wise companion who took it upon himself or herself to accompany another on the soul's journey. And history gives us insight into beautiful lives of faith sustained by friendship. Francis de Sales wrote of friendship as absolutely necessary for people intent on living more devoutly. He believed that a devout life "in the world" needed all the care and support it could get! Mutual commitment to a Christian life and care for each other's growth in that

> *[Our lives] will be enriched by the gift of a listening ear—one who will pay attention to movements of grace and the tremors of change. Listening for the whispers of God is one of the most prized gifts we can offer each other.*
>
> —Larry J. Peacock

life is the main content of spiritual friendship. At its root lies a shared desire for God.[6]

Today spiritual friendship takes many forms. We may discover a group of friends who support us in faith or a particular friend who journeys with us for a short period or over many years. Such friendships vary greatly, as individuals differ. They may arise spontaneously, but if they adopt an intentional structure, they can allow for that careful listening, encouragement, and admonition in which mutual self-disclosure occurs regularly and fruitfully.[7]

Communities of Spiritual Guidance

Christians have discerned the movement of the Spirit in intimate settings of one-on-one guidance throughout their history. But they have also created intentional communities to facilitate growth in the Spirit. The parish or congregation is meant to be such a community. We have noted that in our recent history, discernment has typically been lost in congregational life. Today, however, there is increasingly conscious reflection on the local church and the role of the pastor as spiritual guide, not only to individuals, but also to the congregation as a whole.[8] Considerable interest and attention have been given to the art of discernment as practiced by governing church boards.[9]

More typically, Christians have formed small intentional groupings to provide spiritual encouragement. Monasticism is one long-lived experiment in creating a permanent vessel of spiritual formation. The desert ideal of allowing God to transform the "false self" into the "true self" became institutionalized in the monastic life. The rule of life that governed the monastic community became a living word spoken to guide members of the monastery into the Spirit-transformed life. The rule not only provided an administrative structure for community life; it embodied the spiritual values the monastery sought to foster. For example, the Rule of Saint Benedict (the Western church's most famous monastic rule) allowed such values as silence, prayer, study, stability, and hospitality to be incorporated into the daily life of the monks.[10]

Spiritual guidance went on well beyond the walls of the monastery. There have been many other efforts to guide one another communally. The High Middle Ages saw the rise of the Christian laity. Sometimes women and men who raised families and worked "in the world" joined "third orders," associate groups sponsored by formal religious orders such as the Franciscans or Dominicans. These "third order" associates followed a daily rule modified to suit their obligations. They met regularly with their spiritual mentors for guidance.

Sometimes groups of laypersons or mixed groups of clergy and laity were established for spiritual nurture. One such movement, the Beguines, flourished in the thirteenth century. This movement was mainly for women who sometimes lived in their family homes and sometimes lived together. They shared prayer and good works and grew together into the Christian life. During later centuries in continental Europe, a spiritual movement known as the Modern Devotion arose. Out of it grew groups such as the Brothers and Sisters of the Common Life. These laypeople lived together in small groups, often sharing a similar occupation like textile work. They were part of an ordinary congregation but were more serious than most Christians about the spiritual life. They wrote and circulated devotional manuals, met to read scripture together, and held shared scripture reflections to which they invited guests. And they regularly examined their actions together in light of the gospel.

These same basic components of shared guidance could be found in the churches that grew out of the Protestant Reformation. Calvin encouraged spiritual growth in his congregations through individual care, correspondence, and informal mutual support. His spiritual heirs, the Puritans, were enthusiastic about public sharing of spiritual experience and were encouraged to choose peers to whom they could give account of the workings of God in the soul. The Puritans were great correspondents and journalers, often using their diaries as a way of practicing self-examination. Giving advice and sharing accounts of one's spiritual journey by letter were popular Puritan practices.

We find the most intentional and systematic Protestant effort to encourage spiritual guidance in the early Methodist movement. John

Wesley believed that Christians grow in holiness most effectively in mutually supportive group settings. He devised a system of guidance for every conceivable need within the Christian community. The United Societies were open to anyone and met weekly for prayer, mutual exhortation, and stewardship accountability. The class meetings, smaller units that met in homes under lay leadership, undertook to commit members to a more intentional spiritual discipline. Bands, separate-sex meetings of even smaller numbers, fostered mutual spiritual maturity in a peer setting. Select societies were for those who felt themselves called to the serious pursuit of holiness.[11]

Most churches of the Radical Reformation emphasized group spiritual guidance. The Moravians gathered in small groups for mutual admonition. And the Quakers (Society of Friends) cultivated a style of worship—the silent meeting—that was essentially the practice of corporate discernment. Listening in attentive silence for the Inner Light that could illumine the way of the community was its goal. The Quakers also developed other means of shared spiritual guidance. For example, the Clearness Committee gathered a company of selected listeners or questioners to help individuals clarify God's will in specific moments of decision making.

Today most spiritual guidance takes place with persons meeting face-to-face. However, letters, telephone calls, and even E-mail communication can provide opportunities for exchange among Christians hungry to grow in God. All these models share the common goals of growing in spiritual maturity, discerning God's living spirit, and developing an authentic relationship with God.

The Influence of Culture

One interesting question is the extent to which these various models of spiritual guidance are rooted exclusively in European thought forms and cultural practices. Clearly, Western Christianity has provided much of the spiritual wisdom known to us and still relevant to our churches today. That wisdom is wide and broad but needs further examination in our cross-cultural context. The task of examin-

A Christian community is essential for discernment. The community may be represented by one person who is part of the larger Christian community and brings its faith and values to a particular situation. Or several people may be a community that will focus on the needs of one person by his or her invitation. No one should attempt spiritual discernment by himself or herself without putting decisions to the test of other spiritual friends.

—Danny E. Morris and Charles M. Olsen

ing the influence of culture on spiritual guidance models is relatively new but important. The related question of gender differences has already received some attention. Many now affirm that women bring to spiritual guidance a unique perspective that their male counterparts do not generally share and that issues of power, violence, and anger often alter the way women relate to God.[12]

But the cultural question is still new. Differences in culture influence our image of God and shape our religious experience, which can profoundly affect the practice of spiritual formation. For example, Americans of European ancestry often stress the individual's relationship to the world and God. Persons from cultures outside North America may emphasize the community and the extended family and thus may experience the world and God in a different way. Faith sharing and spiritual formation in Central and Latin America reflect the context of political and economic oppression in that part of the world. Thus God's Word is not solely for personal consolation and salvation but is seen as socially and spiritually liberating for the poor and redeeming for entire classes of people.

Culturally determined patterns of communication also influence spiritual formation. For example, the religious practices of many African Americans are characterized by emotional expressiveness and a strong sense of group solidarity. The dominant one-on-one Western model of spiritual guidance that stresses silence, solitude, and introspection may not be helpful for Christians whose deepest religious experiences have been forged in other settings. Persons from Asian cultures, in which respect for and obedience to authority is deeply embedded, may find the egalitarian model of spiritual friendship unworkable, especially in relation to authority figures such as pastors or teachers. In the context of spiritual guidance, all of these questions need to be considered, not in ways that stereotype people, but in ways that respect the unique experience of each person.[13]

DAILY EXERCISES

Douglas Steere writes of a holy moment in 1950 in the midst of a Quaker meeting at Haverford College. Martin Buber, the renowned Jewish scholar and rabbi, was a guest at the college. He rose from the silence of a Quaker meeting to speak. "[Buber] told us that it was a great thing to transcend barriers and to meet another human being, but that *meeting* another across a barrier was not the greatest thing one man could do for another. There was still something greater. The greatest thing…was to *confirm* the deepest thing he has within him. After this, he sat down as abruptly as he had arisen. There was little more to say." [14]

This week's daily exercises invite us to explore how we see faithful friends and guides in scripture confirming for one another the deepest thing they have within them. How do we experience the same?

EXERCISE 1

Read 1 Samuel 18:1-4; 23:15-18. The stories of David and Jonathan illustrate the gift and joy of genuine friendship. Identify the qualities of spiritual friendship that you see here. Then describe any friendship you have known in your life that embodies such qualities. Who among your friends now helps you find strength in God? How does that happen? Give thanks to God for this person or these persons.

EXERCISE 2

Read 2 Samuel 11:26–12:13. Nathan demonstrates a prophetic dimension of spiritual guidance when he confronts David with the truth about himself. Do you currently struggle with whether to tell a friend or acquaintance a hard truth or to mind your own business? Look for guidance in Nathan's relationship with David and his manner of speaking the truth in love. Take your situation to God in prayer. Listen for whether the Lord is sending you in love to speak, to listen, to learn, or to confess and examine a hidden sin in your life.

EXERCISE 3

Read John 4:1-26. The story of Jesus and the Samaritan woman illustrates Jesus' capacity to see through layers of cultural identity to who persons are in God's "truth." Explore the way Jesus calls the woman to insight, constantly drawing her toward a deeper awareness of "the gift of God" (v. 10) in her midst. Look for when and how Jesus tries to move her beyond conventional or surface ways of seeing him, herself, and God. Notice where Jesus invites her to go from the theological to the personal realm, and how she responds to him.

What insights did this reading bring to you about the nature of spiritual guidance or friendship? Take a moment to be aware of the gift of God in you and to ask for the drink of living water that you need.

EXERCISE 4

Read John 4:1-42. The story of Jesus and the Samaritan woman illustrates communal as well as personal effects of spiritual guidance. The fact that the woman came to the well "about noon" gives us a clue to the possibility of her isolation from the community. Most village women would come to the well in the early morning or late afternoon, not in the heat of the day. This fact, coupled with the woman's marital history and current situation, might suggest a socially unaccepted existence among her own people—somewhat like the way in which Jews viewed Samaritans as unacceptable.

In light of her isolation and lack of acceptance by her community, explore the ripple effects of Jesus' actions as a spiritual guide toward this Samaritan woman. How does Jesus' spiritual guidance impact her relationship to the community? What is the potential impact on the relationship between this Samaritan community and the Jewish community? Record your insights.

EXERCISE 5

Use the model for examen of daily life provided last week (pages 244–45). Or try the one outlined here that reviews your life through the lens of the Lord's Prayer. Enter the process in prayer; ask God to

assist you in remembering your life in truth and grace; record thoughts in your journal.

"Our Father in heaven, hallowed be your name"—*How have you attended to God's holy presence in your life this week? Where and in what ways were you especially aware or unaware of God?*

"Your kingdom come, your will be done, on earth as in heaven"—*In what ways did you seek God's will? In what ways did you succeed or fail in allowing God's yearning for the common good to rule your attitudes and actions?*

"Give us today our daily bread"—*What is the bread, physical and spiritual, that sustained you this week and for which you are grateful to God? What did you do with bread beyond your needs? With whom did you break bread or share your bread?*

"Forgive us our sins as we forgive those who sin against us"—*Did you forgive those who offended or harmed you? What steps remain to restore the peace? Whom did you harm, and what actions did you take to make amends? What steps remain?*

"Save us from the time of trial and deliver us from evil"—*Where was your faith (patience, love, hope) tested this week? In what ways did you fail the test? In what ways were you delivered? What did you learn about your limits and where to find the strength you need?*

"For the kingdom, the power, and the glory are yours, now and forever"—*Give thanks to God for divine blessing and bounty. Name the blessings of this past week and relinquish them to God. Spend time in prayer praising God and rededicating your life to walking with Christ.*

Review your journal entries for the week in preparation for the group meeting.

Part 5, Week 3
Small Groups for Spiritual Guidance

*I*n fourteenth-century Italy, a remarkable woman named Catherine who lived in the town of Siena authored a book entitled *The Dialogue*. It recorded an account of a conversation between God and "a soul." In it Catherine writes that God speaks of the church as a great vineyard in which each individual has his or her own vine garden but in which there are no fences or dividing lines between the gardens. Whatever happens in one's own vineyard, for good or for ill, intimately affects every other vineyard.

Clearly, Catherine of Siena was developing the biblical image of the vine and the branches of which Jesus speaks in John 15. But she did not understand the image in an individualistic way. Not only are we nurtured by a common source—Christ, the Vine—but we are interconnected and thus help nurture one another as well. The fruitfulness of the entire vineyard—the church—is shared by all of us, not only as recipients but as assistant gardeners. Our weeding, pruning, fertilizing, and planting are not only for ourselves; they are for all of us together. Scripture underscores this idea with other metaphors like the church as one body with many members but one Spirit (1 Cor. 12; Eph. 4). Our growth in God is a communal venture!

In a profound sense, whatever spiritual cultivation we do as individuals ultimately affects our families, our communities, and the entire world. This communal dimension is a natural and inevitable

> *At their best, [small prayer, faith, and discernment groups] provide an arena for corporate openness to the Spirit's way, personal support, the perspective of others' views, and opportunities for sharing pain, anxiety, thanksgiving, prayer for others, and surrender to God in faith.*
>
> —Tilden H. Edwards

consequence of the spiritual life. But some methods of spiritual cultivation in the Christian community explicitly recognize that spiritual nurture is a shared undertaking. Several forms of spiritual guidance are available for small groups to explore. Although the following will not exhaust the possibilities, we may distinguish among (1) mutual accountability groups, (2) scripture-focused groups, (3) prayer-focused groups, (4) action-reflection groups, and (5) group spiritual guidance.

While these small-group models are distinct, they share a common goal of helping us open ourselves more generously to the prompting of the Spirit. They may involve elements of study or information gathering, but the primary purpose of such groups is not to help us acquire more information; rather, it is to help change, mold, and shape us more closely to the divine image in which we are originally made. In our present information age that highly values quick access to facts and figures, it is sometimes hard to remember that the spiritual life does not follow this path. We do not acquire a new technique of prayer and expect it to earn the favor or presence of God for us. Instead, we become people of prayer. We do not purchase a how-to book and follow the simple instructions labeled "Five Secrets of the Successful Spiritual Person" or "Ten Guaranteed Traits for Gaining Spiritual Mastery." Spiritual formation more closely resembles a love relationship to which we commit, surrender, and open ourselves. Through this relationship we are challenged, taught, gifted, and loved unconditionally. And by it, we are changed.

The wonderful mystery of the church as a fruitful vineyard is that there are many others like us yearning and struggling to open themselves to the embrace of love. This is not something we do alone.

Mutual Accountability Groups

One way gathered Christians have opened themselves to God is through mutual accountability or covenant groups. The group members agree to practice specific disciplines of the Christian life individually, then meet to support and hold one another accountable.

One popular model is that of covenant discipleship groups. Wesleyan scholar David Lowes Watson has recovered this model from historical Methodist sources.[1] Based on the group practices of the early Wesleyan movement, Watson has shown contemporary Christians the core genius of the early Methodist class meetings. The underlying concept is that people go to God most readily with mutual support and encouragement. A small group of committed Christians (up to seven) agrees to journey together. They look to Wesley's understanding of the Christian life and see that acts of compassion, justice, devotion, and worship are all necessary for such a life. Group members consider specific ways they might carry out such acts: for example, visiting persons who are unable to leave their homes is an act of compassion, daily Bible reading is an act of devotion, advocating for prisoners of conscience is an act of justice, and attending Sunday services is an act of worship. The group members then create a written covenant to which they agree to hold one another accountable. Regular meetings are held in which members give account to one another for the ways they have lived out their shared covenant between meetings. Participants encourage, support, and advise one another. The underlying premise of this model is that practicing these central Christian disciplines is spiritually formative and that we grow together and individually as we practice acts of mercy and piety.

Emmaus groups and other expressions of the Cursillo tradition practice another model. These little discipleship groups of two to six persons meet weekly for an hour around a common format. Members review their awareness of Christ's presence and call to discipleship during the past week and how they responded. Then they share how they are doing with their spiritual disciplines in the area of prayer (personal and corporate), study (scripture and other spiritual reading), and service (in church and community). Finally, they name their plans for walking with Christ in the week to come, closing with prayers for one another and others. The group's purpose is to provide ongoing support and caring accountability for one another's commitment to live wholly in the grace of God and to grow in the self-giving spirit of Jesus Christ.

Another expression of the mutual accountability group is the Renovaré model developed by James Bryan Smith and established by Richard Foster.[2] This ecumenical process for small groups identifies five basic traditions of the Christian life: contemplative, holiness, charismatic, social justice, and evangelical. A small number of people (two to seven) gather to explore these five elements in an outlined set of meetings. The group considers what it might mean to discover (1) a life of intimacy with God, (2) a life of purity and virtue, (3) a life of empowerment through the Spirit, (4) a life of justice and compassion, and (5) a life founded upon the Word. Once formed, the group continues meeting to account for the way participants are living in relation to these traditions and so that group members can share their ongoing faith journeys with one another.

Other types of covenant groups may function differently. They may exist for a specific period of time and serve mainly as a small community in which faith stories can be shared. Generally, they will covenant to honor mutual openness, compassion, encouragement, and confidentiality. The element of mutual commitment to spiritual formation through a written covenant characterizes these groups.

Scripture-Focused Groups

A second type of small group focuses on scripture. Most churches sponsor Bible study groups that have an important place in the life of any faith community. Often, the emphasis in such groups does not go beyond study. Their main purpose is to read and learn about scripture more intentionally. However, a formation group focused on scripture will emphasize shared reflection on the Word. Meditating on scripture is understood to reveal the leading of the Spirit in the lives of participants.[3] The ancient practice of *lectio divina* or meditative reading might guide such a group. You have had many opportunities to experience this practice through earlier daily exercises. As you know, the purpose of slow, reflective reading is to engage our whole selves with the text. We read first simply for content, considering perhaps the meaning of the text in its original communal setting. Then

In small groups, Christ's light shines more clearly. There is a holy mystery in groups as words are spoken that open windows to the soul in another and all sit in awe and wonder. Groups can be the arena for growth in the spiritual life.

—Larry J. Peacock

we allow ourselves to let the text—even one word or image from it—work on us. It settles in us, and we may begin to converse with God about it, turn it over in our hearts, feel it speaking to our lives. Such prayerful "chewing" of the Word often results in a deep, reverent resting in God, a contemplative embrace of the depth of the Word without much thinking or talking. A group that practices *lectio* may focus on each individual's reflections on the Word; or it may merge into shared *lectio*, a prayerful "reading" of scripture as it unfolds in the life of the group.

Prayer-Focused Groups

Still a third type of formation group centers on prayer. These groups vary according to the type of prayer emphasized. The most common form focuses on intercessory prayer, perhaps conscious that the "vineyard without fences" is not merely an encouraging or educational metaphor. We do indeed participate in others' lives at a deep level. The intentions of our prayers, offered on behalf of one another, shape and direct the intentions that circulate in our world. We are interconnected spiritual beings. Acting on the same principle, some prayer groups dedicate themselves specifically to praying for healing of one another and the world.

Also popular today are centering prayer groups, given form by Thomas Keating and others.[4] As you learned earlier in your exploration of prayer, centering prayer is a practice of contemplative praying that takes its inspiration from *The Cloud of Unknowing*, authored by a fourteenth-century English Christian. The practice of centering prayer is structured in twenty-minute periods, twice daily, in which we offer to God a simple, loving word or phrase that captures our deepest sense of divine reality. We allow other thoughts, concerns, or conversation to recede. In silence we offer our word as a "dart of love" that yearns in the direction of divine life. Such prayer empties us to receive God's ever-present love. While many choose to exercise this form of prayer in solitude, centering prayer groups offer instruction and supportive community for this formative practice.

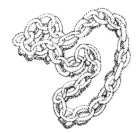

Action-Reflection Groups

A fourth model of group formation is the action-reflection group. Inspired by the rich traditions of social justice that have developed in modern Christian denominations, these groups seek to link action on behalf of the world's poor and oppressed persons with life-challenging reflection. The classic instance of such groups is found in the Latin American base community experience. During the middle of the twentieth century, small groups of the most oppressed and impoverished citizens of Latin America began to reclaim the ancient prophetic vision of scripture: God's plea and preference for the "widow and orphan," the dispossessed, the forgotten, the "little ones." These base communities read scripture in light of their own immediate, desperate situation and sought to hear God's liberating word in it. Then they acted out of that word. The group process that gradually developed was a circular one of action (lived experience), followed by reflection (grounded in scripture), which led to new action. When this process is practiced in situations of privilege, such action-reflection groups often focus on acts of service and justice on behalf of marginalized people. Christians involved in peace work; human rights; action to alleviate hunger, discrimination, or housing shortages can in this way ground their activity in profoundly reflective group sharing that is rooted in scripture, social ethics, and prayer.

Spirituality is a community enterprise. It is the passage of a people through the solitude and dangers of the desert, as it carves out its own way in the following of Jesus Christ. This spiritual experience is the well from which we must drink.

—Gustavo Gutiérrez

Group Spiritual Guidance

A final type of formational group is group spiritual guidance. This small community focuses on helping members with ongoing individual discernment. Group guidance may be practiced several ways. In the first, a clearly identified spiritual guide interacts with each member in turn, in the presence of all. Group members are helped to recognize, celebrate, and respond to the Spirit's movement in their lives, as revealed through accounts of their prayer and life experience since last meeting. In the second form of small group guidance, the identified guide's direction of each individual is combined with reflective input from other group members at specified times. In the third form, group members themselves function as spiritual guides for one another.

In this third variation, as developed by the Shalem Institute for Spiritual Guidance,[5] groups are carefully oriented at the institute for the task they are to undertake. Individuals willingly commit themselves to faithful attendance of meetings, discussion with others about their relationship with God, and commitment to the fundamental process. The process is deeply grounded in the practice of shared silence, the art of listening to one another, and in contemplative alertness to the presence of the Spirit. At each meeting one member acts as facilitator, keeping track of time and alerting the group if it moves away from a contemplative mode, tries to "fix" or "rescue," or becomes distracted. After a period of silence, a member shares for ten to fifteen minutes some aspect of his or her journey with God, especially in relation to prayer, since the group last met. If the speaker wishes response from the group, another shared silence is observed, followed by reflection from any who feel led to respond. The process is repeated for each person in the group. Then they pray for absent members and share reflection on their time together. Typical questions for closure might include the following: How is God working here? How did the process go? What do I/we take from this gathering? The fruit of dwelling together in loving intimacy this way is growth in God and compassion for others.

The church is indeed a thriving vineyard with many engrafted branches taking nourishment from Christ, the Vine. But the nurture and cultivation of that vineyard are never solely individualistic. We prune, water, hoe, and fertilize one another's vine gardens as we cultivate our own and as we actively participate with one another in being formed anew.

In group spiritual direction people learn to listen to God's Spirit at work in them for others in the group. As they take the sharing of others into the resting place of shared silence they seek to respond to what has been disclosed out of that prayerful place. Thus there is a collective wisdom available for each person.

—Rose Mary Dougherty

DAILY EXERCISES

Thomas Hawkins writes, "Our selfhood does come to us as a gift. But it is not a gift that God buries deep within us and that we must then individually uncover. It comes to us through those means of grace that God's prevenience has always provided: our often flawed and sometimes destructive relationships with friends, family, and community....Our spiritual journeys require companions."[6]

The scripture passages in these exercises invite us to explore the power of Christ's presence "where two or three are gathered in my name."

EXERCISE 1

Read Mark 6:30-32. These few verses give us a glimpse into the inward/outward rhythm of Jesus' life with the disciples. After having been dispersed for ministry, the disciples gather around Jesus, report and reflect on their actions, and rest with Jesus in a quiet place in preparation for being sent again in ministry.

To what degree does your life reflect this formative rhythm of life in Christ? What relationships or groups help you maintain the Christ-pattern in a purposeful and life-giving way?

EXERCISE 2

Read Matthew 18:15-20. This passage reflects a model by which church members assist one another in working out differences and in seeking to live the peace of Christ. Notice the aspects of the model that you find appealing, challenging, and/or troublesome. Consider why you feel as you do. (With respect to verse 17, keep in mind the extraordinary love with which Jesus treated pagans and tax collectors!)

Turn your attention to members of your church. How do you (or could you) assist one another in facing hurts, forgiving sins, healing wounds, and celebrating the grace of reconciliation in the community? Where do you see situations that cry out for more deliberate application of Christ's reconciling power in community? Hold the situations in prayer with openness to the leading of the Holy Spirit.

EXERCISE 3

Read John 11:1-44. The story of Lazarus illustrates God's resurrection power in Christ to raise the dead to new life. The story climaxes with three requests for the disciples' cooperation: "Take away the stone," "Unbind him," and "Let him go." Reread verses 38-44 while meditating on how the power of Christ can be present among spiritual friends to bear burdens, unbind fetters, and set one another free for new life. Record your insights.

What practices would characterize a mutual commitment to "take away," "unbind," and "let go free"? What parts of you cry out for the liberation such a group could support?

EXERCISE 4

Read Acts 11:25-30; 13:1-3. These and other similar episodes in Acts give us a glimpse of the way Paul, Barnabas, and their fellow missioners related to one another. When they met together, they were not just a support group; they formed a group committed to supporting the Spirit's ministry in and through one another. The practice of listening prayerfully to the Spirit's leading was central to their relationships and their manner of meeting.

Consider your life in the Spirit. With whom do you (or could you) listen to the guidance of the Spirit? Consider the life of your church. How could you be more deliberate about listening together to the guidance of the Spirit for the church's common life and ministry?

Take a few moments now to listen for and to record in your journal the stirring of the Spirit in you regarding the possibilities and power of fuller reliance on the guidance of the Spirit.

EXERCISE 5: DAILY EXAMEN

Use one of the models for daily examen provided for the past two weeks. Or try the approach described below that is based on Jesus' pattern of meeting regularly with his disciples for reflection and rest (see Mark 6:30-32 and Daily Exercise 1 above). Keep your journal at hand for notes.

Gathering. Imagine gathering at week's end in the company of Jesus with Christian friends. Collect yourself in God's presence. Remember and list people and events that gifted your life this week. Write a brief prayer of thanksgiving.

Reporting. Tell Jesus the story of your week as a disciple. What were the high points and low points? Where did you succeed and fail in living your life as a response to God's call? Where were you tested and delivered? Where did you experience God's presence and prompting? Note actions, attitudes, and experiences that were part of your walk. Reflect on patterns and learnings.

Rest. Spend time with Jesus in quiet and in prayer. Allow him to release you from your failures, heal your hurts, and empower you for the challenges ahead. Listen to Jesus as he affirms your life and sends you forth in ministry for the week to come. Record what you see and hear; write what you understand to be your "sending forth" commission.

Remember to review your journal entries for the week in preparation for the group meeting.

Re-Visioning Our Life As Companions in Christ

*P*erhaps we have inherited the old prejudice that sees spirituality as essentially a private and interior matter, while our life together in worship and service is public. Nothing could be further from the truth! We can aptly define spirituality as the whole personal process of searching for a vital relationship with God. This process has a profoundly introspective dimension. We must look honestly at ourselves and our present relationship with God, paying attention to the deep hunger for meaning that underscores our lives and listening to the heart's longing. But once we have sensed God's promptings, we must respond. We are called to act, living out our spiritual longings in the wider world, our communities, our workplaces, and our families. The spiritual life is a life of call and response. It involves us utterly and cannot be contained in some isolated inward realm. Spirituality is intensely personal, leading us to appreciate that deep solitude and silence through which God often speaks, but it is never private in the sense that it is "just for me."

It would be wise then to look closely at our corporate life in the church as an environment in which spiritual guidance and discernment can and do take place. In fact, the conviction behind this study is that the church is a community of grace and spiritual guidance and that the primary task of congregations is to help people enter into and mature in the Christian life. You do not need to be a pastor or

church professional to consider the role of the church in this regard and to see ways that your congregation can respond more fully to people's search for God and fullness of life in Christ. Each of us—whether a member of the church board, choir singer, Sunday school teacher, Bible study participant, youth group volunteer, or participant in weekly worship—is looking to the church for support and guidance in living a life of faithfulness to Christ. But we are more than receivers. We also participate in how the church responds to people's spiritual needs by the way we choose to share and shape our life together in Christ. We are all invited to re-vision our lives as companions in Christ.[1]

Worship as Guidance

When people think about going to church, the first thing they consider is the Sunday worship service. What are we doing when we meet weekly together? What do we expect, envision, and receive? The Sunday service is first and foremost an occasion for shared worship. I think we have become almost oblivious to the deep resonance of that word *worship*. We come together to acknowledge the astonishing and unfathomable mystery that lies at the heart of life itself. We come with our joys, fears, wounds, dreams, and with one another. When we worship, we acknowledge God's presence in our midst.

Our traditions have given us an infinitely rich reservoir of stories, concepts, and symbols through which we can begin to glimpse and appreciate the mystery that is God. We have words, gestures, rituals, and practices that should enable us to worship with great breadth and beauty. They form bridges by which God enters our lives in intimate and transforming ways. We come to hear the Word proclaimed. Proclamation of God's Word does not merely inform us about scripture and Christian ethical demands. We listen to the Word so that we will be transformed, so that it will become the source of our deepest life, so that in it we will "live and move and have our being." We need to come to the Word as the psalmist suggests, like a thirsty doe seeking a stream. Such thirst ought to be foremost in our minds and hearts

The service of worship builds upon our acceptance of God and moves toward forms through which we open ourselves to God's presence. From the music that plays as the service begins, to the times of quiet within the service, a significant function of worship is that of creating space in which people may experience what it means to make space for God.

—Howard Rice

when we hear the Word preached. The Word is a multifaceted, infinitely deep life source. It cannot be reduced to a single interpretation or viewed as a cipher that only trained specialists can decode. The Word proclaimed, heard, seen, and assimilated is the agent of our transformation.

Our shared worship not only draws our attention to the spiritually vital Word; it also invites us into prayer. Prayer! Not rote phrases rattled off but the cry of the human heart aflame with love, the cry of the parched spirit searching for living water. What we bring to worship is our shared aspiration for God. The outflow of our communal breath—our aspiration—that is prayer. We pray when we sing together the hallowed hymns that give our breathing common shape. We pray when we speak the ancient words that Jesus taught us, words that unfold with endless resonance. We pray when we wait in silence together and attend to the shared beating of our hearts. We pray when we greet one another with a kiss of peace, when we allow the wordless carpet of music to usher us into adoration.

Our worship is orchestrated with gestures and rituals, visual and verbal symbols that invite us to enter into the mystery we long for in a heightened way. To be immersed in baptismal waters is to remember and relive the primal energy of birth, of emerging into a new life. To break bread and share a cup together is to enter into a deeply life-sustaining gesture. We become a community of mutual need and mutual nourishment, feeding on divine sustenance by the Spirit, with and for one another.

The sacraments are not rituals we engage in simply out of habit or mere tradition. They are powerful symbolic doors through whose ample generosity we enter a more complete and meaningful experience of who we are—children of God, nourished by the very source of divine life. If we learn to enter into the power of our symbols, worship can become more than a dutiful activity. Our worship can be a primary source of spiritual guidance, allowing God's Word and our words to give new life.

Education and Administration as Guidance

Although worship is primary, there are many other avenues for members of the gathered church to explore their life together in a spiritually vital way. For example, the church educates through worship and preaching, adult and children's Sunday school, Bible studies and youth groups, and its moral and ethical teachings. Spiritually alive education must be intentionally transformational. It is not enough to conceive of the church as a source of fixed answers or a storehouse of information to be dispensed. The church is the bearer of a broad and rich tradition at the heart of which are the Gospels. From generation to generation the church hands on that Gospel-based tradition. However, for tradition to be genuinely alive, each member of the community must appropriate it in a personal, creative way.

Take, for instance, the practice of Bible study. In many churches this has become the preserve of an "authority," perhaps the pastor because of his or her training in biblical scholarship. Yet as you have already discovered, the Word needs to be more than facts and information to take root in our lives. A spiritually nurturing Bible study might include some historical-critical teachings but also fruitfully incorporates the process of prayer and meditation. In a meditative reading of scriptures, persons may engage all their faculties—thinking, feeling, sensation, and intuition. Doing this allows the text to enter them, to interweave with the story of their own lives, to become a prayer, and perhaps to become a question that takes them deeper into the mystery. True education "educes"—it draws forth from the learner her or his capacity for creativity, reflection, and wisdom. In this way, scripture study can become a significant aspect of spiritual guidance in the church.

The church can also exercise spiritual guidance in its administrative functions. Until recently, most churches approached administration more as a business than as a community of spiritual guidance. Congregational boards and committees usually come to meetings with a mind-set to get a job done or solve a problem. How refreshing it has been to learn of churches that are discovering how meetings can be occasions for working in a worshipful way that makes genuine spiritual discernment possible. Some church leaders now understand committee work and board meetings as times when smaller groups from the larger worshiping community come together to listen prayerfully to God's Word, to one another, and to God's spirit active in their midst. Charles M. Olsen (Presbyterian) and Danny E. Morris (United Methodist), among others, have offered serious attention to "worshipful work" and corporate discernment.[2]

A spiritually alive meeting requires more than opening and closing with prayer. It might, for example, appropriately include time for silence. We have a fine model to observe from the Quakers, who from the start have carried on business meetings as extensions of their silent worship. A meeting opening time also might provide an opportunity for members to share briefly about significant matters in their lives. In part, this sharing helps them release personal agendas early in the meeting and form a caring and compassionate community. Other possibilities include shared prayer and hymn singing, scripture reading, prayerful reflection on where God seems to be moving the group, or open discussions of the spiritual vitality of the church. The idea that church boards, staff meetings, deacons' gatherings, and various committees of the church could provide opportunities for shared discernment is currently quite countercultural. It requires genuine understanding, willingness, and preparation on the part of all involved—but what promise it holds for transforming a congregation's way of life!

Wherever two or three gather in Christ's name, Christ is present. In the midst of conducting business we can have our eyes open to see the Spirit at work through bricks and mortar, dollar signs and newsprint agendas.

—Larry J. Peacock

Outreach and Service as Guidance

Finally, we also can view outreach and service as aspects of spiritual guidance in the church. Action and contemplation are not foes, despite stereotypes to the contrary. In our world, more and more groups dedicated to peace and social justice are considering the deep spiritual resources needed to sustain their action. They are discovering that it is not enough to confront violent structures; they also must cultivate a genuinely nonviolent heart. When church leaders and members reach out to meet the needs of the world, they must not think of it as mere charity—giving money, time, or skills to less fortunate

> *Spirituality must include what we do as well as how we are, include acts of mercy as much as prayer.… To focus all one's spiritual energy inward is to miss meeting Christ in the person of the one who is needy.*
>
> —Howard Rice

persons. Such outreach is truly a practice of spiritual formation. Contact with the world's violence and pain; with poor, oppressed, and forgotten persons, is an opportunity for us to be changed. It is a chance to see God's world through a wider lens than our own limited view. Being open to what God has to say through our works of mercy (feeding the hungry, sheltering the homeless, giving drink to the thirsty, clothing the naked, tending the sick, visiting the imprisoned) can be profoundly transforming. Such ministry will challenge and change us. Often we discover that "the poor" are our most important spiritual teachers and guides. Through outreach and service, we can open ourselves to receive spiritual guidance.

A career woman I know once spent a month at a L'Arche community farm. L'Arche is an organization that brings together persons with mental challenges and persons without such challenges into a shared life experience. This woman went with the idea of helping others, fulfilling her Christian duty by using her gifts on behalf of less fortunate persons. Her experience was exactly the reverse. A city girl, she found herself quite helpless on a farm. She had to be constantly tutored in the most gentle and compassionate way by those she had imagined she would serve. As this woman gradually came to accept her dependence on others, she became aware of all the subtle ways she had learned over the years to mask her neediness. Always having to look good was one way. Always having the right answer was another. Always being competent was a third. She came to see that the tables had turned. The very persons she came to help were helping her. They were her spiritual mentors in the way of God's love and the dignity of each human life.

Behind the notion of the church as a genuine community of spiritual guidance is the unsettling idea that we are a people in process, not a people who have "arrived." We are discerners of God's unfolding will, pilgrims on a journey of individual and communal transformation. Whether church professional or layperson, you can begin to envision the role and meaning of church in this light. Every dimension of our life together is a potential spiritual pathway, an avenue through which we are guided by and with one another toward God.

DAILY EXERCISES

Danny Morris and Charles Olsen have written, "Members of the New Testament church believed that God would guide individuals and communities; they expected to be led by the Spirit."[3]

This week's daily exercises invite us to explore scriptures that point to the practice of discernment in the early church and to consider what it would mean to return more fully to this distinctive way of making decisions together in Christ.

EXERCISE 1

Read Exodus 18:1-27. Jethro advises Moses on how to organize the administration of the faith community based on an important principle for ministry and spiritual discernment: "You cannot do it alone." Outline the main points of Jethro's remedy. Where do you see the principles of Jethro's advice in church life? Where do you see the need for any aspect of Jethro's counsel in your congregation or in the way you carry out your calling?

EXERCISE 2

Read Acts 1:12-26. This is the account of the eleven apostles gathered in an upper room to seek a replacement for Judas. We can find in the story several key insights into the practice of discerning God's will in community. What indications do you see of how they prepared their hearts, when they used their heads, where they relied on God, and how they actually sought God's will?

In light of what you find, describe what you see as the necessary condition(s) for discerning God's will as an individual or as a group. Also name your most serious questions or apprehensions about it. Spend your remaining time prayerfully applying your insights to a question or dilemma in your life.

EXERCISE 3

Read Acts 15:1-29. This story shows the Jerusalem church debating and seeking God's will on an issue of enormous volatility and significance for the development of Christianity: whether Gentile converts had to be circumcised according to the law of Moses. Reread the story with an eye toward words and phrases that describe the atmosphere. Record what you see.

Read the story again slowly with an eye toward attitudes, actions, and grace-filled moments that played a role in the story of how the church moves beyond "no small dissension and debate" to a conclusion that "seemed good to the Holy Spirit and to us." Record what you see. What do these insights add to your understanding of how we discern God's will together?

Take a moment to identify a tough issue or question in your church or community. Hold the parties involved in love and prayer.

EXERCISE 4

Read Acts 15:1-29 again. Then look at the list "Some Principles for Discerning God's Will Together" (page 278). Note how you see these principles at work in the story of the Jerusalem church. Look in particular for where you can imagine "shedding" was required in order to move ahead without dividing the community between winners and losers.

Take a moment to remember the tough issue or question you identified yesterday. What would you and others have to lay down and take up in order to move from dissension and debate toward agreement on God's will in the unity of the Spirit? Remember in love and prayer the persons involved.

EXERCISE 5: DAILY EXAMEN

A daily review of life is a way to examine our thoughts, feelings, and experiences in terms of how God is present and how we are responding. It fosters an awareness of God's presence and call in our daily lives. It is also good preparation for the practice of spiritual guidance in any form. This particular model reads as a conversation with God. Keep your journal at hand to make notes.

God, my Creator and Redeemer, I am totally dependent on you. Everything is a gift from you. I give you thanks and praise for the gifts of this day. Give me also an increased awareness of how you are guiding and shaping my life, and of the obstacles I put in your way.

Be near me now and open my eyes as I reflect (in my journal) on:

*   Your presence in the events of today:

    _____;

*   Your presence in the feelings I experienced today:

    _____;

*   Your call to me:

    _____;

*   My response to you:

    _____.

God, I ask for your loving forgiveness and healing. The particular event of this day that I most want healed is

_____.

The particular gift or grace that I most need is

_____.

I entrust myself to your care and place my life in your strong and faithful hands. Amen.[4]

Remember to review your journal entries for the week in preparation for the group meeting.

Some Principles for Discerning God's Will Together

Preparing—Trust and expect that God is with you and will guide you in all matters as they affect the life and ministry that Christ seeks to express in and through us. Prepare yourselves for the guidance of the Spirit by devoting yourselves constantly to prayer.

Framing—Clearly focus the proposition to be tested or the question to be explored.

Grounding—Define the higher, guiding (or missional) principle or criteria to which your considerations must be faithful.

Shedding—Lay down all motives, agenda, and prejudgments that may limit openness to God; become indifferent to all but God's will.

Rooting—Consider texts from the Bible, wisdom from our spiritual heritage, and experiences from our walk with God that illumine the matter.

Listening—Seek out the voices we need to hear and learn from; listen for God's truth in each one.

Exploring—Consider all of the options and paths within the guiding principle.

Improving—Seek to make each option the best it can be rather than amending down those we don't like.

Weighing—Offer the best possible options to God, one at a time, weighing our readiness as a group to accept a proposal.

Closing—Ask all persons present to indicate their level of acceptance of a proposed path. State and register the wisdom that may lie within lingering reservations.

Resting—Allow time for the decision to rest near our hearts in a spirit of prayer. Notice feelings of assurance or anxiousness, peace or heaviness, consolation or desolation.

Adapted from Danny E. Morris and Charles M. Olsen, *Discerning God's Will Together* (Nashville, Tenn.: Upper Room Books, 1997), 66–67.

Part 5, Week 5
Discerning Our Need for Guidance

The longer I live, the more certain I am of one truth (and the less certain I am of many other truths). The one truth is that God can find us only where we are. Contemporary writer Norvene Vest captures this idea wonderfully when she states,

> Whatever my present circumstances, Christ will meet me there. However confused, bewildering, boring, or chaotic my life, God is involved in it right now. No matter how little or how much I think I love and serve God, God is waiting, ready to deepen our relationship.[1]

In other words, a genuine spiritual life can never be forged in some indefinite future when we get it all together, master some spiritual discipline, find more time, get a new job, or finish raising our children. God cannot reach us where we "ought to be"; God can reach us only where we are precisely because we are accepted and loved not for what we accomplish but simply because we have being. Thus we must root any assessment of our need for spiritual guidance in who we really are—in an honest, genuinely humble knowledge of our desires, strengths, weaknesses, and particular life circumstances.

What do we need in the way of companionship at this time and place? As I look back over my life and focus on the period of my late twenties, I see that it was a time of enormous spiritual growth through which I was guided in a variety of ways. The tapestry of those years is rich and complex, but the main outline is as follows: after a period of

God does not wait for us to have our spiritual acts together before reaching out to us and seeking relationship with us. This should be a point of great relief and freedom for us, for while we may strive for a sense of centeredness and balance, our relationship with God is not dependent upon our success. God's love will remain steadfast regardless.

—Kimberly Dunnam
Reisman

intense upheaval, personal failure, and geographic relocation, I found myself in a religious studies graduate program at a state university. There I met a remarkable professor who had the gift of mentoring students in a manner that went well beyond professional expertise. He was a teacher, and for years after a friend, who sensed the deepest longings of the heart. At the time I was unchurched, yet possessed an aching hunger for God. My professor (who was Lutheran) introduced me to a Franciscan priest at the old Mission Church in town, and the Franciscan gifted me for a long time with a listening ear. Gradually I found myself led into the Roman Catholic communion. There I found a deep structure of liturgy, ritual, history, theology, and spiritual practice that provided the wider spiritual home from which my individual journey could proceed. My university professor, himself engaged in a spiritual quest, also introduced me to a women's community of Cistercian monks with whom I stayed for a period and whose depth of prayer profoundly stamped my spirituality. Through them as well as through my Franciscan guide, parish church, and professor friend, I have continued to meet groups and individuals who have been invaluable companions to me along the way.

Concentric Circles of Guidance

This brief span of several years in my late twenties was eventful and critical. I recall them because they exemplify what Damien Isabell calls the "concentric circles of spiritual direction" in the church.[2]

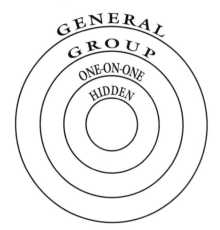

The outer concentric circle is the "General Spiritual Direction of the Church," the whole structure of worship, music, sacraments, and teachings by which the church directs the attention of her children toward God. In my case, my conversion to a Christian communion allowed me to participate in this general, overarching spiritual direction. The second circle is institutional or "Group Spiritual Direction," groups that enable people to grow in faith and take greater advantage of the richness of the church's general spiritual direction. In my case, the very focused Cistercian women's community provided such a structure. Examples of less tightly knit groups would be organized retreat experiences, Cursillo, Emmaus, support groups, scripture-based groups, covenant groups, and so forth. The third concentric circle of spiritual direction is "One-on-One." My Franciscan priest provided such intentional listening and direction for me during a crucial time. The inmost guidance circle is called "Hidden Directors." Isabell quotes Adrian van Kaam who says, "To find ourselves we need to follow the reactions and responses of fellow human beings to the life directives we are manifesting in our behavior." Guides come to us in many guises, as distant heroes or intimate friends, for a brief season or for the long haul. My graduate professor mentor, who later became my friend, would fall into the category of "hidden directors." The sureness with which he sensed and believed in my emerging best self, long before I did, opened doors to the Spirit-life for me.

This slice of my story is in no way normative for anyone else. It does, however, reveal the variety of overlapping ways in which the church can nurture us into greater intimacy with God. At any specific moment we need to assess: What is God drawing me to at this time? What is the deepest hunger of my heart? How can that hunger be fed? What is feasible, realistic, and appropriate for me, given my particular gifts and limitations and the circumstances in which I find myself?

Our greatest need may be for the church's general spiritual guidance. As Christians, we need to be rooted in church communities that genuinely turn our attention to God. One danger in seeking spiritual community is that we will be forever floating from one "spiritual

high" to another, looking for the perfect faith community that will do it for us. Staying with a church, either a denomination or a congregation, even when things are not going according to our preferences or when conflicts arise, is part of growing in love and faithfulness. We do need the deep wisdom of the church, its rhythms and seasons, Word and table, the gathered community. Our individual journeys, when isolated, can be only as broad and wide as our personal limits. With one another, past and present, we begin to taste the unlimited possibilities in God.

If we are already well rooted in a congregation, we may find our need is for more focused spiritual nurture. Then we may look to one of the three inner circles to deepen our walk with Christ. Although these three are not always discrete categories, distinguishing them is helpful.

Let's begin with the role of hidden directors. Sometimes all we need to draw us closer to God is the listening ear, the shared prayer, or the faithful support of another person. In Christian communities there are often unobtrusive persons graced with wisdom and experience who will share their faith with us. They are not necessarily recognized leaders. Although a pastor, educator (as in my case), or church professional may come into our lives at a critical juncture and point the way, a position of leadership is not essential here. Often an older member of a congregation, ripened in life's challenges, may emerge to walk with us for a time. He or she may listen, console, encourage, and pray for us. Or God may touch us and guide us through a Sunday school teacher, a friend, or a virtual stranger in the faith community. These persons may mold us in surprising ways that we may not recognize until years later. This is the gift of the Christian community and of the Holy Spirit's presence among us.

Some forms of spiritual friendship belong among the "hidden" forms of guidance. Special persons may emerge who give us life. This usually happens quite unexpectedly, perhaps in a social gathering or on an airplane—an experience of utterly surprising grace. A friendship may be fairly fluid, marked by the mutual sharing of the fruits of the Spirit in the context of ordinary work or social contact. Such

Never in the history of the church has it been considered necessary for everyone to have their own "spiritual director"....There is so much in the ordinary Christian life of a good parish or of a good faith-sharing group that is formative. There is so much illumination in life itself.

—Carolyn Gratton

a relationship can, however, develop into something more intentional, with get-togethers arranged at regular intervals and careful attention paid to equal time for each of the friends to share. Such a person may become a prayer partner.

There are a few questions (cautions) to consider when discerning your need for spiritual companionship. Informal spiritual friendships, while generally rich and as varied as the Spirit's imagining, are not "supervised" in any way. They are often deeply meaningful. But occasionally, the healing, listening ear of a fellow pilgrim can give way to harmful gossip or inappropriate advice. Some people, sensing they have spiritual gifts, take it upon themselves to be judges. I remember hearing of a charismatically gifted woman who went about warning people that she thought she saw the devil at work in their lives. Her meddling left many frightened and confused. As for friendships, they can sometimes mask serious dependencies or become manipulative. Even the healthiest may ignite deep desires that confuse our primary commitments. They can feed an elitist sensibility—"we are the only holy ones in this church"—or create factions. Being rooted in the wider community of faith is an important antidote to any of these possibilities. No guidance relationship should cut itself off from the larger church or produce the sour fruits of judgmentalism, elitism, narrowness, and/or excessive dependency.

Seeking New Forms of Spiritual Guidance

If our longing is for more intentional and formal spiritual guidance, we may wish to seek out a small group or an individual director. One question we might ask ourselves is temperamental or cultural. In the past, have we found ourselves given life primarily in one-on-one settings or in groups? Extroverted persons usually flourish in a group, while more introverted persons often prefer a one-on-one setting. Regardless of our personality profile, are we looking for a spiritual community or an opportunity to dig deeper on issues that might best be dealt with in an individual encounter? Our ethnic or cultural heritage may dispose us toward a group setting rather than one-on-one.

But the two options are by no means mutually exclusive. We may enjoy the ongoing encouragement of a covenant group, while seeing a personal spiritual guide at the same time.

If we find ourselves drawn to seek out a spiritual guide, we need to consider several issues. First, as mentioned earlier, we need to clarify whether we are truly looking for spiritual guidance—support in discerning God's ongoing will. If we want solutions to a specific life problem, then we would probably do better to seek out pastoral counseling, therapy, or a support group. Second, spiritual direction has emerged as a distinct ministry in today's world. Not all pastors or priests make good spiritual directors, and not all spiritual directors are pastors or priests. Seek referrals from church leaders or trusted individuals to find a spiritual guide. Retreat houses, seminaries, and regional or local church offices for spiritual formation can often advise about spiritual guides in a particular region. A spiritual guide or director is ideally accountable to someone else and has some sort of authorization to undertake the ministry. He or she may have been trained in a recognized program, be on the staff of a house of prayer, or be a member of a religious community.

The manual of ethics of Spiritual Directors International (an ecumenical organization concerned with training and supervision in this ministry) states that anyone claiming to provide spiritual direction should be in direction, working with a supervisor, in consultation with a peer group, or have a network of accountability.[3] Furthermore, not all directors are suited to all persons. Feel free to visit with a potential guide, ask questions about expectations and process, and discern whether that person seems a good "fit." Styles of spiritual guidance differ as do the styles of those seeking guidance. As already suggested, consider ethnic, cultural, denominational, and gender distinctiveness when choosing a spiritual guide. The spiritual guide should respect the conscience and individual spiritual path of each person. Although tremendous intimacy and vulnerability may occur in the guidance process, dependency is never the goal. Having a spiritual guide tell you what to do is never conducive to the freedom of the Spirit. One-on-one spiritual direction may or may not be available in your area.

Each soul is unique: no wisdom can simply be applied without discerning the particulars of this life, this situation.

—Eugene H. Peterson

You may have to decide whether a periodic trip out of town to visit a spiritual guide serves your needs or whether a close-to-home, more frequent group experience is more practical. Finally, there is the matter of mutuality in the spiritual guidance relationship. Do you prefer to focus on your issues with another person, or is a mutual model of guidance from peers, as in some group models, more to your taste?

If a group experience draws you, the first step is to ascertain what sorts of groups are already functioning in your congregation or local area. Next, consider what type of group will feed your spiritual hunger. In Week 3 we explored a variety of models—mutual accountability groups, scripture-focused groups, prayer-focused groups, action-reflection groups, and group spiritual direction. Possibly your need may be for a community of support, and many or most of these group models would nurture you. You may find the kind of group that truly draws you is not available in your local area. You might be instrumental in starting such a group.

Next Steps

Perhaps your question is, "What really does draw me?" Sometimes our deeper needs are revealed to us in unexpected ways. A "hidden director" emerges; a hint comes from a friend; a program catches your attention; a painful longing is awakened as you notice an absence in your life. Anything may point the way to what needs to come next.

If you find yourself drawn to begin a group, several factors are essential. Commitment to regular meetings by a small group (three to ten people) is necessary. For many people, a structured program such as Renovaré or *Companions in Christ* can provide at least initial formation and cohesion for a group. Spiritual formation is not just one more experience or thing to learn. It is a process of self- and other-discovery, of change and challenge, of self-transcendence. It occurs within the context of the Word and the transforming spiritual wisdom of the cumulative Christian community. As such, it needs to refer to the sources of Christian tradition. Group spiritual guidance especially underscores our shared life in Christ.

Discerning your need for spiritual guidance requires that you attend to the particulars of your present life. For a single man with a desire to learn more about prayer, commitment to regular, ten-day prayer retreats may be life-giving. A weekly Wednesday "morning with toddlers faith-sharing" (between nursing and diaper changes) may be the joy of a young mother's life. A long-widowed woman who lives alone in a rural farmhouse may find genuine nurture in a faith-sharing group that offers lively exchange and social companionship, while a busy pastor may relish a periodic solitary retreat interspersed with regular visits to a spiritual guide and augmented by a peer prayer circle.

Whatever discernment we make as to our present need for spiritual companionship, we do well to make it with attention to that deep, silent awareness of which we spoke in Week 1. In that awareness is the knowledge that God is alive and working within us, whispering, nudging, hinting, teasing us into a more loving and joyous embrace of God, self, and one another.[4] "For where two or three are gathered in my name, I am there among them" (Matt. 18:20).

DAILY EXERCISES

The author of Hebrews writes, "See to it that no one fails to obtain the grace of God" (12:15). Susanne Johnson, commenting on this and similar biblical mandates, writes, "By its very nature, the church is an ecology of spiritual care and guidance. It is the decisive context for Christian spiritual formation."[5]

This week's daily exercises challenge you to consider your vision for your church and its possibilities as a community of grace and guidance.

As we listen for the steps of God's Spirit in our midst, and as we seek ways to attune our own steps to these, we will find ourselves taking part, not only with God but also with one another, in the healing of the world.

—Frank Rogers Jr.

Exercise 1

Read Matthew 5:1-12. The late Clarence Jordan made a good case that the Beatitudes are not blessings pronounced on different kinds of people—the meek, the merciful, the pure in heart, and so on. Rather, they are stages in the experience of only one class of people—the "poor in spirit" who are entering the kingdom and growing as children of God who bear the divine likeness as makers of peace among people.

Meditate on the Beatitudes as a stairway of growth in God's blessing. Identify where you find yourself. What would you have to lay down or take up in order to go to the next step? What kind of companionship or guidance would you need for that to happen? Spend some time listening to what God wants to say to you about these questions.

Exercise 2

Read Colossians 1:24–2:7. In this passage, Paul articulates his personal passion and a pastoral goal that motivates all he does: "That we may present everyone mature in Christ." For what do you and your church "toil and struggle"?

Notice phrases and images that illumine what it means to mature in Christ. Rewrite them in your own words. Pay special attention to whether you see the "you" that Paul addresses as individuals, the faith community, or both; and what difference that distinction makes.

EXERCISE 3

Read Hebrews 5:11–6:2. These verses liken some believers to infants who have not yet progressed beyond a diet of milk, even though by now they should be teachers! What kind of spiritual nurture do "milk" and "solid food" consist of? Which is your usual diet?

Imagine your church as a spiritual nutrition center. Design a balanced spiritual diet for persons in your church who want to be "mature" (v. 14). What are the main food groups? Reflect on what it would take for you and other people in the church to represent and provide such a diet. Record your thoughts and feelings.

EXERCISE 4

Read Philippians 1:1-11. Paul begins his epistle by expressing his highest hopes and deepest longings for the church at Philippi. Meditate on Paul's vision and prayer for the people.

Take a few minutes to paraphrase Paul's prayer (vv. 9-11)—or to write a prayer of your own—in a manner that expresses your heartfelt longing "with the compassion of Christ Jesus" for members of your family and faith community. Commit all or part of your prayer to memory. Reflect on what it means to live out your prayer in your family and church.

EXERCISE 5: DAILY EXAMEN

Use a daily/weekly examen provided during a previous week or try this one. The following examen from Marjorie Thompson's book *Soul Feast* is adapted from some examen instructions by Tilden H. Edwards. Keep your journal handy for notes.

> Begin by relaxing your mind. Gently remind yourself of God's presence, and get in touch with your desire to be attentive to that presence during your day. You might offer a simple prayer that the graces of the day will be revealed to your consciousness.
>
> You need not try to find things; simply be "still and open, listening for what might rise from the day." When something surfaces, pay attention to the nature of the grace involved. How was God present? Let yourself feel and express gratitude for the gift.

Then notice how you were present to God or others in the midst of that moment. If you observe that you were unaware of grace, or unresponsive—perhaps holding the reins of ego control—you might breathe a simple prayer like "Lord, have mercy." Let yourself be aware of desire to respond differently another time.

If you observe that you were responsive to, or at least conscious of grace, simply "smile to God with thanksgiving."

Allow something else from your day to rise into awareness; repeat the process. "Thus you are noticing both the hidden presence of God in the day, and your own way of participating in, missing, or resisting that presence."

When you have completed your observations, make note of any responses that seem significant to you. Have you seen something surprising? discovered a pattern in your way of being present to others? received a special sense of grace or gratitude today?[6]

Remember to review your journal entries for the week in preparation for the group meeting.

Closing Retreat for *Companions in Christ*

*P*reparation: As a participant, you will need to spend some time preparing for the Closing Retreat just as you have spent time preparing for weekly meetings. This preparation will not require as much time as a week of daily exercises, but it could involve the equivalent time of two to four daily exercises. You may want a little extra time to review your complete journal notes. You will also want to set aside whatever you feel is adequate time to prepare your creative response to the assignment.

1. Think back over these twenty-eight weeks of personal and group exploration. Review your journal from the beginning.
2. Take some quiet time and open yourself to the Spirit. Allow to surface an image, story, poem, song, or psalm that captures the essence of your whole experience over the course of this time together, or that expresses a particularly significant moment of your journey.
3. Express your image creatively in any way you choose (draw, paint, carve, sew, etc.); write the story, poem, psalm, or song that comes to you; find a similar image, story, poem, psalm, or song in a resource you can bring with you.

Retreat Day

PART 1: CELEBRATION!

9:00   Gathering, fellowship, light breakfast refreshments

9:30   Morning praise

10:00   "Telling Our Story"

11:00   Break

11:20   Reflect on the storytelling process

11:45   Blessing and lunch

PART 2: INTEGRATION

1:15   Midday prayers

1:30   Guided meditation with John 21:1-19

2:00   Personal reflection and journaling with questions

2:30   Share in triads

3:00   Break

PART 3: ANTICIPATION

3:30   Plenary sharing: Looking to our future

5:00   Break for rest, walking, recreation

5:45   Dinner

PART 4: NEXT GENERATION

7:00   Breaking the bread

7:30   Sharing testimonies

8:00   Break

8:15   Closing Communion service

9:15   Good-byes

Materials for Group Meetings

A Few Hymns Categorized by Faces of Grace

PREVENIENT

Come, Sinners, to the Gospel Feast

Come, Ye Sinners, Poor and Needy

I Sought the Lord

Tú Has Venido a la Orilla (Lord, You Have Come to the Lakeshore)

Softly and Tenderly

Pass Me Not, O Gentle Savior

Only Trust Him (Come, Every Soul By Sin Oppressed)

Blow Ye the Trumpet, Blow

I Surrender All

Spirit Song

Turn Your Eyes Upon Jesus

It's Me, It's Me, O Lord (Standing in the Need of Prayer)

Pues Si Vivimos (When We Are Living)

Alas! And Did My Savior Bleed

JUSTIFYING

Rock of Ages

And Can It Be

The Solid Rock (My Hope Is Built)

Blessed Assurance

I Stand Amazed in the Presence

Nothing Between

There Is a Balm in Gilead

It Is Well with My Soul

Just as I Am

A Mighty Fortress

Beneath the Cross of Jesus

Because He Lives

Grace Greater than Our Sin

He Touched Me

Victory in Jesus

Dona Nobis Pacem

Amazing Grace

SANCTIFYING

Love Divine, All Loves Excelling

Spirit of the Living God

Let There Be Peace on Earth

Jesu, Jesu

Be Thou My Vision

Trust and Obey

Have Thine Own Way, Lord

Come and Dwell in Me

This Is a Day of New Beginnings

Something Beautiful

Spirit of the Living God

Take Time to Be Holy

Seek Ye First

We Are Climbing Jacob's Ladder

Make Me a Captive, Lord

Breathe on Me, Breath of God

For the Healing of the Nations

The Voice of God Is Calling

Informational and Formational Reading

Reading for information is an integral part of teaching and learning. But reading is also concerned with listening for the special guidance, the particular insight, for your relationship with God. What matters is the attitude of mind and heart.

INFORMATIONAL READING

1. Informational reading is concerned with covering as much material as possible and as quickly as possible.

2. Informational reading is linear—seeking an objective meaning, truth, or principle to apply.

3. Informational reading seeks to master the text.

4. In informational reading, the text is an object out there for us to control.

5. Informational reading is analytical, critical, and judgmental.

6. Informational reading is concerned with problem solving.

FORMATIONAL READING

1. Formational reading is concerned with small portions of content rather than quantity.

2. Formational reading focuses on depth and seeks multiple layers of meaning in a single passage.

3. Formational reading allows the text to master the student.

4. Formational reading sees the student as the object to be shaped by the text.

5. Formational reading requires a humble, detached, willing, loving approach to the text.

6. Formational reading is open to mystery. Students come to the scripture to stand before the Mystery called God and to let the Mystery address them.

Adapted from information in *Shaped by the Word: The Power of Scripture in Spiritual Formation* by M. Robert Mulholland Jr. (Nashville, Tenn.: Upper Room Books, 2000), 49–63. Used by permission of Upper Room Books.

The Group Lectio Process

PREPARE

Take a moment to come fully into the present. Sit comfortably alert, close your eyes, and center yourself with breathing.

1. Hear the word (that is addressed to you).

First reading (twice). Listen for the word or phrase from the passage that attracts you. Repeat it over softly to yourself during a one-minute silence. When the leader gives the signal, say aloud only that word or phrase (without elaboration).

2. Ask, "How is my life touched?"

Second-stage reading. Listen to discover how this passage touches your life today. Consider possibilities or receive a sensory impression during the two minutes of silence. When the leader gives the signal, speak a sentence or two, perhaps beginning with the words *I hear, I see, I sense.* (Or you may pass.)

3. Ask, "Is there an invitation here?" (for you).

Third-stage reading. Listen to discover a possible invitation relevant to the next few days. Ponder it during several minutes of silence. When the leader gives the signal, speak of your sense of invitation. (Or you may pass.)

4. Pray (for one another's empowerment to respond).

Pray, aloud or silently, for God to help the person on your right respond to the invitation received.

If desired, group members may share their feelings about the process after completing these steps.

Norvene Vest, *Gathered in the Word: Praying the Scripture in Small Groups* (Nashville, Tenn.: Upper Room Books, 1996), 27. Used by permission of Upper Room Books.

Developing Your Breath Prayer

The breath prayer is an ancient way of practicing the presence of God. It is a way to cultivate a posture of constant awareness and availability toward God.

Like prayers of repetition, breath prayers can be phrases from tradition, scripture, or hymnody. We repeat these phrases with our lips, carry them in our hearts, and whisper them under our breath.

The breath prayer is a way to act on your decision to be present to God who is always present to us. Practice your breath prayer at special times when you give God your undivided attention. Continue to say your breath prayer under your breath; let it become a habit of the heart.

Spend a few minutes now in developing and praying your breath prayer. Write it down as a reminder to keep with your journal.

Ron DelBene (pronounced like bane), a contemporary author of books on the spiritual life, has written extensively on creating and using personal breath prayers. The following steps are taken from his book *The Breath of Life: A Workbook*.

STEP ONE
Sit in a comfortable position. Close your eyes and remind yourself that God loves you and that you are in God's loving presence. Recall a passage of scripture that puts you in a prayerful frame of mind. Consider "The Lord is my shepherd" (Ps. 23:1) or "Be still, and know that I am God" (Ps. 46:10).

STEP TWO
With your eyes still closed, imagine that God is calling you by name. Hear God asking you: "(*Your name*), what do you want?"

STEP THREE
Answer God with whatever comes directly from your heart. Your answer might be a single word, such as *peace* or *love* or *forgiveness*. Your answer could instead be a phrase or brief sentence, such as "I want to feel your forgiveness" or "I want to know your love."

Because the prayer is personal, it naturally rises out of our present concerns.... Your response to God's question "What do you want?" becomes the heart of your prayer.

STEP FOUR
Choose your favorite name or image for God. Choices commonly made include God, Jesus, Creator, Teacher, Light, Lord, Spirit, Shepherd.

STEP FIVE
Combine your name for God with your answer to God's question "What do you want?" You then have your prayer. For example:

What I Want	Name I Call God	Possible Prayer
Peace	God	Let me know your peace, O God.
Love	Jesus	Jesus, let me feel your love.
Rest	Shepherd	My Shepherd, let me rest in thee.
Guidance	Eternal Light	Eternal Light, guide me in your way.

What do you do if several ideas occur? Write down the various possibilities and then eliminate and/or combine ideas until you have focused your prayer. You may want many things, but it is possible to narrow wants to those most basic to your well-being. Thus, the question to ask yourself is: *What do I want that will make me feel most whole?* As you achieve a greater feeling of wholeness, serenity will flow into the many areas of your life.

When you have gotten to the heart of your deep yearning, search for words that give it expression. Then work with the words until you have a prayer of six to eight syllables that flows smoothly when spoken aloud or expressed as a heart thought. A prayer of six to eight syllables has a natural rhythm. Anything longer or shorter usually does not flow easily when said repeatedly. Some prayers are more rhythmic when you place God's name at the beginning; other prayers flow better with it at the end.

Ron DelBene, *The Breath of Life: A Workbook* (Nashville, Tenn.: The Upper Room, 1996), 12–13. Used by permission of Upper Room Books.

General Rule of Discipleship

To witness to Jesus Christ in the world,
and to follow his teachings through
acts of compassion, justice, worship, and devotion,
under the guidance of the Holy Spirit.

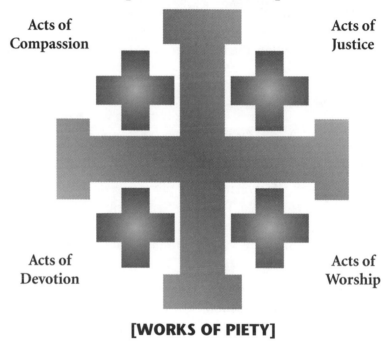

[WORKS OF MERCY]

Acts of
Compassion

Acts of
Justice

Acts of
Devotion

Acts of
Worship

[WORKS OF PIETY]

A GENERAL RULE OF DISCIPLESHIP

"The General Rule is designed to provide faithful disciples with a simple and straightforward method for Christian living in the world. For this…we need both form and power. Without the power of God's grace, our discipleship becomes a mere formality. Without the form of God's law, our discipleship becomes self-indulgent. Accordingly, the

General Rule directs us to follow the teachings of Jesus (form) under the guidance of the Holy Spirit (power)."

WITNESSING TO JESUS CHRIST

"Implicit throughout…is the cardinal privilege and duty of Christian discipleship: witnessing to Jesus Christ.

FOLLOWING THE TEACHINGS OF JESUS

"The next directive is to follow the teachings of Jesus through acts of compassion, justice, worship, and devotion….In these four dimensions of the General Rule, therefore, faithful disciples must not only strive to follow the teachings of Jesus. They must also be ready to hold themselves accountable for doing so."

UNDER THE GUIDANCE OF THE HOLY SPIRIT

"When we have exercised accountability for all of these works of discipleship, the General Rule directs us to accountability for obedience to the Holy Spirit….Whenever Christian disciples meet together in the name of Christ, they will not only watch over one another in love. Something else will happen. The Spirit of God will be present, working in and through the dynamics of the group, to empower them for service in preparing for the coming reign of God, on earth as in heaven….Identifying these warnings and promptings [of the Holy Spirit] sharpens the discernment of faithful disciples. To go further and to share them with one another means a quantum leap forward in their spiritual life, for their discernment and learnings are thereby greatly multiplied."

All the material on pages 298–99 is reprinted from David Lowes Watson, *Covenant Discipleship: Christian Formation through Mutual Accountability* (Nashville, Tenn.: Discipleship Resources, 1991), 77–94, and is used by permission.

Sample Covenant for a Covenant Discipleship Group

Knowing that Jesus Christ died for me and that God calls me to be a disciple of Jesus Christ, I desire to practice the following disciplines in order that I might know God's love, forgiveness, guidance, and strength. I desire to make God's will my own and to be obedient to it. I desire to remain in Christ with the help of this covenant so that I might bear fruit for the kingdom of God.

WORSHIP—*I will worship regularly*
- attending Sunday services
- taking communion at least once each month

DEVOTION—*I will take time to meditate and pray each day*
- remembering each member of this group in my prayers
- reading scriptures or passages from a Christian devotional guide each day
- taking time for silent reflection
- paying attention to God's presence, promptings, and warnings in all aspects of my daily life

JUSTICE—*I will seek to be an agent of God's justice and reconciliation in the world*
- upholding human dignity
- speaking out or acting to alleviate injustice wherever I see it
- practicing responsible stewardship of the world's resources in the context of my personal life and community commitments

COMPASSION—*I will practice love for all people*
- including self, family, friends, colleagues
- including my enemies and the strangers I meet

CALL AND RECOMMITMENT—*I will prayerfully plan the best use of my time and resources*
- responding to God's call in the week to come
- balancing time for work, family, friends, and recreation

I make this covenant, trusting in God's grace to work in me, giving me strength to keep it. When I fail in my efforts, I will trust God's grace to forgive me and sustain me.

_____   _____
Date   Signature

A Covenant Prayer
in the Wesleyan Tradition

I am no longer my own, but thine.

Put me to what thou wilt, rank me with whom thou wilt.

Put me to doing, put me to suffering.

Let me be employed by thee or laid aside for thee,

exalted for thee or brought low by thee.

Let me be full, let me be empty.

Let me have all things, let me have nothing.

I freely and heartily yield all things

to thy pleasure and disposal.

And now, O glorious and blessed God,

Father, Son, and Holy Spirit,

thou art mine, and I am thine. So be it.

And the covenant which I have made on earth,

let it be ratified in heaven. Amen.

From *The United Methodist Hymnal* (Nashville, Tenn.: The United Methodist Publishing House, 1989), 607.

Congregation:
An Ecology of Spiritual Care and Guidance

The concentric circles illustrate how the "church, especially the congregation, is a rich ecology of spiritual care."

"By its very nature, the church is an ecology of spiritual care and guidance. It is the decisive context for Christian spiritual formation. The church offers tacit as well as direct spiritual care and direction as it catches people up in what it is and does."

"The focal setting for spiritual guidance is worship, as we gather to do our liturgy. We initiate, form, and guide Christians through our common prayer and private prayer, through our giving, receiving, rejoicing, confessing, adopting, naming, instructing, washing, anointing, blessing. These are gestures necessary to our formation that the church does *to* us, *for* us, and *with* us."

"Spiritual guidance and care in the congregation must be ongoing and consistent, woven into the fabric of all that happens rather than presented on sporadic occasions as a new program. Many elements of spiritual guidance and care can be initiated and ritualized by pastors and Christian educators who themselves are responsible for breaking the silence about spirituality."

"'See to it that no one fails to obtain the grace of God' (Hebrews 12:15). This charge for ministry and witness is given to the entire company of believers, not simply the clerics. We are to witness to the whole world that the fundamental context of life is the unbounded love and redemptive grace of God."

"To fulfill their vocational call, every Christian already has a spiritual guide in the presence of God's Spirit (1 John 5:7-10). Our task is not to usurp or take over for God, but to help each other pay attention to the motions of grace and the promptings of the Spirit."

"The ultimate context of spiritual formation and guidance, thus, is the environment of grace. *Spiritus creator* is already present, not imported by us, as a creating, converting, guiding presence."

Quotes and diagram on pages 302–3 are taken from Susanne Johnson, *Christian Spiritual Formation in the Church and Classroom* (Nashville, Tenn.: Abingdon Press, 1989), 121–24, 135.

An Annotated Resource List
from Upper Room Ministries®

*T*he following books and videos relate to and expand on the subject matter of the five units of *Companions in Christ.* As you read and share with your small group, you may find some material that particularly challenges or helps you. If you wish to pursue individual reading on your own or if your small group wishes to follow up with additional resources, this list may be useful. The Upper Room is the publisher of all of the books listed, and the number in parentheses is the order number.

PART 1: EMBRACING THE JOURNEY

1. *Hunger of the Heart: A Workbook* (#738) by Ron DelBene is a six-week, small-group resource focused on exploring the spiritual journey. The workbook contains daily readings and suggested prayer exercises. The author helps you and your small group to understand the unfolding dimensions of our life in Christ, or what the author calls the stages of spiritual growth. The video "Finding God" (#722) is used as a part of this study.

2. *Workbook on Becoming Alive in Christ* (#542) by Maxie Dunnam presents material for daily reflection, along with material for group discussion, on the subject of the indwelling Christ as the shaping power of our lives as Christians. This seven-week small-group resource will deepen your understanding of the Christian life and what it means to mature in Christ. Dunnam believes that spiritual formation requires discipline and practiced effort to recognize, to cultivate an awareness of, and to give expression to the indwelling Christ.

3. *Devotional Life in the Wesleyan Tradition* (#740) by Steve Harper explores the nature of the spiritual journey and Christian growth as seen in the writings of John Wesley. The author writes about the disciplines of prayer, scripture, the Lord's Supper, fasting, and Christian community. For Wesley, these disciplines are the means of receiving God's grace in our lives. The workbook has sections for you to reflect upon and record your responses to the material. This is an excellent resource on the significance of spiritual disciplines or means of grace.

4. *Remembering Your Story: A Guide to Spiritual Autobiography* (#781) by Richard L. Morgan is a ten-week study in which participants are helped to remember significant moments in their lives and how God was present to them. It is a creative approach to discernment for the past, present, and future. The accompanying leader's guide is #797. This resource includes many suggestions about how to focus on your memories of important people and events and link those memories with the biblical story.

5. *Called by a New Name: Becoming What God Has Promised* (#802) and accompanying leader's guide (#804) by Gerrit Scott Dawson encourages you to move beyond the names of diminishment given by society and to experience the fresh identities God offers. Through reflection on portions of the book of Isaiah, the author invites you to discover what God names you and to take these names as your own.

6. *Remember Who You Are: Baptism, a Model for the Christian Life* (#399) by William H. Willimon contains one of the very best explanations of the sacrament of baptism and is written in a way that is easy to understand. But it offers much more. The author is interested in helping you to remember your own baptism and to discover a new vision for what it means to be a disciple of Christ. The book presents in a graphic way the fundamentals of the faith.

PART 2: FEEDING ON THE WORD

1. *Shaped by the Word: The Power of Scripture in Spiritual Formation*, rev. ed., (#936) by M. Robert Mulholland Jr. considers the role of scripture in spiritual formation and challenges you to move beyond informational reading to formational reading of the Bible. Mulholland demonstrates how your approach to scripture will in large measure determine its transforming effect upon your life. He examines the obstacles often faced in opening ourselves to God's living word. You will find this a helpful resource as you examine daily patterns of attentiveness to God through scripture, and you will expand your learnings about formational reading.

2. *Heartfelt: Finding Our Way Back to God* (#684) by Gerrit Scott Dawson focuses on ten stories about Jesus from the Gospels as a way for the reader to explore what a vital and transforming relationship with Christ might mean. Reflecting on these biblical stories will help you identify the obstacles in your own relationship with God and understand in a fresh way the full dimensions of a healing and renewing experience with the living Christ.

3. *Opening to God: Guided Imagery Meditation on Scripture* (#768) by Carolyn Stahl Bohler contains a detailed and helpful introduction to the discipline of guided-imagery meditation on scripture. The author includes fifty guided Bible meditations for use with groups as well as detailed guidelines for the person who will be leading the meditations. This approach to scripture offers a creative way to integrate scripture with your own faith journey.

4. *Writing on the Heart: Inviting Scripture to Shape Daily Life* (#713) by Gerrit Scott Dawson addresses the troubling question, "Why is it so difficult for us to live as people whose lives are shaped by the words of scripture?" In this penetrating book, you will discover a simple way to interact with scripture through exploring the scripture passage and identifying with people in the passage, praying for Christ's touch on your life, and then reflecting on a symbolic way to carry the story into daily life.

5. *Gathered in the Word: Praying the Scripture in Small Groups* (#806) by Norvene Vest offers detailed guidelines for small groups to engage in a prayerful approach to scripture. The author presents this process in a creative way by giving instructions and then illustrating with a description of a small group that is using this approach to scripture. It is an excellent resource for groups that wish to pray the scriptures together. You were introduced to this group lectio process in the Part 2, Week 5 group meeting.

6. *The Spiritual Formation Bible: Growing in Intimacy with God through Scripture.* This special Bible edition was developed by The Upper Room and published by Zondervan Press. It is available both in the NIV and NRSV translations with softcover, hardcover, and leather editions. The Bible contains articles on various aspects of spiritual formation and helpful introductions to each book of the Bible. In the margins of the Bible are questions for reflection to guide your prayer and meditation as well as quotations from the spiritual classics.

Annotated Resource List

PART 3: DEEPENING OUR PRAYER

1. *Beginning Prayer* (#676) by John Killinger is a basic resource for persons who are seeking to grow in their prayer life and develop a daily pattern of prayer. The book covers such subjects as attitudes that foster prayer, establishing daily prayer times, selecting a place for prayer, postures of prayer, and specific types of prayer.

2. *Dimensions of Prayer: Cultivating a Relationship with God* (#800) by Douglas V. Steere is a classic on prayer, first published in 1962 and revised in this new edition published in 1997. Steere, in his warm and engaging style, writes about the basic issues of prayer—why we pray, what prayer is, how to pray, what prayer does to us and to our activity in the world. Tilden Edwards says that reading this book is like sitting at the feet of one the wisest spiritual leaders of the twentieth century and hearing what are the important things he has learned about prayer over a lifetime.

3. *Teach Me to Pray* (#125) by W. E. Sangster is another classic on prayer that focuses on the importance of prayer in the life of a Christian and on ways to develop a strong and intimate prayer life with God. Sangster wrote a section of this book on practical questions about prayer, a section on how to form prayer groups, and a section on how we learn to "live in Christ." This book has been recently revised and updated.

4. *Alone with God: A Workbook* (#799) by Ron Delbene is a small-group resource designed to be used for six weeks. The purpose is to guide persons into a daily discipline of prayer and listening to God through scripture. In many ways this workbook functions in the same way as the daily exercises in *Companions in Christ*. The author has included suggestions for a daily pattern of prayer and scripture reading, as well as material for six group sessions. The workbook will help you learn how to be more attentive to God's presence in your life.

5. *The Workbook of Living Prayer* (#718) by Maxie Dunnam is a six-week study on prayer. It includes material for daily readings and prayers with reflection suggestions. The tremendous popularity and widespread use of this workbook demonstrate its effectiveness in a variety of settings and attest to the essential, time-tested nature of the teachings it contains about prayer. The author gives special attention to what we learn from Christ about the life of prayer.

6. *Responding to God* (#783) by Martha Graybeal Rowlett is a resource that helps us understand prayer as a response to God's grace in our lives. This book and accompanying leader's guide contain a suggested model for daily prayer and material for ten weeks of study on the various facets of prayer. It includes chapters on our understanding of God, the forms of prayer, the difference prayer makes in the life of the believer, and why some prayers go unanswered. The leader's guide (#926) also offers suggestions on using the book for different time frames, such as six weeks, twelve weeks, or a weekend retreat.

7. *The Breath of Life: A Simple Way to Pray—A Workbook* (#766) by Ron Delbene is a five-week study on how to pray without ceasing by using a breath prayer. You were introduced to the breath prayer in Part 3, Week 2 of *Companions in Christ*. A video on learning the breath prayer entitled "Learning the Breath Prayer" (#725) is used for one of the group sessions. The workbook includes material to be used by each participant on a daily basis as well as guidance for the group meetings.

PART 4: RESPONDING TO OUR CALL

1. *The Spiritual Classics, Series 1* (# 832), *Series 2* (#853), and *Series 3* (#905) offer a collection of contemporary translations of some of the best spiritual writing in the Christian tradition. By reading the writings of Christians across the centuries, you will receive help in discerning your own call and what

faithfulness means. The resources can be ordered as a series or by individual booklets. The first series includes the writings of John Cassian (#831), John Wesley (#827), Teresa of Avila (#828), Augustine (# 830), and Thomas Kelly (#829). The second series includes the writings of Julian of Norwich (#833), Toyohiko Kagawa (#836), Evelyn Underhill (#837), Thomas à Kempis (#835), Francis and Clare (#834). The third series includes the writings of John of the Cross (#904), the Desert Mothers and Fathers (#902), William Law (#901), John Woolman (#900), and Catherine of Siena (#903). Each book includes an introduction to the life story of the writer, fourteen excerpts from their writings, and a special section on how to read the classics in a devotional way.

2. *Then Shall Your Light Rise: Spiritual Formation and Social Witness* (#816) by Joyce Hollyday gives concrete expression to the relationship between spiritual growth and the life of action and witness. The author believes that as you become more attentive to God's love in your life, you also become more attentive to the needs of people in your community and throughout the world. Through personal story and biblical reflection, you are led to a deeper understanding of how actions of compassion help you grow in faith and see God more clearly.

3. *As If the Heart Mattered: A Wesleyan Spirituality* (#820) by Gregory S. Clapper offers a summary of Wesley's understanding of the essentials of the Christian life. Clapper believes that Wesley's major contribution centers on his view of what constitutes "heart religion" or a faithful seeking of transformation at the very core of life. Wesley was concerned with religion that reorders the loves and fears of everyday life. Clapper writes, "Wesley's view was that if Christianity does not affect a person on this most elemental level, then it has not really taken root."

4. *Yours Are the Hands of Christ: The Practice of Faith* (#867) by James C. Howell helps you find ways actively to express your faith in daily life and make your commitment to Christ evident in today's world. Howell believes that Christians long to make a difference in the world as a response to the call of discipleship. By considering all that Jesus did as a teacher, a healer, and a compassionate servant, the author challenges you to be the hands and love of Christ in the world.

5. *Rediscovering Our Spiritual Gifts: Building Up the Body of Christ through the Gifts of the Spirit* (#633) by Charles V. Bryant offers a practical look at how the gifts of the Holy Spirit can renew the lives of individuals and Christian communities. The author provides ways for you to discover your spiritual gifts. A separate workbook (#771) accompanies this book and provides suggestions for use in a group setting. The author has also provided a spiritual gifts inventory that can be used by individuals (#819).

6. *Neglected Voices: Biblical Spirituality in the Margins* (#891) by John Indermark explores some lesser-known biblical figures like Rahab, Puah, and Simon Magus who have much to teach you about the importance of faithfulness in all times and places. The author seeks to help you open to the possibilities in your own life and the lives of those around you. The leader's guide (#890) presents material for six weekly meetings.

7. *Prayer, Stress, and Our Inner Wounds* (#501) by Flora Slosson Wuellner describes several types of pain—physical pain, painful memories, forgotten wounds, the pain of uncertainty, and the pain of stress and anxiety. Wuellner reminds us that the first step for transforming the world's pain is to look with honesty at our own pain and begin to open the door to God's love. The passion to heal was central in Jesus' ministry and this book helps us confront our own needs in the confidence of Christ's healing presence.

PART 5: EXPLORING SPIRITUAL GUIDANCE

1. *Learning to Listen: A Guide for Spiritual Friends* (#677) by Wendy Miller introduces spiritual friendship, presenting a practical guide to beginning and strengthening such a friendship. The author gives helpful

suggestions about finding a spiritual friend, planning your time together, and how the practice of personal spiritual disciplines enriches your spiritual friendships.

2. *A Guide to Spiritual Discernment* (#779) by Rueben P. Job is designed for individuals or groups to use for a period of forty days in preparation for major decisions. The daily readings, prayers, and liturgies are arranged to help you reflect on God's presence and activity in your life and how to open yourself more fully to God's guidance. This resource could be used by a church group facing a large issue requiring serious discernment or by an entire congregation facing a difficult decision. One of the benefits of such a resource is the sense of unity it engenders as persons prepare to seek God's will together.

3. *Discerning God's Will Together: A Spiritual Practice for the Church* (#808) by Danny E. Morris and Charles M. Olsen suggests ways to implement a decision-making approach in church gatherings that is built on prayer and discernment. You were introduced to this basic process in Part 5, Week 4 of *Companions in Christ.* Morris and Olsen believe that church members are weary of the way church business is handled when it does not seem connected with the deeper meanings of their life and faith. This book outlines ten movements in a process designed to help groups seeking to be open to God's will for them. It describes such a process as it might occur in a small group, a congregation, or a church gathering.

4. *Finding a Spiritual Friend: How Friends and Mentors Can Make Your Faith Grow* (#857) by Timothy Jones is an excellent book for persons who want to understand more about the expectations and dynamics of spiritual friendship and ways to strengthen such friendships. The author writes convincingly that interdependence is at the heart of the faith community. We need one another for strength and guidance as we seek to grow in faithfulness. As an added benefit there are biblical reflections interspersed with the chapters. Although this resource does not contain guidance for small group sessions, the book does provide personal questions for reflection at the end of each chapter.

5. *Discovering Community: A Meditation on Community in Christ* (#870) by Stephen V. Doughty kept a weekly appointment with his journal to answer the question, "Where this past week have I actually seen Christian community?" In his work with over seventy congregations, he found an abundance of times and places where he witnessed genuine community. Out of these experiences, he helps you understand what fosters Christian community and what blocks it. This resource can help to bring a renewed sense of personal calling and commitment to shared ministry for individuals and congregations.

6. *The Pastor as Spiritual Guide* (#846) by Howard Rice positions the specific tasks of pastoral ministry in the larger framework of spiritual guidance. Rice explores preaching, teaching, and administration in the church as opportunities to nurture spiritual growth in members. In developing the image of pastor as spiritual guide, the author examines other prominent images of ministry and shows how these models do not satisfy the full dimensions of leadership. This resource offers a challenging understanding of the role of the congregational leader because it is built on a clear understanding of the mission of the church, namely, the formation of Christian disciples. This resource will make interesting reading as you complete Part 5 of *Companions.*

7. *Communion, Community, and Commonweal* (#737), edited by John Mogabgab, is a compilation of articles to deepen an understanding and practice of spiritual leadership. Part One explores the rhythm of listening and responding to God that is essential to leadership. Part Two focuses on the core disciplines needed by faith communities of remembering, celebrating, communicating, and guiding. Part Three examines the mission of the church and your own discipleship. You will find an article by Parker Palmer on clearness committees of special interest.

Notes

PART 1: EMBRACING THE JOURNEY

Week 1   The Christian Life As Journey
1. Walter Brueggemann, *Praying the Psalms* (Winona, Minn.: Saint Mary's Press, 1982), 16–24.

Week 2   The Nature of the Christian Spiritual Life
1. While the church has traditionally attributed the writing of this letter to the Apostle Paul, many reputable scholars attribute it to a strong, second-generation Pauline community.
2. Elizabeth O'Connor, *The New Community* (New York: Harper & Row, 1976), 58.

Week 3   The Flow of Grace and the Means of Grace
1. Dallas Willard, *The Spirit of the Disciplines* (San Francisco: HarperSanFrancisco, 1991), 158.
2. Marjorie Thompson, *Soul Feast* (Louisville, Ky.: Westminster John Knox Press, 1995), 69–70.
3. Ibid., 9–10.

Week 4   Sharing Journeys of Faith
1. Augustine, *Confessions* 3.6, trans. Henry Chadwick (New York: Oxford University Press, 1991), 41.
2. Augustine, *Confessions* 3.6, trans. R. S. Pine-Coffin (New York: Penguin Books, 1961), 61.
3. *Martin Luther: Selections from His Writings*, ed. John Dillenberger (Garden City, N.Y.: Anchor Books, 1961), 11.
4. Ibid., 11–12.
5. Mother Teresa, *Mother Teresa: In My Own Words*, comp. José Luis González-Balado (Liguori, Mo.: Liguori Publications, 1989), 24.
6. Ibid., 99.
7. Deborah Smith Douglas, "Evelyn Underhill at Pleshey," *Weavings: A Journal of the Christian Spiritual Life* 14 (January–February 1999): 19.
8. Ibid., 20.
9. Ibid.

Week 5   Living As Covenant Community
1. Tilden H. Edwards, *Living in the Presence* (San Francisco: Harper & Row, 1987), 61.
2. Dietrich Bonhoeffer, *Life Together*, trans. John W. Doberstein (New York: Harper & Row, 1954), 30.
3. Clifford Williams, *Singleness of Heart* (Grand Rapids, Mich.: William B. Eerdmans, 1994), 116.
4. Robert Wuthnow, ed., *"I Come Away Stronger": How Small Groups Are Shaping American Religion* (Grand Rapids, Mich.: William B. Eerdmans, 1994), 15.
5. Ibid., 105.
6. Ibid., 153.
7. Morton T. Kelsey, *Companions on the Inner Way* (New York: Crossroad, 1983), 8.

PART 2   FEEDING ON THE WORD

Week 1   Why Do We Call the Bible God's Word?
1. Thomas Merton, *Opening the Bible* (Philadelphia, Pa.: Fortress Press, 1970), 18.
2. M. Robert Mulholland Jr., *Shaped by the Word: The Power of Scripture in Spiritual Formation*, rev. ed. (Nashville, Tenn.: Upper Room Books, 2000), 27, 30.

Notes

Week 2   Studying Scripture As a Spiritual Discipline

1. At Qumran the dissidents from the Temple cultus required all who entered the community to take a binding oath to study and abide by the law of Moses (*Manual of Discipline* 5.7–20). They scheduled round-the-clock study for the community.
2. Richard J. Foster, *Celebration of Discipline: The Path to Spiritual Growth*, rev. ed. (San Francisco: Harper & Row, 1988), 62.
3. Thomas Merton, *Spiritual Direction and Meditation* (Collegeville, Minn.: The Liturgical Press, 1960), 44.
4. Ibid., 46.
5. Jean Leclercq, *The Love of Learning and the Desire for God: A Study of Monastic Culture*, trans. Catharine Misrahi (New York: Fordham University Press, 1961), 87–90.

Week 3   Meditating on the Word

1. Merton, *Spiritual Direction and Meditation*, 51.
2. Douglas Burton-Christie, *The Word in the Desert: Scripture and the Quest for Holiness in Early Christian Monasticism* (New York: Oxford University Press, 1993), 107–133.
3. Merton, *Spiritual Direction and Meditation*, 64.
4. Ibid., 95.
5. Elizabeth Canham, unpublished article on *lectio divina*.
6. Merton, *Spiritual Direction and Meditation*, 75.
7. John Cassian, *Conferences* 10.11, trans. Owen Chadwick, The Library of Christian Classics, vol. 12 (Philadelphia: The Westminster Press, 1958), 244.
8. Teresa of Avila, *The Life of Teresa of Jesus, The Autobiography of St. Teresa of Avila*, ed. E. Allison Peers (Garden City, N.Y.: Image Books, 1960), 133.
9. Douglas V. Steere, *Traveling In*, ed. E. Glenn Hinson, Pendle Hill Pamphlet 324 (Wallingford, Pa.: Pendle Hill Publications, 1995), 19.
10. Teresa of Avila, *The Life of Teresa of Jesus*, 137.
11. Bonhoeffer, *Life Together*, 82.
12. Ibid., 83.
13. Ibid., 84.

Week 4   Directing Imagination

1. Ignatius of Loyola, *The Spiritual Exercises of St. Ignatius*, trans. Anthony Mottola (Garden City, N.Y.: Image Books, 1964), 37.
2. Richard Baxter, *The Saints' Everlasting Rest*, ed. E. Glenn Hinson, The Doubleday Devotional Classics, vol. 1 (Garden City, N.Y.: Doubleday, 1978).
3. John Bunyan, *Grace Abounding* 46, ed. E. Glenn Hinson, The Doubleday Devotional Classics, vol. 1 (Garden City, N.Y.: Doubleday, 1978), 230.
4. Baxter, *The Saints' Everlasting Rest* 13, 21; 141.
5. Ibid., 14, 2; 142.
6. Quote adapted into modern English idiom from the original text in Richard Baxter, *The Saints' Everlasting Rest* (Philadelphia: Presbyterian Board of Publication, 1847), 306–307.
7. Henri J. M. Nouwen, *Behold the Beauty of the Lord: Praying with Icons* (Notre Dame, Ind.: Ave Maria Press, 1987), 15.

Week 5   Group Meditation with Scripture

1. Bunyan, *Grace Abounding* 77; 237.
2. John Bunyan, *The Pilgrim's Progress*, ed. E. Glenn Hinson, The Doubleday Devotional Classics, vol. 1 (Garden City, N.Y.: Doubleday, 1978), 348.

3. In *A History of Christianity: Readings in the History of the Church*, vol. 2, ed. Clyde L. Manschreck (Englewood Cliffs, N.J.: Prentice-Hall, 1964), 31.

4. Those who would like a more extensive discussion of group meditation will find much help in Norvene Vest's *Gathered in the Word: Praying the Scripture in Small Groups* (Nashville, Tenn.: Upper Room Books, 1996); see especially 17–27.

5. Some may wonder whether the monks did not use primarily the Psalms for *lectio divina*. I believe the answer to that is no. The psalms were chanted in the Opus Dei, the Daily Office monks gathered for eight times a day. During the four hours scheduled for *lectio divina*, they usually meditated on other scriptures and other writings. We probably owe wonderful illuminated manuscripts such as the Lindisfarne Gospels and the Book of Kells to *lectio*.

PART 3   DEEPENING OUR PRAYER

Week 1   Prayer and the Character of God

1. Thompson, *Soul Feast*, 31.

2. Augustine, *Confessions* 10. 27. 38, trans. J. G. Pilkington, Nicene and Post-Nicene Fathers, First Series, vol. 1 (1886; reprint, Peabody, Mass.: Hendrickson Publishers, 1994), 152–53. Adapted by Keith Beasley-Topliffe.

Week 2   Dealing with Impediments to Prayer

1. Jean-Pierre de Caussade, *Abandonment to Divine Providence*, trans. John Beevers (New York: Image Books, 1975), 72.

2. Douglas V. Steere, *Dimensions of Prayer* (Nashville, Tenn.: Upper Room Books, 1997), xx.

Week 3   Prayers of Petition and Intercession

1. Steere, *Dimensions of Prayer*, 69.

2. Maria Boulding, *The Coming of God* (Collegeville, Minn.: The Liturgical Press, 1982), 7–8.

Week 4   Praying As We Are

1. Harvey D. Egan, "Negative Way," in *The New Dictionary of Catholic Spirituality* (Collegeville, Minn.: The Liturgical Press, 1993), 700.

2. James Finley, as quoted by Allan H. Sager, *Gospel-Centered Spirituality* (Minneapolis, Minn.: Augsburg Fortress, 1990), 37.

3. Urban T. Holmes III, *A History of Christian Spirituality: An Analytical Introduction* (New York: Seabury, 1980), 4–5.

4. For a more detailed description of the four types, see Corinne Ware, *Discover Your Spiritual Type* (Bethesda, Md.: The Alban Institute, 1995).

5. Ibid., 43.

6. Ibid., 44–45.

7. Karl Rahner, *Encounters with Silence*, trans. James M. Demske (Westminster, Md.: The Newman Press, 1960), 15–16.

8. Dom Chapman, as quoted in Richard Foster's book *Prayer: Finding the Heart's True Home* (San Francisco: HarperSanFrancisco, 1992), 7.

Week 5   Psalms, the Prayer Book of the Bible

1. Thomas R. Hawkins, *The Unsuspected Power of the Psalms* (Nashville, Tenn.: The Upper Room, 1985), 37.

Week 6   Exploring Contemplative Prayer

1. William H. Shannon, "Contemplation, Contemplative Prayer," in *The New Dictionary of Catholic Spirituality*, 209.

2. Augustine, *Confessions* 1.1, ed. Keith Beasley-Topliffe, Upper Room Spiritual Classics, Series 1 (Nashville, Tenn.: Upper Room Books, 1997), 12.

Notes

3. Teresa of Avila, *The Interior Castle* in *The Collected Works of St. Teresa of Avila*, vol. 2, trans. Kieran Kavanaugh and Otilio Rodriguez (Washington, D.C.: Institute of Carmelite Studies, 1980), 283.
4. Teresa of Avila, *The Book of Her Life* in *The Collected Works of St. Teresa of Avila*, vol. 1, trans. Kieran Kavanaugh and Otilio Rodriguez (Washington, D.C.: Institute of Carmelite Studies, 1976), 80.
5. Teresa of Avila, *The Interior Castle*, 430.
6. Brother Lawrence of the Resurrection, *The Practice of the Presence of God*, trans. John J. Delaney (New York: Image Books, 1977), 68.

PART 4 RESPONDING TO OUR CALL

Week 1 Radical Availability
1. Oswald Chambers, *My Utmost for His Highest* (London: Simpkin Marshall, 1937), 120.

Week 2 Living Reliance
1. Ray Summers, *Behold the Lamb: An Exposition on the Theological Themes in the Gospel of John* (Nashville, Tenn.: Broadman Press, 1979), 188–89.
2. Lesslie Newbigin, *The Light Has Come: An Exposition of the Fourth Gospel* (Grand Rapids, Mich.: William B. Eerdmans, 1982), 197.
3. Ibid., 198.
4. Thomas F. Torrance, *Scottish Theology* (Edinburgh: T & T Clark, 1996), 58.

Week 3 Bearing the Fruit of the Vine
1. Newbigin, *The Light Has Come*, 200.
2. Ibid.
3. Andrew Murray, *With Christ in the School of Prayer* (Old Tappan, N.J.: Fleming H. Revell, 1953), 43.
4. Ibid., 44.

Week 4 Gifts of the Spirit
1. John Calvin, *Institutes of the Christian Religion*, trans. Ford Lewis Battles, Library of Christian Classics, vol. 20 (Philadelphia: The Westminster Press, 1960), 537–41.
2. Thomas F. Torrance, *The Trinitarian Faith* (Edinburgh: T & T Clark, 1993), 228.
3. Ibid.
4. Calvin, *Institutes of the Christian Religion*, 540–41.
5. Ibid.

Week 5 The Body of Christ Given for the World
1. Gustav Nelson, "A New Model for a New Century," *Presbyterian Outlook* (30 June 1997): 7.

PART 5 EXPLORING SPIRITUAL GUIDANCE

Week 1 How Do I Know God's Will for My Life?
1. Thompson, *Soul Feast*, 103–5.
2. Margaret Guenther, *Holy Listening: The Art of Spiritual Direction* (Cambridge: Cowley Publications, 1992), 43.
3. Ben Campbell Johnson, *Invitation to Pray*, rev. ed. (Decatur, Ga.: CTS Press, 1993), 18–22.

Week 2 Spiritual Companions
1. A contemporary exploration of desert spirituality is found in Henri Nouwen's now classic *The Way of the Heart: Desert Spirituality and Contemporary Ministry* (New York: Seabury Press, 1981).
2. *The Wisdom of the Desert*, trans. Thomas Merton (New York: New Directions, 1960), 25–26.
3. *Desert Wisdom*, ed. and illus. Yushi Nomura (Garden City, N.Y.: Doubleday, 1982), 84.
4. Guenther, *Holy Listening*.
5. Howard Rice, *The Pastor As Spiritual Guide* (Nashville, Tenn.: Upper Room Books, 1998), 80–81.

6. Wendy M. Wright, *A Retreat with Francis de Sales, Jane de Chantal and Aelred of Rievaulx: Befriending Each Other in God* (Cincinnati: St. Anthony's Messenger Press, 1996).
7. Tilden H. Edwards, *Spiritual Friend* (New York: Paulist Press, 1980).
8. Howard Rice, *Ministry as Spiritual Guidance* (Louisville, Ky.: Westminster John Knox Press, 1991).
9. Charles M. Olsen, *Transforming Church Boards into Communities of Spiritual Leaders* (Bethesda, Md.: The Alban Institute, 1995). Also Danny E. Morris and Charles M. Olsen, *Discerning God's Will Together* (Nashville, Tenn.: Upper Room Books, 1997).
10. Cf. Esther de Waal, *Living with Contradiction: Reflections on the Rule of St. Benedict* (San Francisco: Harper & Row, 1989).
11. David Lowes Watson, *Covenant Discipleship: Christian Formation through Mutual Accountability* (Nashville, Tenn.: Discipleship Resources, 1994).
12. Kathleen Fischer, *Women at the Well: Feminist Perspectives on Spiritual Direction* (New York: Paulist Press, 1988).
13. Susan Rakoczy, ed., *Common Journey, Different Paths: Spiritual Direction in Cross-Cultural Perspective* (Maryknoll, N.Y.: Orbis Books, 1992).
14. Douglas V. Steere, *Together in Solitude* (New York: Crossroad, 1982), 33–34.

Week 3   Small Groups for Spiritual Guidance

1. Watson, *Covenant Discipleship.*
2. James Bryan Smith, *A Spiritual Formation Workbook* (San Francisco: HarperSanFrancisco, 1993).
3. Vest, *Gathered in the Word.*
4. Thomas Keating, *Invitation to Love: The Way of Christian Contemplation* (New York: Continuum, 1994).
5. Rose Mary Dougherty, *Group Spiritual Direction* (New York: Paulist Press, 1995).
6. Thomas R. Hawkins, *Sharing the Search* (Nashville, Tenn.: The Upper Room, 1987), 19, 25.

Week 4   Re-Visioning Our Life As Companions in Christ

1. A wonderful resource for doing just that is Howard Rice's *The Pastor As Spiritual Guide* (Nashville, Tenn.: Upper Room Books, 1998).
2. See Olsen, *Transforming Church Boards*, and Morris and Olsen, *Discerning God's Will Together.*
3. Morris and Olsen, *Discerning God's Will Together*, 25.
4. Adapted from an unpublished work by Kathleen Flood., Nashville, Tenn., April 2000, and used by permission. This examen is inspired by some writings of Ignatius of Loyola.

Week 5   Discerning Our Need for Guidance

1. Norvene Vest, *No Moment Too Small: Rhythms of Silence, Prayer, and Holy Reading* (Kalamazoo, Mich.: Cistercian Publications, 1994), 6.
2. Damien Isabell, *The Spiritual Director: A Practical Guide* (Chicago: Franciscan Herald Press, 1976).
3. Spiritual Directors International, 1329 Seventh Avenue, San Francisco, CA 94122-2507.
4. A helpful resource in discernment is *A Guide to Spiritual Discernment*, comp. Rueben Job (Nashville, Tenn.: Upper Room Books, 1996).
5. Susanne Johnson, *Christian Spiritual Formation in the Church and Classroom* (Nashville, Tenn.: Abingdon Press, 1989), 121.
6. Marjorie J. Thompson, *Soul Feast*; adapted from Tilden H. Edwards, *Living in the Presence: Disciplines for the Spiritual Heart* (San Francisco: Harper & Row, 1987), 84.

Sources and Authors of Marginal Quotations

PART 1   EMBRACING THE JOURNEY: THE WAY OF CHRIST

Week 1   The Christian Life As Journey

James C. Fenhagen, *Invitation to Holiness* (San Francisco: Harper & Row, 1985), 10.

Evelyn Underhill, *The Spiritual Life* (New York: Harper & Row, n.d.), 36.

Henri J. M. Nouwen, *The Inner Voice of Love* (New York: Doubleday, 1996), 39.

Week 2   The Nature of the Christian Spiritual Life

Augustine, *Confessions*, trans. Maria Boulding (Hyde Park, N.Y.: New City Press, 1997), 39.

Julian of Norwich, *Showings,* trans. Edmund Colledge and James Walsh (New York: Paulist Press, 1978), 263.

Ben Campbell Johnson, *Calming the Restless Spirit* (Nashville, Tenn.: Upper Room Books, 1997), 50.

Steve Harper, *Devotional Life in the Wesleyan Tradition* (Nashville, Tenn.: The Upper Room, 1983), 54.

Week 3   The Flow and the Means of Grace

Martin Luther, *Preface to the Letter of St. Paul to the Romans*, trans. Andrew Thornton, 1983, (27 May 1999) <http://www.ccel.org/l/luther/romans/pref_romans.html> (7 July 2000).

Joyce Rupp, *May I Have This Dance?* (Notre Dame, Ind.: Ave Maria Press, 1992), 118.

Maria Boulding, *The Coming of God* (Collegeville, Minn.: The Liturgical Press, 1982), 2.

John Wesley, "The Means of Grace" in *The Works of John Wesley*, vol. 5 (Grand Rapids, Mich.: Zondervan Publishing House, n.d.), 189.

Week 4   Sharing Journeys of Faith

Dwight W. Vogel and Linda J. Vogel, *Sacramental Living* (Nashville, Tenn.: Upper Room Books, 1999), 52.

Frederick Buechner, *Whistling in the Dark* (San Francisco: Harper & Row, 1988), 104.

Richard L. Morgan, *Remembering Your Story* (Nashville, Tenn.: Upper Room Books, 1996), 21.

Week 5   Living As Covenant Community

Mary Lou Redding, "Meeting God in Community," *The Spiritual Formation Bible* NRSV (Grand Rapids, Mich.: Zondervan, 1999), 1498.

Dietrich Bonhoeffer, *Life Together* (New York: Harper & Row, 1954), 26.

Joseph D. Driskill, *Protestant Spiritual Exercises* (Harrisburg, Pa.: Morehouse, 1999), 74.

The Rule of the Society of St. John the Evangelist (Cambridge, Mass.: Cowley Publications, 1997), 8.

PART 2   FEEDING ON THE WORD: THE MIND OF CHRIST

Week 1   Why Do We Call the Bible God's Word?

John Cassian, *Conferences*, Book 14 in *The Spiritual Formation Bible* NRSV (Grand Rapids, Mich.: Zondervan, 1999), n.p.

Thomas à Kempis, *Imitation of Christ* in The *Spiritual Formation Bible* NRSV (Grand Rapids, Mich.:

Zondervan, 1999), n.p.

Martin Luther in *The Spiritual Formation Bible* NRSV (Grand Rapids, Mich.: Zondervan, 1999), n.p.

Week 2   Studying Scripture As a Spiritual Discipline

Matthew Henry, *Commentary on the Whole Bible* (27 May 1999) <http://www.ccel.org/h/henry/mhc2/MHC00001.HTM> (21 July 2000), Preface to Volume 1.

Dietrich Bonhoeffer, *Meditating on the Word* (Nashville, Tenn.: The Upper Room, 1986) 44.

Elizabeth J. Canham, *Heart Whispers* (Nashville, Tenn.: Upper Room Books, 1999), 30.

M. Robert Mulholland Jr., *Shaped by the Word* (Nashville, Tenn.: Upper Room Books, 2000), 116.

Week 3   Meditating on the Word

John Calvin, *Golden Booklet of the True Christian Life* (Grand Rapids, Mich.: Baker Book House, 1955), 19.

Richard J. Foster, *Celebration of Discipline* (San Francisco: Harper & Row, 1978), 26.

Norvene Vest, *Gathered in the Word* (Nashville, Tenn.: Upper Room Books, 1996), 11.

John Wesley, *Works*, vol. 14, 253.

Week 4   Directing Imagination

Eugene H. Peterson, *Subversive Spirituality* (Grand Rapids, Mich.: William B. Eerdmans, 1997), 132.

Richard Baxter, *The Saints' Everlasting Rest* (New York: American Tract Society, 1824), 339-340.

Ibid., 349.

John Killinger, *Beginning Prayer* (Nashville, Tenn.: Upper Room Books, 1993), 67.

Avery Brooke, *Finding God in the World* (San Francisco: Harper & Row, 1989), 43.

Week 5   Group Meditation with Scripture

Mary Jean Manninen, *Living the Christian Story* (Grand Rapids, Mich.: William B. Eerdmans, 2000), 6.

Vogel and Vogel, *Sacramental Living*, 18.

Vest, *Gathered in the Word*, 13.

PART 3   DEEPENING OUR PRAYER: THE HEART OF CHRIST

Week 1   Prayer and the Character of God

Martha Graybeal Rowlett, *Responding to God* (Nashville, Tenn.: Upper Room Books, 1996), 29.

Margaret Guenther, *The Practice of Prayer* (Cambridge, Mass.: Cowley Publications, 1998), 16.

George MacDonald, *The Diary of an Old Soul* (London: George Allen & Unwin, 1905), 17.

Boulding, *The Coming of God*, 20.

Douglas V. Steere, *Dimensions of Prayer* (Nashville, Tenn.: Upper Room Books, 1997), 12.

Week 2   Dealing with Impediments to Prayer

Killinger, *Beginning Prayer*, 16.

Teresa of Avila, *The Interior Castle*, trans. Kieran Kavanaugh and Otilio Rodriguez (New York: Paulist Press, 1979) 53.

John Calvin, "Of Prayer" in *Institutes of the Christian Religion*, trans. Henry Beveridge (27 May 1999) <http://www.ccel.org/c/calvin/prayer/prayer.html> (14 July 2000), sec. 50.

Thomas R. Kelly, *A Testament of Devotion* (New York: Harper & Row, 1941), 60.

Week 3   Prayers of Petition and Intercession

Emilie Griffin, *Clinging: The Experience of Prayer* (New York: McCracken Press, 1994), 5.

Henri J. M. Nouwen, *The Genesee Diary* (New York: Image Books, 1989), 145.

Toyohiko Kagawa, *Meditations on the Cross* as cited in *Living Out Christ's Love: Selected Writings of Toyohiko Kagawa*, ed. Keith Beasley-Topliffe (Nashville, Tenn.: Upper Room Books, 1998), 57.

William Law, *A Serious Call to a Devout and Holy Life* (Philadelphia: The Westminster Press, 1948), 308.

Week 4   Praying As We Are
Kenneth Leech, *True Prayer* (San Francisco: Harper & Row, 1980), 3.

Timothy Jones, *The Art of Prayer* (New York: Ballantine Books, 1997), 122.

Catherine de Hueck Doherty, *Soul of My Soul* (Notre Dame, Ind.: Ave Maria Press, 1985), 113.

Week 5   Psalms, the Prayer Book of the Bible
Walter Brueggemann, *Praying the Psalms* (Winona, Minn.: Saint Mary's Press, 1982), 17.

Kathleen Norris, *The Psalms*, (New York: Riverhead Books, 1997), viii.

Larry R. Kalajainen, *Psalms for the Journey* (Nashville, Tenn.: Upper Room Books, 1996), 10.

Week 6   Exploring Contemplative Prayer
Thomas Merton, *Contemplative Prayer* (Garden City, N.Y.: Image Books, 1971), 89.

Tilden H. Edwards, "Living the Day from the Heart," from *The Weavings Reader* (Nashville, Tenn.: Upper Room Books, 1993), 58.

Mother Teresa, *A Life for God: The Mother Teresa Treasury*, comp. LaVonne Neff (London: Fount, 1997), 17–18.

Henri J. M. Nouwen, *Making All Things New* (San Francisco: Harper & Row, 1981), 57.

PART 4   RESPONDING TO OUR CALL: THE WORK OF CHRIST

Week 1   Radical Availability
Jean-Pierre de Caussade, *The Joy of Full Surrender* (Orleans, Mass.: Paraclete Press, 1986), 91.

Donald P. McNeill et al., *Compassion* (Garden City, N.Y.: Image Books, 1983), 35.

Brother Roger of Taizé, *His Love Is a Fire* (London: Geoffrey Chapman Mowbray, 1990), 58.

Week 2   Living Reliance
Howard Thurman, *Deep Is the Hunger* (Richmond, Ind.: Friends United Press, 1951), 198.

Evelyn Underhill, *The Ways of the Spirit* (New York: Crossroad, 1993), 100.

Thomas R. Hawkins, *A Life That Becomes the Gospel* (Nashville, Tenn.: Upper Room Books, 1992), 70-71.

Week 3   Bearing the Fruit of the Vine
Jacqueline McMakin with Rhoda Nary, *Doorways to Christian Growth* (Minneapolis: Winston Press, 1984), 204.

Roberta C. Bondi, *To Pray and to Love* (Minneapolis: Fortress Press, 1991), 31–32.

Andrew Murray, *With Christ in the School of Prayer* (Grand Rapids, Mich.: Zondervan, 1983), 106.

Robin Maas, *Crucified Love* (Nashville, Tenn.: Abingdon Press, 1989), 71.

Week 4   Gifts of the Spirit
Andrew Murray, *The New Life: Words of God for Young Disciples* (1998) <http://www.ccel.org/m/murray/new_life/life25.htm> (25 July 2000), chap. 22.

Ibid.

Charles V. Bryant, *Rediscovering Our Spiritual Gifts* (Nashville, Tenn.: Upper Room Books, 1991), 27.

Joan D. Chittister, *Wisdom Distilled from the Daily* (San Francisco: Harper & Row, 1990), 46.

Week 5   The Body of Christ Given for the World
Stephen V. Doughty, *Discovering Community* (Nashville, Tenn.: Upper Room Books, 1999), 110.
Bryant, *Rediscovering Our Spiritual Gifts*, 56.
Thomas R. Hawkins, *Sharing the Search* (Nashville, Tenn.: The Upper Room, 1987), 44.
Elizabeth O'Connor, *Eighth Day of Creation* (Waco, Tex.: Word Books, 1971), 8.
Bryant, *Rediscovering Our Spiritual Gifts*, 57.

PART 5   EXPLORING SPIRITUAL GUIDANCE: THE SPIRIT OF CHRIST

Week 1   How Do I Know God's Will for My Life?
Suzanne G. Farnham et al., *Listening Hearts: Discerning Call in Community* (Harrisburg, Pa.: Morehouse, 1991), 14.
Danny E. Morris and Charles M. Olsen, *Discerning God's Will Together* (Nashville, Tenn.: Upper Room Books, 1997), 16.
Jeannette A. Bakke, *Holy Invitations: Exploring Spiritual Direction* (Grand Rapids, Mich.: Baker Books, 2000), 223.
William A. Barry and William J. Connolly, *The Practice of Spiritual Direction* (New York: The Seabury Press, 1982), 8.
Hawkins, *A Life That Becomes the Gospel*, 36.

Week 2   Spiritual Companions
William A. Barry, *Spiritual Direction and the Encounter with God* (New York: Paulist Press, 1992), 92.
Kenneth Leech, *Soul Friend* (San Francisco: Harper & Row, 1977), 37.
Larry J. Peacock, *Heart and Soul*, (Nashville, Tenn.: Upper Room Books, 1992), 24.
Morris and Olsen, *Discerning God's Will Together*, 39–40.

Week 3   Small Groups for Spiritual Guidance
Tilden H. Edwards, *Spiritual Friend* (New York: Paulist Press, 1980), 96.
Peacock, *Heart and Soul*, 26.
Gustavo Gutiérrez, *We Drink from Our Own Wells* (Maryknoll, N.Y.: Orbis Books, 1984), 137.
Rose Mary Dougherty, *Group Spiritual Direction: Community for Discernment* (New York: Paulist Press, 1995), 36.

Week 4   Re-Visioning Our Life As Companions in Christ
Howard Rice, *The Pastor As Spiritual Guide* (Nashville, Tenn.: Upper Room Books, 1998), 97.
Peacock, *Heart and Soul*, 12.
Rice, *The Pastor As Spiritual Guide*, 132.

Week 5   Discerning Our Need for Guidance
Kimberly Dunnam Reisman, *The Christ-Centered Woman* (Nashville, Tenn.: Upper Room Books, 2000), 18.
Carolyn Gratton, *The Art of Spiritual Guidance: A Contemporary Approach to Growing in the Spirit* (New York: Crossroad, 1993), 107.
Eugene H. Peterson, *Working the Angles* (Grand Rapids, Mich.: William B. Eerdmans, 1987), 104.
Frank Rogers Jr., "Discernment" from *Practicing Our Faith*, ed. Dorothy C. Bass (San Francisco: Jossey-Bass Publishers, 1997), 118.

COMPANION SONG
Piano Accompaniment Score

Lyrics by Marjorie Thompson

Music by Dean McIntyre

Optional cut for short version: omit measures 19-34.

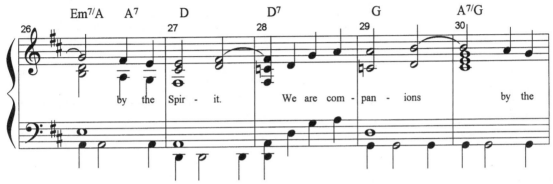

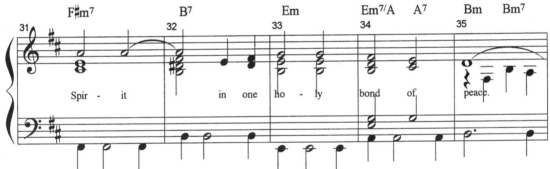

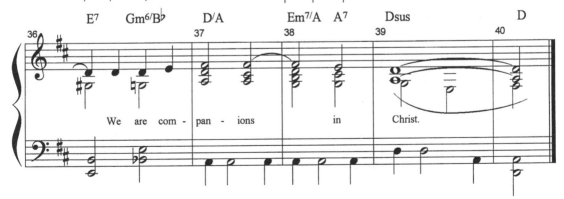

Companions in Christ Authors

 Gerrit Scott Dawson is the senior minister of First Presbyterian Church in Lenoir, North Carolina, and author of three books published by The Upper Room®: *Heartfelt, Writing on the Heart,* and *Called by a New Name.* His other writings include the books *Love Bade Me Welcome* and *I Am with You Always,* as well as articles for *Weavings®* and *D̄evo'Zine®*.

 Adele J. Gonzalez is Assistant Director of the Office of Lay Ministry in the Roman Catholic Archdiocese of Miami, Florida. She is a lay associate of the Sisters of St. Francis and has served as a migrant worker advocate, hospital chaplain, spiritual director, retreat director, and formation director. Her writings include journal articles and chapters dealing with ministry to Hispanics in two different books.

 E. Glenn Hinson retired as professor of spirituality and the John Loftis Professor of Church History at Baptist Theological Seminary in Richmond, Virginia, having taught previously at Southern Baptist Theological Seminary. A prolific author and frequent lecturer, Hinson is a member of the *Weavings®* Advisory Board, teaches in the Academy for Spiritual Formation®, and has written two Upper Room Books®, *Love at the Heart of Things* and *Spiritual Preparation for Christian Leadership.*

 Rueben P. Job is a retired United Methodist bishop, former editor/publisher of The Upper Room®, and the founding director of the Pathways Center for Christian Spirituality in Nashville, Tennessee. His titles for Upper Room Books® include *A Guide to Prayer for Ministers and Other Servants, A Guide to Prayer for All God's People, A Guide to Spiritual Discernment,* and *Spiritual Life in the Congregation.*

 Marjorie J. Thompson is an ordained Presbyterian minister, spiritual director, retreat leader, and director of the Pathways Center® for Spiritual Leadership in Nashville, Tennessee. She is the author of two books, *Family The Forming Center* (Upper Room Books®) and *Soul Feast,* along with articles for *Weavings®* and other journals.

 Wendy M. Wright, professor of theology at Creighton University in Omaha, Nebraska, is a noted writer in the field of contemporary spirituality. Her articles can be found in *Weavings®* and other leading journals of the spiritual life. She has published several books, including a trilogy on the seasons of the Christian year for Upper Room Books®: *The Rising, The Vigil,* and *The Time Between.*